RED OAKS & BLACK BIRCHES

THE SCIENCE AND LORE OF TREES

BY REBECCA RUPP

A Garden Way Publishing Book

STOREY

Storey Communications, Inc.
Schoolhouse Road
Pownal, Vermont 05261

COVER AND TEXT DESIGN by Judy Eliason
COVER WOOD ENGRAVING AND DECORATIVE TEXT ART by Charles Joslin
EDITED by Jill Mason

The name Garden Way Publishing is licensed to Storey Communications, Inc. by Garden Way, Inc.

Printed in the United States by BookCrafters

First Printing, August 1990

Library of Congress Cataloging-in-Publication Data

Rupp, Rebecca.
    Red oaks & black birches : the science and lore of trees / Rebecca Rupp.
        p.   cm.
    "A Garden Way Publishing book."
    Includes bibliographical references and index.
    ISBN 0-88266-620-7 (pbk)
    1. Trees.   2. Trees—Folklore.   3. Trees—United States.
4. Trees—United States—Folklore.   I. Title.   II. Title: Red oaks and black birches.
QK475.R78   1990
582.16—dc20   90-55043
                                                        CIP

For Randy, who cuts the firewood
And for Joshua, Ethan, and Caleb,
who stack the woodpile

"Men seldom plant trees until they begin to be wise."
John Evelyn, 1664

CONTENTS

INTRODUCTION

*e*ighth-graders of my generation were made to memorize, in English class, Joyce Kilmer's "Trees," a poem that begins with the innocent sentiment, "I think that I shall never see /A poem lovely as a tree," and ends, humbly, with, "Poems are made by fools like me / But only God can make a tree." All of us found it a wholly embarrassing little ditty, though about what you would expect from a man willing to admit in print that his first name was Joyce. The saving grace of the thing, to our uncivilized minds, was that it lent itself readily to parody, as in Ogden Nash's "I think that I shall never see / A billboard lovely as a tree." There was a kid in the back row in Miss Walker's class who came up with much worse.

"Trees," according to the *Encyclopedia Britannica*, is one of the best-known (not best) poetic effusions of the twentieth century. Joyce Kilmer, whose first name was actually Alfred, published it in *Poetry* magazine in 1913, when he was twenty-seven years old. He followed it up with similar poems on such topics as stars, snowmen, and roses, but none of them caught the public fancy like the egregious trees. Kilmer didn't get much chance to improve upon his first literary hit: he was killed a mere five years later, in action in France during World War I. He left behind two books of poetry and two of literary essays, neither of which are much remarked upon today. "Trees" remains his poetic legacy.

Kilmer came from New Brunswick, New Jersey, so the trees that inspired him to rhyme were presumably North American trees — an immense assortment of some twelve hundred different species, scattered among an estimated 150 different forest types, from the spruce-heavy boreal forests of Labrador to the steamy bald-cypress swamps and piney woods of the Gulf of Mexico. Kilmer joined a long line of American tree admirers, stretching back to the awestruck early explorers and to the homely Reverend Francis Higginson, first minister of Salem, Massachusetts, who wrote in 1630, "Here is good living for those who love good fires."

Fuel for those good fires was cut from the vast virgin forests of the East, four hundred thousand square miles of trees, some of which — so dense that it blocked out the sun — was known to the nervous pioneers as "black forest." The ax-happy settlers, surrounded by what looked like limitless woods, were prolific in their use of trees. A farmhouse with two fireplaces burned thirty to forty cords of wood a year — which meant an annual acre of forest downed just to keep warm. New England alone, one source calculates, consumed about 260 million cords of firewood between 1630 and 1800. By the 1790s, so much original forest was gone that a perceptive few were urging the creation of forest preserves; and Benjamin Lincoln, a general in the recent Revolutionary War, was proposing programs of acorn-planting to replace vanished trees. Such prophets were right, but ineffectual: today less than two thousand square miles remain of forests so great that the very smell of them carried many miles out to sea.

Nowadays 34 percent of the land area of the United States is forested — which gives us proportionately fewer trees than the U.S.S.R. (51 percent) or Canada (45 percent), but considerably more than Australia (6 percent), Syria (2.5 percent), or Egypt, which has no forest land at all. Such forests still provide one-third of the world with its fuel — and all of the world with such necessaries as oxygen, rain, newspapers, and lumber.

Collectively the world's forests produce over twelve billion tons of wood each year. Wood is an awesomely complex construct of chemicals, cells, and tissues, put together in such elaborate fashion that perhaps only God indeed could have made such a thing. Roughly half of it consists of cellulose, the major component of plant cell walls and by far the most abundant plant product on earth. Cellulose, like starch, is a monstrous sugar, made up of long chains of glucose molecules, each solidly connected to its neighbor by a chemical bond impervious to human digestive enzymes. This bond is the reason that people can't live on grass (like cows) or wood (like termites) — though in cold fact, neither cows nor termites could make do on their respective diets without their populations of gut bacteria, which actually do all the hard work of reducing cellulose to usable form.

In the tree, cellulose is the major constituent of wood fibers. Pure cellulose, extracted chemically from wood chips, is the most important substance obtained from digested wood. We wear it, as rayon, and peer through it or wrap things in it, as cellophane. (Five trees, properly processed, states chemist John Emsley, could clothe one human being for a lifetime.) Modified cellulose once went into celluloid, an ivory-like preparation developed in the 1870s for the fabrication of false teeth. In dentures, it was less than successful; highly flammable, it had a tendency to burst into flame in the wearer's mouth. (Toothless smokers were particularly at risk.) It did better in billiard balls and piano keys.

Today, less dramatically, modified cellulose figures in steering wheels, eyeglass frames, ping-pong balls, and screwdriver handles, serves as thickener in such otherwise slurpy substances as ice cream, mayonnaise, hand lotion, instant pudding, and paint, and puts the oomph in laundry detergents. Wood chemists, who feel that cellulose has yet to reach its full potential, have high hopes for developing cellulose-based equivalents of nylon and plastics, which nowadays come from Arabian oil.

All plants, from the miniature duckweed to the massive sequoia, contain cellulose; *lignin*, however, is the distinguishing feature of solid wood. Chemically a nightmarish snarl of ring-shaped molecules, lignin functions in the tree as chemical cement, binding the cellulose-heavy wood fibers together. Lignin keeps our wooden houses standing and our wooden furniture on its feet, holds tree trunks firmly erect, and — accumulating undesirably in the stalks of elderly broccoli and asparagus — renders vegetables too tough to eat. It's lignin that gives off the distinctive sawn-wood smell of carpenters' shops. The word comes from the Latin *lignum*, which, unsurprisingly, means "wood." Lignin is a sticking point in the manufacture of paper; wood pulp producers throw away thirty million tons of it each year. What little isn't discarded goes into highway blacktops or pastes for laying linoleum — or is processed to make *vanillin*, as in vanilla, reportedly the world's most popular flavoring.

The tree, in all its chemical and physical glory, is commemorated annually on Arbor Day, a largely ignored national holiday that falls on the last Friday in April. Arbor Day was established in 1872, a brainstorm of the Nebraska state legislature — though the holiday went into effect a bit belatedly, since by the 1870s, over-eager settlers had already chopped down most of Nebraska's trees. The first year repentant Nebraskans planted a million trees; within sixteen years, six hundred million. The rest of the country, impressed by this performance, gradually followed suit. Today Arbor Day is an established feature of the federal calendar, but not enough so for anybody to get the day off. Which goes to show that for a society dependent on some four hundred pounds of wood products per person per year to maintain our present luxurious lifestyles, we still take trees pretty much for granted.

"A country without children would face a hopeless future," wrote Teddy Roosevelt (father of six), "a country without trees is almost as hopeless."

"If a tree dies," wrote botanist Carolus Linnaeus simply, "plant another in its place."

OAK

*A*ccording to the *Guinness Book of World Records,* Roy C. Sullivan, former Shenandoah park ranger, is the only human being known to have been struck by lightning seven times and lived to tell the tale. Mr. Sullivan has lost one big toenail and a pair of eyebrows to lightning, has had his hair set on fire twice, and has been admitted to the hospital once for chest and stomach burns. He professes total bafflement over his continued attraction for lightning, which *Guinness* lists, incidentally, under "Human Achievements: Stunts and Miscellaneous Endeavors" instead of the preceding "Accidents and Disasters."

Other than in Mr. Sullivan's boots, perhaps the worst place to be during an electrical storm is under an oak tree. The mighty oak gets blitzed by lightning more than any other tree, which unfortunate faculty, some scholars theorize, led the ancient Greeks to consecrate oaks to Zeus, a notorious hurler of lightning bolts, and the ancient Norse to associate them with Thor, the obstreperous god of thunder. One reason the hapless oak is singled out for all this heavenly fury is its bark, a rough, ridged production three to four inches thick.

Under usual circumstances, bark — a sort of botanical armor plate — is a plus for a tree, protecting it from temperature extremes, dehydration, and insect damage. Bark is formed by the *vascular cambium,* a busy sheath of actively dividing cells that is responsible for the tree's annual increase in girth. The cambium, rather like a magician whose right hand doesn't know what the left hand is doing, produces *xylem*—water-conducting tubules—to the inside, and *phloem*—food-conducting tubules—to the outside. The xylem, once its days of usefulness are over, is destined to solidify into heartwood. The phloem, less gracefully, is doomed to end as bark. In each successive year the cambium adds new cells to increase its own circumference, thus neatly accommodating itself to the expanding tree trunk. The phloem, unhappily, lacks this expansive facility and, as new phloem cells are produced, the older layers are shoved outward, crushed, split, and shed, somewhat like the old skin on a growing snake. This battered and elderly phloem thus becomes a primary component of bark.

Just beneath the bark lies the *periderm*, a protective inner skin whose *raison d'être* is to shield the delicate and essential cambium from harm. (Those who carve their initials on trees insouciantly slice through it.) The periderm, in turn, is composed in part of a second cambium, called the cork cambium or *phellogen*, which divides to form clusters of air-filled cells known to the scientifically precise as *phellem* and to casual commoners as cork. The phellogen continually enlarges itself to keep pace with the growing tree — sloughing off, in the process, the aging cork of yesteryear. The manner in which this is done varies from species to species, and in large part determines the distinctive look of various barks. Smooth-barked trees like the beech, for example, have a long-lived phellogen which remains close to the surface, forming a continuous girdle-like sheath around the tree. Rough-barked trees, like our prototypic oak, have, in succession, numerous short-lived phellogens. Each produces a new batch of cork, forcing the older layers above it to stretch, crack, and eventually pull apart under expansive pressure, forming rough and ragged ridges. Some trees, such as pines and sycamores, scatter small cork cambia spottily about their trunks, each of which eventually multiplies, expands, and rips apart, creating barks patterned with reptilian scales (pine) or colorfully peeling patchworks (sycamore) of dead corky tissue.

While cork is a standard component of bark, most trees produce it only in small and unexciting quantities. An exception is the cork oak, *Quercus suber*, a native of the Mediterranean region. Aficionados of Munro Leaf's *Ferdinand the Bull* may recall the flower-sniffing Ferdinand lounging about beneath a fine specimen of *Q. suber*, from which bottle corks dangle in clusters like grapes. Though an enchanting picture, the cork, in actual fact, develops in continuous layers around the tree trunk. Eventually these layers may reach eight inches or more in thickness. By the time a given *Q. suber* is about twenty-five years old, enough cork has built up to permit stripping without damage to the tree. This first crop — "virgin cork" — is generally considered shoddy stuff and is ground up to make composition cork, the cork of floor matting and bulletin boards. Subsequent harvests, usually at nine- to ten-year intervals, yield the higher-quality cork used for champagne stoppers and beer-barrel bungs. The ancient Greeks and Romans were familiar with *Q. suber*, using it not only to seal their wine jars, but also, fashionably, for shoe soles, and, practically, for fishing floats.

Cork makes a fine fishing float both because it is light — over half the volume of cork is thin air — and because it is waterproof, rendered so by a waxy water-repellent chemical called *suberin*. It is also airtight, and thus, when wrapped around the tree, necessarily contains breathing pores — *lenticels* — that allow air to reach the underlying living tissues. In the absence of such air holes, cork-bound trees would smother where they stand. The lenticels are visible on the sides of bottle corks as dark brown dots — or, if you slice the cork crosswise, as horizontal channels. All corks are cut in this horizontally aligned fashion. If the air channels opened vertically, corks would no longer be airtight and bottles of bubbly would no longer fizz. Furthermore, given non-airtightness, it would no longer be possible in jubilant moments to shoot champagne corks into the air — the record distance for which is 102 feet, 11 inches, set in 1979 in the effervescent state of California. Modern engineers, in a more serious mood, have used cork for insulating spaceships.

However, to return to lightning. The havoc a bolt of lightning wreaks on its arboreal victim depends to a large extent on how wet the tree is. A truly sopping tree may get off relatively scot-free.

Electricity, of course, travels readily through water, which is why you should never drop a space heater into the bathtub. Lightning, zinging out of the atmosphere at over sixty miles per second, will strike the uppermost branches of the tree and, if the tree is uniformly wet, will follow the surface water film down the outside of the trunk to the ground. Real trouble occurs, however, when the tree is partially dry. Such is usually the case of the unfortunate oak, whose rough and ridged bark plates prevent water from running smoothly and evenly down the tree. Here the lightning bolt whips along the rain-soaked branches until it hits the end of the water slick; then, seeking the next-best downward path, it enters the liquid sap channels inside the tree trunk. These channels are very narrow — anywhere from forty to three hundred microns in diameter, the largest barely visible to the naked eye. The heat of the travelling lightning — 50,000 degrees Fahrenheit, five times hotter than the surface of the sun — promptly vaporizes the sap, which, trapped in its tiny tubes, expands violently. The resultant explosion blasts the luckless oak to oblivion, leaving behind a shredded stump coated with caramel from fast-fried photosynthetic sugars. The unappealing implication here is that at the first sign of approaching storm, ardent tree lovers, cautiously clad in rubber boots, should dash out and hose down their oak trees.

Standing under a tree, oak or otherwise, is an emphatic no-no during a thunderstorm, and even standing near a tree may prove sizzlingly unwise. Lightning from the base of the trunk may enter the root system and continue barrelling along underground. *Along* is the key word here. While mature oak trees do possess a main taproot (reminiscent of a giant carrot) and a number of downward-pointing vertical roots called sinkers, the majority of tree roots extend horizontally beneath the soil surface, often sixty feet or more from the main base of the tree. These are the killers when it comes to lightning. An unsuspecting storm-watcher perched on such a subsurface root can be zapped by electricity from the feet up. People have walked away from such bottoms-up lightning strikes with nothing worse to show for it than a melted zipper in their pants, but it's nothing to count on. The best place to spend a thunderstorm, safety-conscious citizens agree, is indoors — preferably in bed, with a glass of brandy.

Barring abrupt termination by lightning, the average oak lives to be about 450 years old. "Generations pass while some trees stand," wrote Sir Thomas Browne, in melancholy reflection on the longevity of human beings, "and old families last not three oaks." Extrapolating from Browne's calculation, old families do somewhat better in comparison to other trees. They survive, for example, twenty-two paper birches, thirteen Southern poplars, seven loblolly pines, six American elms, or four Eastern hemlocks. The oak, in the arboreal scheme of things, is a fairly long-lived tree, outlasting a long string of lesser plants. Still, the assertion of seventeenth-century forester John Smith that some contemporary English oaks dated to the first dry summer after the Flood was unduly optimistic. Old as oaks grow, they don't hold a candle to the California redwood, whose average lifespan is one thousand years, the giant sequoia (twenty-five hundred years), or the Methuselan bristlecone pine (upwards of three thousand years).

As a family, the oaks evolved about ninety million years ago, probably in Asia. According to *Hortus III*, the ultimate in botanical reference books, there are about four hundred and fifty different species of oak worldwide. Sixty-eight (or so) are indigenous to North America and some fewer to Europe, where a considerable number of plant species were eliminated by a glacial squeeze about ten thousand years ago in the last Ice Age. Among oaks, the chief glacial survivor in northern Europe is the English oak, *Quercus robur*, the wood of which built the British throne, Shakespeare's second-best bed, and the *Mayflower*. The name *robur* comes from the Latin, meaning, interchangeably, either "strength" or "oak" — as in the modern word *robust*. The "English" designation, though appropriate on the basis of exploitation, is a bit insular in view of the tree's range. *Q. robur* grows not only on English soil, but all across western Europe to the Caucasus Mountains of Russia, and in a strip across northern Africa.

Still, despite this catholic scatter, *Q. robur* over the centuries has become as much a symbol of England as John Bull, roast beef, and the stiff upper lip. *Q. robur* was the oak held sacred by the Druids, those ancient dignitaries dubbed "oak priests" by later generations for their association with forest groves. Queen Elizabeth I was reputedly sitting under a *Q. robur* when the messenger arrived from London with the glad news of her accession to the throne; the historic tree became known as Queen Elizabeth's Oak, and its remains, shored up with ropes and cement, are preserved at Hatfield House. Elizabeth's descendant, Charles II, owed his life to a *Q. robur*: he hid in one after the fatal Battle of Worcester, thus evading capture by Cromwell's soldiers. Upon his restoration to the throne some four years later, Charles, properly grateful, declared a Royal Oak Day, to be celebrated annually on May 29th by wearing oak leaves in hats, hanging oak branches over doors and windows, and generally rejoicing.

The oak's intervention in the affairs of kings showed more romance than political acumen. Charles proved an unsatisfactory monarch, given to wild parties and heavy personal expenditures. He is remembered for coining the phrase "God will never damn a man for allowing himself a little pleasure," and accordingly left behind him fourteen illegitimate children and vast debts.

The oak's economic performance, in contrast, was superb. During the two hundred years that Britannia ruled the waves, she did so by the grace of *Q. robur*, which was used for the keels and sheathing of the world-famous British fleet. So solid were these ship timbers that during World War II, Winston Churchill's London bunker was shored up with the century-old oak ribs of one of Lord Nelson's flagships. With the continuing growth of the British Empire and its supporting navy, however, the British oaks were soon in painfully short supply. One estimate suggests that England was probably only about 20 percent forested by the time of the Norman Conquest, and those forests, barring the stretches selfishly preserved for the royal hunts, continued to shrink into the twentieth century. Many upright citizens short-sightedly viewed this as a trend to the better. The decline of the English oaks, a Dr. Thomas Preston informed Parliament in 1791, "is not to be regretted, for it is a certain proof of national improvement; and for Royal Navies countries yet barbarous are the right and only proper nurseries."

In the seventeenth and eighteenth centuries, the country yet barbarous that had been awarded naval nursemaid status was colonial America. The closest American equivalent to the familiar *Q. robur* was the Eastern white oak, *Q. alba*, which the tobacco planters of Jamestown were slicing up with their wind-driven sawmill and shipping back home by 1625. *Q. alba* got a mixed reception in the old country. While chronic timber shortages had created an eager market for imported wood, Britons persisted in the belief that there was no oak to touch the true British — *Q. robur* — oak. This superstition held firm for over a century. It was eventually dispelled by the construction of the *Constitution* — "Old Ironsides" — a ship so strong and well built that cannonballs were said to roll off it like water off a duck's back. Old Ironsides featured a keel and gun deck of white oak, respectively cut in New Jersey and Massachusetts, and a hull of live oak (*Q. virginiana*) from Georgia, covered with a skin of copper sheathing made by Paul Revere. The spectacular naval success of Old Ironsides with its live oak hull created such enthusiasm for *Q. virginiana* that President John Quincy Adams attempted to limit promiscuous public consumption by establishing the first national forest reserve, near Pensacola, Florida, in 1828. The reserve, actually less an attempt to preserve a unique forest environment than a sharp-eyed effort to keep the navy's timber out of the hands of southern lumber barons, was short-lived — it bit the dust five years later during the Jackson administration.

The legendary toughness of oaks, both English and American, led to an association of oak with muscle-bound masculinity. The unconquerable British seaman, wrote David Garrick in 1770, had a "heart of oak." Nineteenth-century romantic gardener William Shenstone, whose famed garden at Leasowes was the first to feature winding garden paths in place of the usual gravelled straightaways, dubbed the oak "the perfect image of manly character." This annoyingly sexist sentiment is echoed by the state of Maryland, whose state tree, the white oak, is complemented by the Maryland motto: "Manly

Deeds, Womanly Words." Five other states, however, boast state oaks of various kinds without resort to overtly manly imagery: Connecticut ("He Who Transplanted Still Sustains"), Georgia ("Wisdom, Justice, and Moderation"), Illinois ("State Sovereignty — National Unity"), Iowa ("Our Liberties We Prize and Our Rights We Will Maintain"), and New Jersey ("Liberty and Prosperity"). While the oak is historically a macho tree, there is a touch of oak symbolism on the distaff side. In early Victorian times, villages in Cheshire — the home district of Alice's grinning cat — celebrated May Day by hanging tree branches on houses to show how the residents were regarded by their neighbors. A birch branch denoted a pretty girl; an alder branch, an incorrigible scold. An oak branch so hung indicated a good woman. And oak, according to the Victorian language of flowers, represented hospitality. (The Victorian bouquet-maker's symbol of strength was a leafy sprig of fennel.)

The American settlers, a wood-conscious group if there ever was one, quickly learned the high and low points of their predominant regional oaks. Most botanists tend to divide the vast number of North American oaks into two categories, termed, like the opposing sides in the Wars of Roses, the white and the red. White oaks are roughly distinguished from red by their leaves — smoothly lobed instead of bristle-tipped — and their acorn gestation period. White oak acorns take one year to mature; red oak acorns two. Dendrologist Alan Mitchell in his *Trees of North America* is more precise: his oaks are classed as white, red, chestnut, willow, and live, with fleeting mention of the Chinese evergreen oaks, which sport big hard leathery leaves like rhododendrons.

Front runner among American white oaks is the aforementioned Eastern white, the great-granddaddy of oak trees, which may, if lucky, survive to the ripe old age of eight hundred years. Its round-lobed leaves are somewhat variable in shape, reminiscent of Rorschach blots. They emerge, colored blush-pink, in the spring, proceed through summer's bright green, and turn crimson, scarlet, and rust in the fall. The wood, tough, tight, and durable, was once the prime choice for bridges, barns, ship planking, and wagon beds, and, impermeable to water, was favored for whiskey casks, beer kegs, cider barrels, and old oaken buckets. Yankee peddlers, along with their notorious wooden nutmegs, supplied the gullible with wooden pumpkin seeds carved from white oak.

Oak was also the preferred wood for plank roads. Plank roads — miles of sawn planks, spiked to parallel stringers — were constructed in the early nineteenth century, in the transition period between the muddy trench of earlier decades and the gravel road, invented by Scotsman John Macadam, of later. At least one medical authority swore by them. A Dr. Frank Johnson, in a promotional pamphlet for the oak-and-pine "Nicolson Pavement," wrote in 1867: "Wood is better than stone for pavement, for any pavement that increases the destruction of shoe, horse, vehicle, chaise or decreases comfort and convenience is not economical though it costs nothing and lasts forever." An oak plank road was built to last twelve years, but in actual practice seldom lived up to expectations, warping, splitting, buckling, and cracking well before the intended expiration date. Geographer George Perkins Marsh compared American plank-road travel unfavorably to progress on camelback across the Sahara Desert.

White oaks of the east also include the bur oak, *Q. macrocarpa*, which bears the biggest acorn of any American oak — whoppers measuring 2 x 1½ inches were plucked off a tree in Tulsa, Oklahoma — and the overcup oak, *Q. lyrata*, a southerly tree whose acorns are nearly swallowed up by their surrounding cups. The post oak, *Q. stellata*, whose acorns are attractive, but unremarkable, is named for its colonial function of producing fence posts. It is distinguished by Maltese-cross-shaped leaves.

Western white oaks include the largest of the American oaks, the California white or valley oak (*Q. lobata*), from whose branches the Spanish padres once hung their mission bells. Its range is restricted to the Golden State from the Trinity River in the north to Los Angeles in the south. A large and attractive tree, the valley oak produces long skinny acorns and a wood so useless that the early settlers referred to it scornfully as the "mush oak." Nowadays the valley oaks are fast disappearing to make way for housing developments. Often they are reduced to wood chips and shipped off to the papermills of Japan, a practice painfully reminiscent of sending old racehorses to the glue factory.

Similarly struggling against human population pressures is another western-dwelling white oak, *Q. douglasii*, commonly known as the blue oak. Another California native, it was used by the forty-niners to fuel their campfires and shore up their gold mines. To the north grows the Oregon white oak, or Garry oak (*Q. garryana*), which ranges from British Columbia south to San Francisco Bay. The Garry oak, a useful tree, is characterized by very dark — nearly black — leaves. It is also all too often hung with mistletoe.

So are other oaks: in ancient England, the Druids harvested the mistletoe hanging from their sacred stands of *Q. robur* for use in religious ceremonies. The revered oak was believed to invest its resident mistletoe with above-average spiritual powers. The mistletoe so prized by the Druids was *Viscum album*, the Old World mistletoe, but immigrants to the New World soon identified an American look-alike, *Phoradendron serotinum*. Both are semiparasites. Since their leaves contain chlorophyll, they are able to produce their own photosynthetic sugars; however, they obtain water, minerals — and a sturdy support — from their hosts. Mistletoe seed is dispersed by birds, who are fond of the translucent white mistletoe berries. The encased seeds are not eaten. Instead, by virtue of their sticky outer coating, they adhere to the bird's beak or feet, and are subsequently cleaned off by scraping on a handy tree trunk. The deposited seed germinates, developing a fibrous organ called the *haustorium* that parasitic plants use to absorb nutrients from their hosts. The haustorium penetrates the cambium of the host tree and eventually plugs into the xylem vessels, thus tapping into a ready source of water and minerals. Despite the traditional association of mistletoe with oaks, it actually parasitizes many widely different species, some sixty-two in North America. Other victims include the persimmon, the red maple, and the black walnut.

The mistletoe that drapes the forests of the West is a different

— and nastier — kettle of fish. The western mistletoes, commonly known as dwarf mistletoes, belong to the genus *Arceuthobium*. Unlike *P. serotinum*, their green and leafy eastern cousin, the dwarf mistletoes lack chlorophyll. Lacking personal food-making capacity, the dwarf mistletoes live wholly by snatch-and-grab. All are highly invasive, penetrating and draining the inner tissues of host trees like sneak thieves siphoning fuel out of their neighbors' gas tanks. Most of their evil activities proceed invisibly. The dwarf mistletoes emerge into the light only as a series of scaly spikes, which comprise the mistletoe version of sexual organs. Once fertilized, the female spikes develop swollen seed capsules at the tips. The seeds are distributed by explosion: when ripe, water pressure builds up within the enclosing spike until the capsule bursts, ejecting the sticky seeds at speeds of up to sixty miles per hour. The whizzing seeds can land as far as one hundred feet from the mistletoe host, sticking to and eventually infecting new trees. Most dwarf mistletoes are picky when it comes to hosts: *Arceuthobium douglasii*, for example, associates almost solely with the Douglas fir; *A. americanum* zeroes in on the lodgepole pine. Collectively, the assorted dwarf mistletoes infect coniferous forests across the United States, including an estimated 40 percent of the commercial timberlands of Oregon and Washington. They account for more timber destruction than any tree disease in the United States. Nobody kisses under them at Christmastime.

The custom of decking the family halls with (leafy) mistletoe is an ancient one. The Druids hung mistletoe in their homes to invoke kindly spirits from the forest; the Scandinavians hung it in their doorways to fend off evil spirits. The custom of using the mistletoe as a Christmas kissing bough was established in England long before it caught on in perennially Puritan America. Nathaniel Hawthorne, author of *The Scarlet Letter*, first came across the kissing bough in Liverpool in the Christmas of 1855, and reportedly was shocked by its licentious and continual use. Shocking or no, by the turn of the century, the mistletoe bough was a standard American Christmas trapping. Often sold by the "ball" — a thick cluster just as cut from the tree, occasionally weighing upwards of thirty pounds — mistletoe was markedly popular among fathers of marriageable daughters. Particularly desirable was imported English mistletoe, said to be more effective than the American variety, and therefore twice as expensive. Originally kissees were supposed to pluck a berry off the ball with every kiss. It's a custom that seems to have fallen by the wayside, perhaps because mistletoe berries are known to be poisonous to people.

On the red oak side of the coin is the northern red oak, *Q. rubra*, found as far north as Quebec and Nova Scotia, which makes it the most cold-loving of the eastern oaks. Red oak was considered about as good as white by colonial woodworkers, who used it for general construction and, among other things, for sugar and molasses barrels. The pin oak, *Q. palustris*, which flourishes from New England southwest to Tennessee and Oklahoma, is named for its notoriously tough branches, once used to pin barn beams. Nowadays it's the commonest tree in Central Park.

The black oak, *Q. velutina*, is, confusingly, a red oak and ranges from Maine south to Florida and west to Texas. The scientific name *velutina* derives from the velvety surface of the shoot, leaf, and leafstalk. The fuzz on the upper side of the leaf soon falls off, however, leaving it shiny, stiff, and parchment-like. The black oak is also referred to as the yellow-bark oak or quercitron, and this, with its earlier scientific name, *Q. tinctoria*, indicates its colonial use as a dyestuff. The inner bark of the black oak is a bright orange-yellow, and can be used fresh or dried and powdered, to produce yellow-dyed woollens, cottons, and linens.

Though doubtless used for decades by American home dyers, quercitron was officially "discovered" — and named — by an Englishman, Dr. Edward Bancroft, sometime before the Revolutionary War. The new American yellow proved excellent, ten times more effective by weight than the more commonly used European weld or dyer's wood, and four times better than fustic, also called yellow wood or dyer's mulberry, which was imported from Brazil. Parliament was so impressed with Dr. Bancroft's yellow that, in 1785, they awarded him exclusive rights to use it in dyeing and calico-printing processes. Quercitron proved to be one of the world's major vegetable dyes and remained in commercial use well into the twentieth century. Used alone or in combination with other dyestuffs, quercitron was used to produce not only a range of yellows, but drabs, smoke, olive, snuff, orange, yellowed reds, and cinnamon browns.

The blackjack oak, *Q. marilandica*, is perhaps the oddest of the red oaks, with bizarre splayed leaves shaped like duck feet. It is also an eastern oak, ranging from New York to Texas. The only western red oak is the California black, *Q. kelloggii*, a denizen of California and Oregon, whose elongated striped acorns are eaten every October by Stellar's jays, the raucous black-crested western relatives of the eastern bluejay.

The best known of the willow oaks, which have long slim leaves reminiscent of the true willow, is *Q. imbricaria*, the shingle oak, which furnished tight roofs for many colonial cabins. The chestnut oaks, which have tapering, shallowly lobed leaves reminiscent of chestnuts, include the chestnut oak, *Q. prinus*, which ranges from Delaware to Florida and Texas, and the chinkapin oak, *Q. muehlenbergii*, with a slimmer and even more chestnut-like leaf, found from Maine to Minnesota and south to Texas and Florida. *Q. prinus* is sometimes called the basket oak, since the wood splits easily into splints, ideal for the weaving of baskets. Splint baskets of chestnut oak were used for toting cotton in from the fields in the southern plantation days. *Q. prinus* acorns, exaggeratedly touted as "large and sweet as the best chestnuts" by early colonial recruiters, never measured up to their original press, but the leaves were a hit with colonial cows, who gorged on them whenever they got the chance. For this reason, the chestnut oak, among cow owners, was referred to as the cow oak.

The live oaks are evergreen. It's these trees that shaded many a plantation owner's home and a dozen of them gave the name to Ashley Wilkes' estate — Twelve Oaks — in *Gone With the Wind*. Best known of the live oaks is probably the aforementioned *Q. virginiana*, of Old Ironsides fame. *Q. virginiana* ranges from Virginia to Florida, and west through Texas, a sixty-foot tree often generously hung with gray beards of Spanish moss. Neither Spanish nor moss, *Tillandsia usneoides* is a bizarre relative of the pineapple. Scientifically it is known as an *epiphyte*: a plant that lives without soil, absorbing water and nutrients directly from the air. Unlike the intrusive mistletoes, Spanish moss does not develop roots or other protrusions that penetrate its host, but depends on a host solely for support. Limp but self-sufficient, Spanish moss can thrive on telephone wires. Physically Spanish moss is a grayish green tangle of threadlike growths, often up to twenty-five feet long. During the first half of the twentieth century, Spanish moss was a prized stuffing material, used in upholstered furniture and in automobile seat cushions. It was also boiled to make a tea, said to aid women in childbirth, and was stuffed into shoes to alleviate high blood pressure.

The coast live oak, *Q. agrifolia*, is a California native. A prime source of firewood, it was almost the sole heat source for the chilly houses of San Francisco well into the twentieth century, the next-best available option being Australian coal. The tree reaches heights of one hundred feet and bears spiny-toothed leaves reminiscent of holly. Alan Mitchell suggests that the scientific name *agrifolia* ("field-leaved") may be the result of a taxonomer's spelling error. The intent may have been *aquifolia* ("holly-leaved"), which makes more sense. The canyon live oak, *Q. chrysolepsis*, is more widely distributed, extending from Oregon south along the California Coast Range and the Sierra Nevada to the Mexican border. Its wood is so hard that it was familiarly known as "maul oak" from its use in splitting redwood and cedar shakes.

Given the ubiquitousness of the American oak family, it is hardly surprising that the country should be littered with commemorative oak trees: treaty oaks, council oaks, boundary oaks, and witness oaks, under which various well- or ill-considered public declarations were made. Evangeline and her fellow Acadians disembarked under an oak in St. Martinville, Louisiana, in 1758; Aaron Burr was tried for treason under the oaks of Washington, Mississippi, in 1807; the Republican Party was founded under a grove of white oaks in Jackson, Michigan, in 1856. The pirate Jean Lafitte is said to have buried his treasure under, around, or near the Lafitte Oaks of Louisiana's Jefferson Island in the bad old profitable days of the early 1800s; if so, it has not yet been unearthed, despite considerable investigative digging by the local citizenry. A bur oak near Council Grove, Kansas, served for years as a post office drop on the wagon train trail. For a decade or so, it was the only known letter cache between Junction City, Kansas, and Santa Fe, New Mexico. Andrew Jackson camped under an oak en route to the Battle of Horseshoe Bend; George Armstrong Custer camped under an oak en route to the Little Big Horn; Davy Crockett camped under an oak — in Crockett, Texas — en route to the Alamo. Several oaks still stand on Gettysburg's Cemetery Ridge that once marked the target of George Pickett's heroic, if somewhat maniacal, charge on July 3, 1863. Mark Twain wrote "The Celebrated Jumping Frog of Calaveras County" under an oak in Tuolumne County, California.

Among the most famous of historic oaks was Hartford, Connecticut's now-defunct Charter Oak. The Charter Oak was already over two hundred years old in 1685 when James II became king of England. It stood in that year on the grounds of the Wyllys place, reputedly spared by the resident Wyllyses because the local Indians venerated the tree and begged that it be preserved. In the autumn of 1686 the king's newly appointed colonial governor, Sir Edmund Andros, arrived in Hartford, and, full of administrative new-broom-ishness, demanded the surrender of the liberal charter under which Connecticut had operated so happily since 1662. The Charter, among other concessions, granted Connecticut all the lands "from the said Narragansett Bay on the east to the South Sea [the Pacific Ocean] on the west." Connecticut citizens, understandably, were devoted to it. Providentially, in a meeting between Governor Andros and a number of outraged citizens — on Halloween night, the story goes — a gust of wind blew the candles out. Under cover of darkness, a quick-witted colonist named Jeremiah Wadsworth pinched the charter and secreted it in the hollow of the old oak tree. (Wadsworth family tradition skips the tree and holds that the document was stashed all along in the Wadsworth cellar.) Andros, piqued, promptly dissolved the colonial government. His victory in this battle of wills, however, was short-lived; he was recalled to England in 1688, upon the abdication of King James. The Charter then resurfaced and served Connecticut as a constitution until 1816, by which time it was obvious that Connecticut wasn't going to extend any farther west than its present border, just short of the Hudson River. Wadsworth received a twenty-shilling reward for his pains, and a measure of immortality, somewhat marred by vagaries about his Christian name, which some historians list as Joseph.

The Charter Oak survived until 1856, when it blew over in a windstorm, to the great sorrow of Hartford citizens. The tolling of church bells and the playing of funeral dirges marked its passing, a white marble memorial tablet was erected at the place where it once stood, and the adjacent street was nostalgically renamed Charter Oak Avenue. The wood of the downed landmark went into a vast assortment of memorabilia, including picture frames, gavels, and a couple of chairs for the Connecticut State House.

Among extant historical oaks, perhaps the best known is the Wye Oak of Talbot County, Maryland, which according to the American Forestry Association, is America's largest specimen of *Q. alba*. Now over four hundred years old, the Wye Oak, when last measured, was 102 feet tall and nearly 30 feet around the trunk, with a canopy spread of 158 feet. The tree still produces six to seven thousand acorns each year, which seeds, lovingly harvested by the Maryland Forest Service, are distributed to hopeful growers of champions.

The average oak produces about five thousand acorns annually, with a bumper crop every three to four years. From a small percentage of such little acorns, great oaks do manage somehow to sprout and grow. "When one considers how oaks reproduce," writes naturalist David Rains Wallace, "simply by dropping on the ground a large seed that half the animals in the neighborhood would like to eat, it seems a bit miraculous that trees of the genus *Quercus* have survived as long as they have." Statistically it seems miraculous, too: One study, cited by Richard Ketchum in *The Secret Life of the Forest*, tracked the fates of some fifteen thousand acorns, offspring of one spectacularly prolific tree. Of these, 83 percent were gobbled by deer, squirrels, and other animals; 6 percent were attacked by weevils and insect larvae; and about 10 percent were "naturally imperfect." Less than 1 percent actually sprouted, and of those that did, over half died as seedlings. Such an infant mortality rate seems doubly depressing in view of the oak's slow growth rate — an oak can take up to a century to reach full maturity. Eighteenth-century estate owners refused to plant them in favor of faster-growing conifers, which made an elegant show in less than half the time. An old English country saying points out that withy and sallow — willow wands — would buy a horse before oak would buy a saddle.

Most oaks begin bearing acorns by about ten years of age. Acorns, like beechnuts, hazelnuts, and sweet chestnuts, are true nuts — botanically, one-seeded fruits with a hard, woody outer layer corresponding to the flesh of culinary fruits. Most of the other munchies included in Christmas mixed-nut bowls are, botanically speaking, not nuts at all. Almonds, walnuts, pecans, and hickory nuts are all surrounded by a fleshy layer while on the tree and as such are the equivalents of the stones of drupe fruits, like peaches and plums. Brazil nuts, which really do come from Brazil, are officially seeds: twelve to twenty individual "nuts" are borne in clusters packed within woody pods about six inches in diameter. These arboreal cannonballs weigh about five pounds apiece and are usually collected after they have fallen to the ground. The harvesters, with a nervous eye to the sky, carry protective shields. Cashews, like Brazil nuts, are non-nuts of South American origin. Cashews, scientifically, are the seeds of drupe fruits, but their closest relative is not the delectable plum but the detestable poison ivy. Cashews never appear on supermarket shelves in the shell because their shells contain an irritating poison-ivy-like oil. The peanut, simultaneously the most familiar and most bizarre of non-nuts, is the seed of a tropical legume. The peanut blossoms, after fertilization, bend downward and literally drill themselves into the soil — a behavior believed to have developed as an escape mechanism, a means of protecting the developing seeds from voracious peanut-eaters. The dry shells enclosing the "nuts," which develop underground, correspond to the pods of peas and beans.

Acorns, though viewed somewhat coldly by modern eaters — food historian Waverley Root states flatly that acorns are "best eaten indirectly by man, in the form of pork" — supported countless prehistoric and primitive civilizations. Plutarch, who lived in the first century A.D., by which time all but the hungriest scorned acorns, claimed that when primitive man first chanced to taste the fruits of the oak tree, he danced about in joy, calling the oak "life-giver, mother, and nourisher." Of like mind were the Indian tribes of California, where, according to present-day estimates, a population of 150,000 flourished on a staple diet of acorns.

As staple diets go, acorns are an excellent choice. Like most nuts, they are good sources of B vitamins and protein. Most nuts, however, are also notoriously high in fat, which is why Brazil nuts (67 percent fat), pecans (71 percent), walnuts (59 percent), and the like are off-limits to those in the throes of a weight-reducing diet. Acorns and chestnuts are exceptions to this pudgy rule: both, in lieu of fat, contain substantial complex carbohydrate reserves, primarily in the form of starch. Chestnuts, for example, contain a mere 2 percent fat and approximately 42 percent carbohydrate; acorns, at 5 percent fat, contain an average of 68 percent carbohydrate, and David Bainbridge, a plant researcher and acorn enthusiast from Riverside, California, has identified varieties with carbohydrate contents of nearly 90 percent.

In view of these nutritional plus points, it seems surprising not that the California Indians lived on acorns, but that more of us don't. The reason is that most acorns are at best bland, often tasteless, and at worst mouth-puckeringly bitter. The bland varieties — generally termed "sweet" — are produced on trees of the white oak class, such as the Eastern white, chestnut, chinkapin, and live oaks. Red-type oaks, on the other hand, such as the red, black, and willow oaks, all produce acorns that are usually inedibly bitter due to their tannin content.

Chemically tannins can be separated into two main classes: the hydrolyzable, easily broken down by water to yield alcohols and acids; and the condensed, water-resistant chains of cyclic compounds. Luckily much of the tannin content of acorns falls into the former class and can thus be leached out in water. The California Indians routinely ground their (bitter) acorns into flour — millstone holes used for this purpose can still be found in California rocks — then put the flour in leaf-lined pits in the sand along river banks and poured hot water over it to remove the offensive tannins. Whole acorns can be leached similarly in repeated changes of hot water until the water ceases to turn brown. Acorn flour can be used in cakes, breads, noodles, pancakes, and muffins; ground acorns or acorn chunks, according to Dr. Bainbridge, can be used in place of chickpeas, peanuts, and olives in numerous recipes.

Bainbridge, who corresponds with a nationwide network of acorn-tasting volunteers, is actively pursuing a search for the ideal acorn. He himself has tracked down some markedly flavorful varieties, described as having overtones of chocolate and cashew. Some are sweet enough to be roasted and straightforwardly eaten like chestnuts. Still, acorns aren't to everyone's taste. Euell Gibbons, that indefatigable consumer of wild foods, stated bracingly that "even unleached acorns of some species are worth the attention of someone who is really hungry" — but, when it came down to brass tacks, was unable to win over the other members of his camping party until the acorns were leached, roasted, and dipped in clarified sugar.

Acorns can also, again according to Dr. Bainbridge, be treated with pickle brine, or with lye, in the same manner that raw olives are prepared for market. Like bitter acorns, raw olives hot off the tree are almost painfully inedible. Bitterness in olives is due to an evil-tasting glucoside called *oleuropein*, which, since the days of ancient Rome, has been leached out of the fruit by prolonged soaking in lye solution. (The extracted oleuropein was used by the Romans for weedkiller, leather lubricant, and axle grease.) This procedure works equally well for the tannins in acorns.

As the very latest in modern acorn-leaching techniques, Bainbridge recommends soaking the ground nuts in a solution of sodium bicarbonate (baking soda). The idea derives from the work of Dr. N. R. Reddy, a food scientist at the Virginia Polytechnic Institute, who discovered that 60 percent of the tannins can be removed from legumes, such as dried beans and peas, by soaking them for twelve to fifteen hours in sodium bicarbonate (about one tablespoon to a quart of water). As well as eliminating tannins, which, consumed in bulk, can lead to anemia and growth retardation, the baking soda was shown effective in reducing leguminous flatulence factors — which, in the vernacular, means it degassed the beans.

Some acorns are pressed to yield a cooking oil; high-fat varieties contain up to 30 percent oil. Acorn oil figures in the national cuisines of Algeria and Morocco, and is said to be equivalent in flavor and quality

▼

ACORN COFFEE

Take sound and ripe acorns, peel off the shell or husk, divide the kernels, dry them gradually, and roast them in a close vessel or roaster, keeping them continually stirring; in doing which special care must be taken that they be not burnt or roasted too much, both which would be hurtful.

Take of these roasted acorns (ground like other coffee) half an ounce every other morning and evening, alone mixed with a dram of other coffee, and sweetened with sugar, with or without milk.

This receipt is recommended by a famous German physician, as a much esteemed, wholesome, nourishing, strengthening nutriment for mankind; which, by its medicinal qualities, has been found to cure slimy obstructions in the viscera, and to remove nervous complaints when other medicines have failed.

Remark: Since the duty was taken off, West India coffee is so cheap that substitutes are not worth making. On the continent the roasted roots of the wild chicory, a common weed, have been used with advantage.

— Family Receipt Book, 1819

to high-grade olive oil. The same, regrettably, cannot be said of acorn "coffees" — a variety of which Scarlett O'Hara and compatriots choked down during the Civil War. Europeans make an analogous brew from *Q. robur*, known as *Eichel kaffee*, and the resourceful Turks make a spiced acorn-based drink called *raccahout*, which is supposedly comparable to hot chocolate. Dr. Bainbridge hypothesizes acorn beer, an idea which is not as far-fetched as it first sounds: the early American "bread beers" were often brewed with a proportion of acorn or chestnut flour, which was said to give a "very distinct nutty flavor" to the beer.

Wine can be made from oak leaves, picked by our forebears for that purpose in the spring when they reached "the size of a mouse's ear." Boiling water was poured over the leaves, which were soaked for a day, then strained. The oak-leaf water was then combined with sugar, lemon juice, yeast, and water, and allowed to ferment. Similar wines were made with grape leaves, potato leaves, spinach, and lettuce.

Tannins have their useful places in the sun. Their primary function, from the tree's point of view, is defensive: Tannins are chemical weapons against insect attack. Concentrated in leaves, bark, and seeds, they act as feeding repellents, as off-putting to munching insects as they are to human beings. They do not, however, appear to deter deer, raccoons, bears, mice, wild turkeys, pheasants, quails, crows, or squirrels — the last, with an apparently iron digestive system, also capable of downing daffodil bulbs and *Amanita phalloides*, the destroying-angel mushroom. Domestic animals similarly thrive on tannin-laden acorns. The medieval English domesday books estimated land values based on the number of pigs a given area's oak mast would feed. Colonial American farmers relied on acorns to feed their roving livestock; California settlers bragged about the hams from their acorn-stuffed hogs.

Human beings use tannins in leather-making, specifically in tanning, the process of treating raw skins to render them resistant to water, heat, and degradation by microorganisms. It also turns the skins tan, hence the name. No one is sure precisely when tanning was discovered, but it has certainly been around for several thousand years. Professional-looking leather sandals thirty-three hundred years old have been unearthed from Egyptian archaeological sites. Tanning techniques have changed little since those sandals were made. Basically animal skins were treated to remove hair, then soaked in a concentrated solution of tanniferous plants. Sources of tanning solutions have traditionally included the barks of sumac, chestnut, spruce, and willow, and in Europe, pomegranate; but the tannin-rich bark of various oak species has always topped the list.

Tannins of whatever source operate in the same fashion, binding to certain regions of the collagen fibers in animal skins. On the molecular level, animal skins are made of highly organized collagen fibrils, tightly packed, precisely oriented, and — in this shoulder-to-shoulder, backs-to-the-wall orientation — resistant to the depredations of microbes. In certain regions of the skin, however, this ordered phalanx of fibrils falls apart, and these chemically disorganized areas are ripe for fungal or bacterial attack. Tannins circumvent such attacks by getting there first, impregnating the susceptible weak points, and chemically bonding to the collagen molecules within. Leather is thus rendered essentially immortal, hence the longevity of the motorcycle jacket.

Tannins are also used as mordants, which facilitate the binding of pigment molecules to fibers in dyeing, and as astringents in medicine, and they are added to the mud in drilling operations to increase viscosity. Historically, tannins have been an essential ingredient of ink, which in most large households was homemade up until the eighteenth century. In inks, tannins act to fix the pigment to the paper and to prevent fading. Prime sources of tannins for ink were oak galls, dark warty excrescences of the tree created in response to insect infestations. The galls, in which the tree brings out its heaviest anti-insect ammunition, contain up to 17 percent tannic acid, and were thus much in demand for the ink and dyeing trades. An eleventh-century recipe for black ink, of the sort with which King John eventually and grudgingly signed the Magna Carta, called for "12 lbs of oak galls pounded, 5 lbs of gum pounded, 5 lbs or less of green sulphate of iron, 12 gallons of rain water boiled each day till sufficiently done, letting it settle overnight."

If the verdict has been less than favorable on the acorn, which grows on the oak, human society — or at least its upper crust — has shown almost unanimous enthusiasm for the truffle, which grows under the oak. The truffle — "a rather ugly, but delicious, fungus" — grows anywhere from a couple of inches to a foot underground, near the roots of oak or beech trees. Truffles come in black, brown, gray, purple, and white, and the United States boasts some thirty different varieties, none of them anything to raise a gourmet's blood pressure. The only one of these ever to be exploited commercially is the Oregon white truffle, found through Oregon, Washington, and British Columbia in association with the Douglas fir. Its major drawback is its shelf life — three days, max — which prevents much widespread consumption.

The prizes among truffles come from France, originally from the region of Perigord, where the terms "black diamond" and "black pearl" were coined to describe the delectable black truffle, *Tuber melanosperm*. Henry IV (two wives, six mistresses) attributed his "prowess in the bedroom" to Perigord truffles; Balzac credited them with his creativity; and Napoleon fed them to Josephine in hopes of producing a son. Louis XIV, an irrepressible glutton, supposedly consumed a pound a day.

A craze for truffles swept Paris in the eighteenth century, creating such a gap between demand (voracious) and supply (limited) that truffles were escorted into the city under armed guard. Their already outrageous price skyrocketed and a number of status-conscious nobles beggared themselves in the effort to throw banquets featuring the highly desirable truffled turkey — "a luxury," wrote gastronome Brillat-Savarin, "found only on the tables of the greatest lords and of kept women." The taste for truffles did not trickle down to the lower and more virtuous socioeconomic levels: in 1848, when the pantries of the Tuileries were pillaged by peasants, the truffles were left behind, judged unfit to eat.

Today the top truffle territory in France is the southern province of Quercy — named from the Latin *quercus*, for its truffle-promoting oak trees. Detection of these elusive mushrooms, ranging in size from that of a walnut to that of a tangerine, is a mysterious art, historically the province of pigs, dogs, (female) virgins, Sardinian goats, Russian bear cubs, or simply experienced truffle trackers with highly developed senses of smell. Enterprising farmers have been attempting to establish home truffle plots since at least the nineteenth century, by planting acorns from known "truffle oaks" and hoping — usually futilely — that a *Tuber melanosperm* crop would follow. The impetus for solving the secret of truffle cultivation has increased in recent years, with the decline of the annual truffle haul. The European truffle harvest, which totalled 450 tons in 1925, had dropped to 20 tons in 1986. Beginning in the 1970s, French agronomists have been attempting to combat this decline, by seeding truffle spores in plantations of young oak saplings. Initial results were unexciting: a crop of twenty truffles from seventy-five hundred acres of 150,000 oak seedlings.

Another — oakless — approach to modern truffle production is that of Californian Moshe Shifrine, an immunologist, who has spent the last thirty years researching techniques for raising truffles in petri plates. To date, Shifrine has identified a successful growth medium for infant truffles, and has boosted his laboratory truffle output to sixty pounds per week. Shifrine's test-tube truffles are harvested after only a year's growth, which means that they are tiny; truffles unearthed in the wild have usually spent seven years reaching maturity. Thus they are marketed — under the trade name "La Truffe" — as truffle paste, powder, juice, and oil, but not as whole truffles.

For the present, truffles remain out of reach of the common pocket. Which may be just as well: Pliny, whose attitude toward truffles seems to have been suspicious, wrote, "We know for a fact that when Lartius Licinius, an official of praetorian rank, was serving as Minister of Justice at Cartagena in Spain a few years ago, he happened when biting on a truffle to come on a denarius contained inside it which bent his front teeth. This clearly shows that truffles are lumps of earthy substance balled together."

A final note for oak lovers: poison oak, that maddeningly allergenic native of North America, is no relative of the true oak tree. Named for its oak-like leaves, poison oak (*Rhus toxicodendron*) is a cousin of sumac, poison ivy, the mango, and the cashew. Thomas Jefferson, who may have found reason to regret it, thought it appropriate for planting as ornamental shrubbery.

CHESTNUT

"*U*nder the spreading chestnut tree / The village smithy stands," wrote Henry Wadsworth Longfellow in 1842, which poem — titled "The Village Blacksmith" — was to become what is surely the most quoted verse about chestnut trees in American history. The chestnut tree so immortalized was a real tree, spreading lushly over Brattle Street in the town of Cambridge, Massachusetts. In 1879, thirty-seven years after its entry into literature, the tree was cut down to make way for a widening of the roads in the increasingly urban Boston area, and a chair made from its wood was presented to Mr. Longfellow as a gift on his seventy-second birthday. The chair was later analyzed by a more cynical and less poetic generation, and its wood found to be European horse chestnut.

Ironically, in Longfellow's day, the true American chestnut — *Castanea dentata* — was still in its prime. Of the four chestnut species native to North America, only *C. dentata* was a sizeable tree — eighty feet tall on the average, and four feet or so in diameter — though monsters far exceeding the norm were often found and reported upon. In 1880, the proud citizens of Seymour, Indiana — a town some hundred miles south of Indianapolis — measured a chestnut tree twenty-two feet in girth. A comparable late-nineteenth-century chestnut in the vicinity of New York Harbor was so mammoth it was popularly referred to as "the elephant."

By the time a chestnut is about ten years old, it begins bearing the large sweet nuts for which the tree is named. The scientifically sanctioned *Castanea* derives from the Greek word for chestnut, *kastanon*. Both names, in turn, come from the town of Castan in eastern Thessaly through which, legend has it, the sweet chestnut first entered western Europe. The fruit of the chestnut tree is a fat green bur, off-puttingly studded with sharp porcupine-like spines. The bur splits open spontaneously in the fall to release the two or three mature seeds, ½ to ¾ inch long, spit-polished brown, and usually flattened on one side from the confining pressure inside the protective seed case. In their heyday, these seeds, described as mild, rich, and mouthwateringly sweet, fed a vast range of wildlife, plus a considerable number of people and their associated domestic animals. The Iroquois Indians of New York ground chestnut kernels in wooden bowls, then boiled the crushed nuts in water until the chestnut oil rose to the surface. The oil, carefully skimmed off, was used as a seasoning; the boiled nut meal was dried and pounded into a starchy flour. The European settlers also ate American chestnuts, raw or roasted, and converted them into a flour that was used, among other things, for the brewing of beer.

Thomas Jefferson, usually a proponent of foods American, grew "French chesnuts" at Monticello. He may have used them to stuff his native turkeys, or perhaps served them whole and roasted at the end of formal dinners. It was customary in the late eighteenth century for the aristocratic repast to round off with nuts, fruit, and wine, the chestnuts presented to the replete diners in tureen-shaped porcelain chestnut baskets, topped with pierced lids to allow for escaping steam. Martha Washington's *Booke of Cookery*, a venerable family heirloom by the time Martha acquired it, includes chestnuts in a recipe for mutton pie: "put to yr shread meat a reasonable proportion of chestnuts halfe roasted & about halfe a pound of bacon cut in small pieces." The pie, elegantly described in Martha's *Booke* as a "Pasty Royall," was indeed fit for a king. Along with the "shread meat" — a large leg of mutton's worth — the bacon, and the chestnuts, the Pasty contained sweetbreads and kidneys, "neats tongues slyced," egg yolks, garlic, "mushrumps," "harty choak bottoms, graps, & sparragus," with an option for pickles, oysters, cockles, and sausages. Less elegant is "Possum with Chestnuts," a dish described in Jerry Mack Johnson's *Country Scrapbook* as an "old receipt": it involves skinning and dressing a possum, then stuffing the animal with equal amounts of applesauce, bread crumbs, and chestnuts.

The American chestnut holds the distinction of being the only plant used by an Indian tribe as a specific against whooping cough. The Mohegans reportedly treated the disease with a tea brewed from chestnut leaves, this doubtful remedy said to have been gleaned from the white settlers, who in turn picked it up from an "unknown source." A Dr. C. F. Millspaugh, who wrote a comprehensive guide to American medicinal plants in 1887, defended the chestnut tea technique on the grounds that the extract had a "sedative action on the nerves of respiration" — a scientific theory scotched once and for all in 1942 by the *Dispensatory of the United States*, which deemed it a "superstition." Dried chestnut leaves do contain 9 percent tannic acid, and chestnut teas thus do have some medicinal value as mild astringents.

The chestnut, when the Pilgrims landed, was the most common hardwood forest tree from Maine to the Gulf of Mexico. In Appalachia, three out of five wild trees were chestnuts, and in the last century, 25 percent of all lumber cut from hardwood trees in the East was chestnut. Chestnut is a rich and lovely wood with a pronounced grain, similar in appearance to oak, but browner, without oak's famous golden-yellow tinge. As such it went into panelling and an array of fine and not-so-fine furniture, from cribs and cradles to coffins. Chestnut bark, neatly cut in squares, furnished early pioneer houses and barns with shingles. Chestnut heartwood, remarkably resistant to rot, was a popular choice for such heavy-weather items as fence posts, stable floors, mine timbers, and, eventually, railroad ties and telegraph poles. A good bit of it is still around today and still holding firm: "Today," wrote Ted Williams several years ago in *Yankee* magazine, "chestnut siding from many 18th-century barns smokes under the Skilsaws of those astonished renovators who proclaimed it to be rotten."

The fences in which *C. dentata* figured so prominently were no mean repositories for wood. "Every man must secure his corn and meadow against great cattle," proclaimed a Massachusetts order of 1642, and "if any damage be done by such cattle, it shall be borne by him through whose insufficient fence the cattle did enter." Sufficient fences in the days of colonial settlement took many forms. Earliest perhaps was the stockade fence, a closely packed fortification of towering pointed stakes of the sort that enclosed Jamestown and Plimouth Plantation, and protected the brand-new buildings of Harvard University from encroaching savages. Such structures, however, were for the protection of people rather than crops, and most farmers satisfied themselves with less impressive barriers. Simplest of these was the stump fence, a row of durable chestnut or oak stumps, aligned and upended with their twisted roots in the air, looking, according to one historian, like a "frozen witches' Sabbath." A chestnut stump fence would last over a generation, but the labor involved in erecting it was immense: the stumps had to be dug or chopped out of the field with hand tools, then dragged to the edge of the field by oxen. In general, colonial farmers much preferred to leave their stumps solidly *in situ*, planting their crops around them. Witness the case of the Coventry common. Sometime in the 1820s, the story goes, the Harmon brothers of Coventry, Vermont, donated some land to the village for use as a common, "on the condition that the citizens should clear it of stumps and smooth the surface." No one took it upon himself to do so, so frustrated village officials forced the issue, cannily ruling that anyone publicly becoming "the worse for liquor" should pay for his crime by digging out one stump. The common was cleared in record time, and from then on in the environs of Coventry a pint of rum was considered standard payment for excavating a stump.

Less effortful was some form of the post-and-rail fence, the posts of chestnut or the similarly rot-resistant cedar, the rails of oak or ash. Even easier was the famous snake or worm fence, a zigzag construction of overlapping rails that required no tedious posthole-digging. These typically American structures were viewed askance by foreign visitors — "the most ungraceful-looking things I ever saw," wrote the touring Captain Basil Hall in the 1820s, following his first good look at the worm fences of upstate New York. They also consumed tremendous amounts of wood. On the average, an acre of woodland fell to fence ten acres of farmland. By the 1880s, according to the Iowa Agricultural Report, the United States was crisscrossed by some six million miles of wooden fence, at an estimated cost of $325 per mile. "The stripping of forests to build fortifications around personal property," tartly observed a late-eighteenth-century London newspaper, "is a perfect example of the way those people in the New World live and think."

The demise of the American chestnut, however, was not brought about by the rail-splitter's ax. The once ubiquitous tree was laid low in the early days of this century by *Endothia parasitica*, a devastating parasitic fungus that arrived in this country, according to best retrospective guess, in 1895 with a shipment of Chinese chestnut trees destined for planting in New York's Botanical Garden. The fungus travelled fast. Chestnuts near the Bronx Zoo were dying in 1904; by 1907 trees were biting the dust one hundred miles north, in Poughkeepsie, New York, and one hundred miles south, in Trenton, New Jersey. By the 1920s, *E. parasitica* had shown up in Pennsylvania and Maryland; a decade later it reared its ugly head in Ohio and North Carolina. By the 1940s, the day of the American chestnut was over. *Hortus III*, which describes *C. dentata* as the hardiest of the chestnuts and the producer of the best-quality nuts, now characterizes the species as "almost extinct." The riddled tan-brown wood known as "wormy chestnut," popular for fancy veneers and picture frames, comes from victims of fungal blight. It is all that is left of what — at $700 to $1,000 per thousand board feet — should have been $400 billion worth of chestnut lumber.

E. parasitica, the evil genius behind this botanical blitzkrieg, enters the tree through wounds in the bark and rapidly spreads, zeroing in on the cambium, the sheath of actively dividing cells that encircles the tree trunk. Eventually the fungus begins to ooze out through the bark, producing fruiting bodies — "nasty-looking yellowish pustules" — which swell into curved horns, each capable of spewing out five million spores. Death occurs by starvation. The fungus essentially girdles the tree, cutting off the flow of food.

E. parasitica generally limits its destructive activity to the above-ground portion of the tree, leaving the roots untouched. From the still-active roots, hopeful chestnut sprouts continue to emerge, forming youthful circles around the corpse of the parent tree. They seldom make it through puberty, however, usually succumbing to blight before their fruit-bearing years. Many different trees have the ability to send up shoot "suckers" of this sort from the roots, among them oaks, maples, willows, poplars, and the spectacular giant redwoods of California. The chestnut's ability to reproduce itself in this fashion led the cottagers of Kent in England to cultivate the trees for coppicing (from the old English term *coppice*, meaning a grove of trees maintained for periodic cutting), regularly harvesting the slender saplings to serve as hop poles for the hops that flavored the famous Kentish beer.

An intrepid traveller, *E. parasitica* has also spread to the chestnut trees of Europe, apparently arriving in 1917 in Genoa, Italy, with a shipment of American mine timbers. During the destructive years of World War I, while European botanists were occupied on other fronts, the fungus ran amok among the European chestnut trees. However, while damaging, *E. parasitica* did not manage to obliterate *C. dentata*'s European cousins. Instead, the European trees appeared to develop what is referred to as "field resistance": infected trees recovered from their bouts with the disease and survived. Bark samples from such resistant survivors, first analyzed in the 1960s by French agronomist Jean Grente, revealed a weakened form of the fatal fungus, white in color rather than orange. The white fungus was deemed hypovirulent — less poisonously potent — than the feisty orange version. The hypovirulent fungus is itself infected with a molecule of double-stranded RNA, presumably a virus. It is not known where this virus came from or how it spreads, though there is some evidence that it travels via asexual fungal spores called *conidia.* Some researchers hope that this hypovirulent fungus with its debilitating viral partner may be a case of two evils cancelling each other out — a microscopic version of Jonathan Swift's verse:

> *So, naturalists observe, a flea*
> *Hath smaller fleas that on him prey;*
> *And these have smaller still to bite 'em;*
> *And so proceed ad infinitum.*

White fungus has "cured" American chestnut trees in controlled laboratory experiments, and in a few scattered locations — Michigan, West Virginia, Tennessee — isolated stands of mature living chestnut trees carrying the hypovirulent strain of fungus have been identified. Such trees are often no longer the soaring and militarily erect chestnuts known to our grandparents. Struggle with near-terminal disease shows: often recovered trees bulge with wound tissue surrounding former sites of fungal infection. The trees, like victims of elephantiasis, are swollen and grotesque, but indisputably alive. With luck, chestnut experts state, hypovirulent *E. parasitica* may be the American chestnut's ticket to survival.

The European sweet chestnut, the tree that gave chestnut blight a run for its money, is scientifically termed *Castanea sativa. C. sativa* bears sweet nuts, which, though reasonably tasty, are markedly less flavorful than the lost nuts of *C. dentata*. These are the imported chestnuts that appear on supermarket shelves at Christmastime, to be roasted, if not on an open fire, at least on cookie sheets in an electric oven. Usually these are called Spanish chestnuts, but most actually come from Italy, today the world's top chestnut producer, with 1.7 million acres of chestnut trees yielding an annual six thousand metric tons of nuts.

C. sativa is mentioned in the Bible — Jacob, still on the farm after working his seven plus seven years for Rachel, put chestnut "rods" in the barnyard water trough to make his livestock fertile. The Romans are credited with cultivating the chestnut and distributing it all over Europe in the wake of their burgeoning Empire. One reputedly Roman-planted tree in Sicily — known as the "chestnut of a hundred horses" because of its gargantuan girth — survived until

1850 and was still producing nuts when it was destroyed by volcanic eruption. The famous plan of the Benedictine monastery of St. Gall, established around A.D. 820, included elaborate gardens and orchards, with plots specifically blocked off for chestnut trees, along with apples, pears, plums, quinces, almonds, hazelnuts, walnuts, service trees, bay trees, peaches, mulberries, and figs. English household accounts of the twelfth and thirteenth centuries record deliveries of immense quantities of chestnuts, and the romantic garden of the "Romaunt de la Rose" — a popular French poem of the late thirteenth century, translated into English by Geoffrey Chaucer — featured chestnuts:

> *And many hoomly trees ther were,*
> *That peaches, coynes [quinces], and apples, bere.*
> *Medlars, ploumes, peres, chesteynes . . .*

Medieval chateaux were built with chestnut beams, reportedly because spiders will not spin webs on chestnut wood, which thus saved the medieval servant the next-to-impossible task of sweeping cobwebs off a fifty-foot ceiling.

"Chestnuts of all wilde nuts are the best and meetest to be eaten," wrote William Langham in *Garden of Health*, a natural-foods tome of 1577. Chestnuts were a common treat in Shakespearean England: the three witches in *Macbeth* stirred up a storm at sea because a sailor's wife rudely refused to share hers. Similarly they were a popular treat across the Channel in seventeenth-century France, where the playwright Molière (1622-1673) was the first to speak warningly of pulling one's chestnuts out of the fire.

The French, according to food historian Waverley Root, distinguish two forms of edible chestnut: the *châtaigne*, a small, inferior nut, usually fed to animals, ground to make chestnut flour, or consumed by very hungry people during time of famine, and the far tastier *marron*, Molière's roasting chestnut. The *marron* was the chestnut of the upper-class table, eaten raw or roasted, in chestnut stuffings, or as *marrons glacés*, elaborately candied chestnuts.

Preparation of the traditional *marrons glacés* involves sixteen separate steps, the process reportedly developed sometime during the reign of Louis XIV, to feed the Sun King's sweet tooth.

Châtaignes were less elegant fare. Before the days of potato promoter Jean Parmentier, chestnuts served as the staple food of the poorer peasantry. Today that nourishing but unexciting fare is immortalized in the phrase "jeuner à l'eau et à la châtaigne" ("to dine on water and chestnuts") — the French equivalent of our rockbottom menu of bread and water. On the island of Corsica, birthplace of Napoleon and home of the poorest of the French poor, chestnuts historically have played such a central part in the regional diet that the chestnut tree has been dubbed the "Corsican bread tree." Napoleon's somewhat unreliable memoir of the Corsican revolt of 1774 (the great man was five years old at the time) describes the establishment's battle plan: "Somebody proposed the singular plan of cutting down or burning all the chestnut trees, whose fruit was the food of the mountaineers: 'You'll force them to come to the plains to beg for pease and bread.'" According to Waverley Root, the current Corsican expression "They eat out of the drawer," which describes penny-pinching grocery shoppers, harks back to the old days of deprivation, when wild chestnuts, gathered in the woods, were spread out to dry in bureau drawers.

Home-grown chestnuts in the United States these days are generally Chinese. The Chinese chestnut, *C. mollissima*, is resistant to chestnut blight, and as such has been much crossed with *C. dentata* in attempts to produce a blight-free, sweet-nutted hybrid. The Chinese trees are smaller than the late lamented American chestnut, and multiply boled, as opposed to *C. dentata*'s single straight pillar-like trunk. Judicious hybrid selection has in many cases, however, provided chestnut-growers with the best of both worlds: blightless timber-type trees with tasty nuts. Prominent among the Chinese-American successes is the optimistically named 'Revival' chestnut, the first chestnut in America to receive a plant patent from the United States government. 'Revival' boasts among its forebears both *C. mollissima* and a remarkable American chestnut specimen, stumbled upon in 1953 by an observant Ohioan named James Carpenter while out pheasant-hunting. Carpenter's chestnut was a mature and eye-catchingly healthy tree, towering in lonely magnificence over a grove full of the blighted bodies of its relatives. Carpenter, impressed, collected nuts and scionwood from his tree and shipped them off to Robert Dunstan. Dunstan, a North Carolina professor of linguistics, was also an amateur horticulturist; his hobby had earlier led to the first successful mating of French wine grapes with American muscadines. His 'Revival' chestnut has to date shown no trace of blight infection and bears consistent annual crops of massive nuts.

Essentially inedible — without herculean preparative proce-dures — are the nuts of the European horse chestnut, *Aesculus hippocastanum*, Longfellow's famous tree. The designation "horse" is said to denote coarse and unpalatable, unfit for human consump-tion. (Perversely, in the Victorian language of flowers, horse chestnut blooms were held to symbolize luxury.) Alternatively, the "horse" moniker may come from the unusual shape of the leaf scar left on the branch after the leaf has fallen: horseshoe-shaped and complete with small circular markings reminiscent of nail holes. Or, according to tree expert Alan Mitchell, the name may have been applied by the ancient Greeks, who reportedly used the seeds to cure coughing in horses.

The European horse chestnut is a popular shade tree in the United States, grown from Salem, Massachusetts, to Santa Fe, New Mexico, appearing in Salt Lake City and in New York's Central Park. It's a glorious tree in spring, producing foot-tall pyramidal clusters of white flowers splotched with yellow at the base — the "chestnut flambeaux" of the A. E. Housman poem. The flowers at the top of the pyramid are entirely male, the protruding stamens tipped with red pollen; the flowers at the bottom are kinkily bisexual, possessing both stamens and pistils. Following pollination — by bees — and fertilization, the flowers turn orange and then crimson before the petals fall. The seeds that result from fertilization are a seductively gleaming mahogany color, enclosed in prickly green husks.

Horse chestnut wood is creamy-white to pale yellow and has the ability to crack or fracture without generating vicious splinters. For this reason — splinterlessness — it traditionally has been the wood of choice for artificial limbs. Long John Silver's peg leg was most likely whittled from horse chestnut, and chances are that the sound of horse chestnut prostheses clumping along the pavement led to the late-nineteenth-century expression "lame as a tree," which meant badly crippled. For the same reason — clean splinterless breaks — the horse chestnut tree can be particularly lethal to shelter under during storms. Large branches have a tendency to crack off neatly at the base and abruptly plummet to the ground.

The American alter ego of Europe's horse chestnut is the buckeye — so-named for its nuts, dark brown with a whitish spot, resembling the eye of a deer. The buckeyes include some fifteen different species of trees and shrubs. Most grow east of the Rockies; one, the California buckeye (*A. californica*) is native to the west coast. Alan Mitchell describes this last as an "odd little tree" of the California coastal mountains and the Sierra foothills, characterized by scaly pinkish gray bark and five-fingered compound leaves that turn a bizarre black in fall. The large seeds are borne in pear-shaped pinkish brown fruits and were eaten "after considerable preparation" by the local Indians. The considerable preparation is required to rid the nuts of *aesculin,* a bitter and poisonous substance that has found some modern use, one authority states dauntingly, as a fish stupefier. Bookbinders have favored a paste made from aesculin-impregnated buckeye starch because it is shunned by book-nibbling insects; and depressed members of at least one California tribe ate the nuts in the untreated state to commit suicide. The detoxification process involved roasting the nuts in a pit lined with hot stones for up to ten hours, then shelling and thinly slicing them, and placing them in a container in running water for up to five days. The nuts are highly nutritious, containing about 23 percent protein, which made all this trouble worthwhile.

Perhaps best known of the American horse chestnuts is *A. glabra,* the Ohio buckeye. Though the designated state tree of Ohio (the Buckeye State, "With God, All Things Are Possible"), *A. glabra* has a wide range outside Ohio boundaries, from Pennsylvania to Tennessee, and from Iowa south to Arkansas. The country's largest Ohio buckeye, perversely, is found in Kentucky. (Ohio, in retaliation, boasts the biggest Kentucky coffeetree.) Only Ohioans, however, are popularly referred to as "Buckeyes," a nickname that, legend has it, originated with the local Indians in the late eighteenth century. In 1788, the story goes, to celebrate the opening of the first court in the Northwest Territory, a parade was held, headed by the High Sheriff, with drawn sword, mounted on a white horse. The effect was so impressive that Indian spectators began referring to the sheriff as "Hetuck" or "Big Buckeye," a name soon stretched to encompass other important Ohioans. Among subsequent Big Buckeyes was William Henry Harrison, the ninth president of the United States, whose bid for election in 1840 involved the distribution of walking sticks made of buckeye wood as campaign emblems. Harrison, sadly, made little show as president. His was the shortest term in American history: he died after only thirty days in office, of pneumonia contracted while delivering his inaugural address, without an overcoat, in the chilly Washington March.

Buckeye wood, which does not split easily, was used in whole-log form to build midwestern cabins and, hollowed out, to fashion cradles and troughs. More extensive use may have been precluded by the unpleasant smell of the bruised bark — nasty enough to earn the epithet "fetid" or "stinking" buckeye. Barkless, and presumably nonodoriferous, buckeye shavings were used to weave summer hats, to shade those Buckeyes at work in the cornfields. The nuts were believed to have medicinal virtue: a buckeye carried in the pocket, legend held, would cure — or at least alleviate — rheumatism. C. F. Millspaugh, whose view of American medicinal plants seems to have been a bit sanguine, touted the buckeye nut as a narcotic — "10 grains are equal to 3 grains of opium" — a claim so far unsubstantiated by modern science. The Indians are said to have used the pulverized nuts by mixing them with fat as a remedy for hemorrhoids.

Early Ohio farm wives used buckeye nut kernels to make a "vegetable soap" for doing the family laundry. A number of different plants yield such soap-like substances, capable of foaming up when shaken with water. Chemically known as *saponins*, these substances are closely related in molecular structure to steroid hormones. Most publicized of the saponins is certainly *diosgenin*, extracted from two Central American species of yam, and used to synthesize the active principal of the birth control pill. For soap seekers, the prime source of saponin historically was *Saponaria officinalis*, the pink-flowered herb commonly known as Bouncing Bet. More suds-oriented alternative names include soapwort, scourwort, fuller's grass — from its medieval use by fullers for soaping newly woven woollen cloth — foam dock, and My Lady's Washing Bowl. It was also referred to, far less accurately, as world's wonder, from its supposed ability to alleviate poison ivy and syphilis. Soapwort-derived saponin is a far gentler product than true soap and its use is periodically resurrected nowadays for such painfully delicate cleaning jobs as the washing of museum tapestries. Horse chestnut nuts — colloquially known as "conkers" — contain up to 5 percent saponin, and were thus satisfying sources of soap for midwestern housewives. During World War II, horse-chestnut-derived saponins were used as foaming agents in anti-Blitz fire extinguishers.

Despite the similarity of their names, the chestnut and the horse chestnut are not closely related. The horse chestnuts are members of the small (two genera) Horse Chestnut family, *Hippocastanaceae*. The true chestnuts are members of the more populous (six genera) Beech family, *Fagaceae*, along with the beeches, the oaks, and the chinquapins (or chinkapins). Chinquapin, from an Algonquian word referring to the edible nuts, is a somewhat confusing designation, as are many names botanical. The true chinquapins, according to *Hortus III*, differ from the true chestnuts in having furry shoots and leaves — a condition referred to by the inhuman *Hortus* as *tomentose* — and in bearing only a single nut in each spiny seed case. At least one chinquapin is officially a chestnut, *Castanea pumila*, a smallish tree found anywhere from Pennsylvania south to Florida and Texas.

Its sweet nuts — 45 percent starch, 2.5 percent protein — are edible, and at least one Indian tribe, the Cherokees, used a solution of steeped chinquapin leaves as an external wash to treat chills and fevers. Non-chestnut chinquapins belong to the genus *Castanopsis*, the major American representative of which, the giant chinquapin (*C. chrysophylla*) of the west coast, is considered a botanical link between the chestnuts and the oaks.

A chestnut, of no expressed species, has been defined as a stale story or outworn jest since the 1880s, according to Eric Partridge's *Dictionary of Slang* — a meaning conferred, linguistic authorities hypothesize, with respect to a too-much-repeated funny story featuring a chestnut tree. Nobody nowadays remembers what it was.

BEECH

$\mathcal{U}$p until 1916 a tree survived in Washington County, Tennessee, bearing the carved inscription "D Boone cilled a bar on tree in year 1760." The "D Boone" was the then twenty-six-year-old Daniel, frontiersman extraordinaire, who topped off his adventurous career by hiking from Defiance, Missouri, to the future site of Yellowstone Park at the age of eighty-five; the "bar" was almost certainly the American black bear (*Ursus americanus*). The tree was *Fagus grandifolia*, the American beech. The beeches, first cousins to the oaks and chestnuts, include some ten species, seven or so native to eastern Asia, two to Europe, and one, *F. grandifolia*, to North America. All are distinguished from other members of their family *(Fagaceae)* by their flowers — the male or staminate flowers are borne in yellow-green clusters dangling from long stems, rather than on furrily cylindrical catkins; the female or pistillate flowers bloom in pairs on short stalks.

To most casual observers, however, the crucial beech feature is the smooth pearl-gray bark. Beech bark is thin — seldom more than half an inch thick — stretchy, and smooth, covering the tree's trunk and branches like skin. This very smoothness has been, for centuries, an almost irresistible temptation to man toting a pocket-knife. In classical times, Roman couples cut their initials in the bark of *F. sylvatica*, the European beech — a custom attested to by the surviving Latin proverb "Crescent illae; crescetis amores," or "As these letters grow, so may our love." Shakespearean lovers did the same, a practice immortalized by the Bard himself in *As You Like It* when Orlando, wandering through the Forest of Arden, penknife presumably in hand, rhapsodizes to his beloved, "O Rosalind! these trees shall be my books, / And in their barks my thoughts I'll character." It has been, in fact, suggested that *book* and *beech* have a common linguistic origin. The earliest *buches* of northern Europe are said to have been the smooth boles of beech trees upon which the early literati scratched inscriptions. The term eventually expanded to encompass more portable forms of literature. Such arboreal record-keeping is made possible by the rapid formation of wound cork, the tree's equivalent of the scab that forms over human skinned knees. Tears, cuts, or incisions in the bark are quickly sealed over by the cork cambium, leaving distinctive scars visible for decades or even, in the case of the beech tree, centuries.

Historic beech trees are often so designated because of their accompanying graffiti. The Presidents' Tree of Takoma Park, Maryland, for example, is so named for its incised list of all the presidents' names from George Washington to Andrew Johnson (plus, in a prophetic P.S., Lt. General Ulysses S. Grant), along with the autograph of the carver, Samuel Fenton. Fenton was reportedly stationed in the Washington area with the Union forces deployed to protect the Capitol during the Civil War. The assignment, apparently, was not a busy one. Another such tree is the Old Benchmark Beech near Covington, Louisiana, an old boundary marker with two centuries' worth of surveyors' notations carved on its gray bark. Mississippi boasts the Union Beech, near Michigan City, adorned with the names, initials, and regimental numbers of bored Yankees stationed at the local federal garrison.

The scientific name for the beech genus, *Fagus*, comes from the Greek *phagus*, meaning "to eat." The edible parts of the beech tree are the nuts, small sweet triangular morsels enclosed, in pairs or triplets, in a spiny bur. The bur splits open on its own in October, releasing its tasty contents. The kernels, up to 22 percent protein, were an important inclusion in the diet of many Indian tribes, and some tribes also valued the nuts for their oil content. At 50 percent fat, the nuts could be pressed for cooking oil, long-lasting and slow to develop rancidity. The early settlers fattened their Thanksgiving turkeys and their hogs on beechnuts. (The proverbial fondness of hogs for beechnuts may be why A. A. Milne provided his Piglet with a home in a beech tree in the children's classic *Winnie-the-Pooh*.) The settlers also roasted and ground beechnuts to prepare what surely must have been an abysmal coffee substitute, and occasionally mashed, dried, and ground the kernels to make a flour, which was used in combination with cereal grain-based flours in bread-making. The nuts were eaten either raw or roasted, despite food historian Waverley Root's lukewarm endorsement: "edible for man, who usually leaves it to the animals." At least some portion of the population must have found them delectable, however — enough so that a burgeoning business founded in Canajoharie, New York, in 1891, as a purveyor of hams and bacon, adopted the name Beech-Nut Company as indicative of tasty succulence. (The tasty and succulent Beech-Nut gum was added to their inventory in 1911.) Medicinally, the Indians used a decoction of beech leaves as a frostbite remedy, the preparation plastered over the afflicted body part. The pioneers used beech leaves to stuff their mattresses, in preference to straw, which rapidly became brittle and musty-smelling.

The late passenger pigeons positively doted on beechnuts, which they consumed at the rate of half a pint of nuts per pigeon per day. Total beechnut consumption is difficult to calculate since no one is certain how big the original passenger pigeon population was. Early explorers agree that it was awesomely large: William Wood spoke of "Millions of Millions"; Jacques Cartier of "countless myriads"; Samuel de Champlain of "countless numbers." Audubon, in the course of his bird-painting expeditions, saw a flight of pigeons in Kentucky that lasted three full days in undiminished numbers. Roosting pigeons, piling on top of each other several birds deep, accumulated in such numbers that they broke the branches off trees. Later they were equally destructive to telegraph wires. Boastful pioneers, aiming randomly into the bird-filled sky, recorded downing up to 132 pigeons with a single shot. Pigeons were so ubiquitous that they formed a major part of the colonial diet, variously roasted, smoked, salted, dried, or pickled in apple cider. Some people ate pigeon morning, noon, and night, a practice leading to a superstition in nineteenth-century Ontario that pigeon-eating caused cholera. Peter Kalm, who observed "incredible flocks" in upstate New York, deemed pigeon "the most palatable of any bird's flesh I have ever tasted." Some Indian tribes, nonetheless, are said to have shunned pigeon in favor of skunk.

Modern ornithologists put the probable pigeon population of sixteenth-century America at three to five billion. Such numbers, at a guess, would have consumed somewhere between twenty-six and forty-three billion bushels of nuts and seeds each day. Beechnuts took top place on the hungry passenger pigeon's food list, followed by acorns, chestnuts, elm seeds, birch catkins, wild black cherries, rose hips, berries — and eventually, cultivated grains. The vast forests of pre-Pilgrim America were a paradise for pigeons. Prince Maximilian von Wied Neuwied, gamely touring the Midwest in the summer of 1833, commented on the beech forests: "the most splendid forests I had yet seen in America" — and as a homesick afterthought, added that they reminded him of the scenery back home in Germany. The cutting of the forests by pioneer farmers is believed to have been a factor in the demise of the pigeon, combined with overhunting and the pigeons' own specialized habits. Like the depleted buffalo, the passenger pigeons were highly social creatures, unable, scientists hypothesize, to survive in the increasingly smaller flocks. The final passenger pigeon, named Martha after Martha Washington, died in the summer of 1914. Now stuffed and displayed in the Smithsonian, she's the only glimpse most of us will ever have of the vanished five billions known to early observers as "blue meteors."

The American beech, more resilient than the pigeons, survived the depredations of the pioneers. An elegant, attractive, and ornamental tree, it reaches — eventually — heights of over one hundred feet and makes, for those lucky enough to have a great-grandfather who planted one, an exceptional shade tree. The European beech (*F. sylvatica*), though in the opinion of some tree connoisseurs a darker, coarser, and aesthetically inferior production, was one of the earliest imported tree species established in the American colonies — most likely because the settlers were familiar with the qualities and uses of the home-style beech wood. Several cultivars of the European beech are grown now as ornamentals, among them the copper (or purple) beech, named 'Purpurea,' whose "variously muddy brownish black purple foliage," writes Alan Mitchell, manifestly not a fan of copper beeches, "disfigure[s] so many garden landscapes." The copper beech first came to public notice in Switzerland in the 1680s. European beech cultivars, like sneakers, are available in a wide range of shapes, sizes, and colors, among them the fastigate beech, 'Fastigiata,' a svelte pillar-like tree whose branches grow almost vertically upright like those of the Lombardy poplar; and the weeping beech, 'Pendula,' whose branches droop dismally toward the ground. There is also a fountain-shaped beech ('Borneyensis') and a bizarre twisted beech with corkscrew-like branches appropriately called 'Tortuosa.'

The classical beech leaf is about four inches long (up to six inches in the heftier American species, hence *grandifolia*, "large-leaved"), and elliptical, with paired veins and toothed edges — resembling, says one mnemonic-minded author, the waves on a "beach." The generic leaf is green (yellow in the fall), but more creative beeches produce purple or copper-red leaves, purple leaves daintily edged with pink, green-and-white spotted leaves edged with pink, and green-and-yellow variegated leaves. There is a plumply round-leaved beech ('Rotundifolia') and a fern-leaf beech ('Laciniata'), the leaves with deeply scalloped lobes.

Beech is a moderately hard reddish wood, compared by some to sycamore (but less prone to splitting) and by some to maple (but lighter). Blue beech, traditionally one of the strongest woods available to American carpenters, is not a beech at all, but a hornbeam (*Carpinus caroliniana*), a member of the Birch family. The common name derives from its smooth bluish gray beech-like bark; its legendary toughness gave it a second nickname: American iron-wood. True beech wood was traditionally used for making chair and table legs in Europe and colonial America. In southern England, craftspersons known as "bodgers" spent summer and autumn camped in the beech forests carving vast stockpiles of chair legs.

Beech was never a popular wood for major construction, since it has a marked tendency to warp during seasoning, but, as an odorless and tasteless wood, it was commonly used for food containers. As such it was the province of the white cooper, who specialized in small household pieces — butter tubs, buckets, nested boxes, churns — variously made of beech, pine, maple, birch, and hickory. The white cooper also turned out the ubiquitous rum kegs, or "rundlets," so-named from an old English measure, equalling about eighteen modern gallons. Larger containers for liquids — whiskey barrels and cider casks — were made by the wet or tight cooper, who used white oak; barrels for dry goods — flour, sugar, grain — were made by the dry or slack cooper, whose woods were red oak, chestnut, maple, hickory, ash, and occasionally elm.

Beech has little resistance to rot if left in contact with the soil, so was at the bottom of the list for fence posts. However, it wears well and takes on a high polish, according to the sages of the American Forestry Association, when "subjected to friction underwater" — a physical phenomenon that occurs, for example, when wood floors are scrubbed down with a stiff brush. According to *A Book of Country Things* — Walter Needham's nostalgic story of his Vermont grandfather, born in 1833, and a "one-man education" in self-reliance — beech was the nineteenth-century wood of choice for anything that took a great deal of scouring, like a threshold, or, in fact, for anything subject to frequent friction, like the soles of clogs or the wooden bodies of carpenter's planes.

A beech tree planted near a house, one story holds, will protect that dwelling place from lightning — a superstition with at least a dribble of truth in it since beech trees are struck by lightning statistically less often than other species. The reason for this is believed to be the high oil content of the beech tree trunk.

In the Victorian language of flowers, beech boughs, for no discernible reason, stood for prosperity.

MAPLE

*D*uring the early years of the 1970s, a good many New England maples crossed the Pacific Ocean in response to the Japanese bowling alley boom. The trees that furnished lanes and pins for the neophyte bowlers of Tokyo were sugar maples, *Acer saccharum*, also known, for their notable strength and hardness, as rock maples. Including the sugar maple, there are thirteen maple species native to the continent of North America, and some two hundred in existence worldwide. The Roman legions toted spears and lances made from maple wood; medieval magicians recommended maple as the material of choice for skewering the hearts of vampires. The early American colonists, more prosaically, preferred maple for small housewares: rolling pins, bread boards, butter prints and molds, ladles, spoons, and chopping bowls. Cobblers used maple lasts and cabinetmakers prized it for furniture, especially for chairs.

Much of colonial woodenware — or "treenware," from the old-fashioned plural of tree — was whittled from the wood of *Acer saccharum*, today still the chief source of commercial maple wood. It's an imposing tree, reaching heights of up to 130 feet, and is found anywhere from Nova Scotia west to Minnesota, and south through Missouri into the mountains of Tennessee and North Carolina. Its seeds are borne in pairs, in a form commonly known as a maple key, and formally as a double samara. The samara, ordinarily a single-seeded winged fruit, contains two seeds if manufactured by a maple tree, and is shaped roughly like a sagging airplane propeller. The sugar maple leaf, generally taken as the prototype for the entire maple family, is three-lobed, irregularly toothed, and four to six inches wide. Colored red, it's the emblem of Canada.

The sugar maple shares portions of its generous range with the black maple (*A. nigrum*), which, if not exactly coal black, is at least darker than the sugar maple; the silver maple (*A. saccharinum*), which has silvery-bottomed leaves; the red maple (*A. rubrum*), which bears clusters of bright-red flowers in early spring; and the striped maple (*A. pensylvanicum*), which has gray-and-white striped bark.

The striped maple bears the distinction of a misspelled scientific name: Linnaeus, busily speciating trees in 1753, plumped for too few *n*'s in *Penn*. The striped maple is also called the moosewood, because moose like to munch on its sappily sweet branches; the whistlewood, because the young bark slips easily off the twigs, the better for the making of whistles; and the goosefoot maple, because of the flipperlike shape of its leaves. More formally, it is considered one of the snakebark maples, some twenty species of smallish (under thirty-five feet tall) trees. All, except the striped maple, are natives of China or Japan; *A. pensylvanicum*, geologists hypothesize, was stranded on our shores following the separation of the continental plates. Along with its isolated habitat and mangled moniker, the striped maple features unusual leaves. The largest of any of the maples, these three-lobed dark-green leaves measure some nine inches long by eight inches wide, over twice the size of the leaves of its better-known relative, the sugar maple.

While the eastern half of the United States holds the monopoly on North American maples, there are a couple of notable westerners. Among them is the Rocky Mountain maple (*A. glabrum*), a smallish tree ranging from Montana and South Dakota south to Arizona. A variant form of this tree, the Douglas maple, grows even further west, found from southern Alaska southward into Washington and Oregon. It was the bark and wood of this tree from which the Thompson Indians of British Columbia prepared a decoction reportedly effective at curing the nausea "brought on by the odor of a corpse." The

West also boasts the ashleaf maple or boxelder (*A. negundo*), a tree whose "extraordinary native range" covers the country from New York to California, with side trips into Mexico and Guatemala. The ashleaf maple, true to its name, is characterized by strikingly un-maple-like leaves, each composed of three, five, or seven variously lobed individual leaflets. The western Indians were said to make sugar from the sap of the boxelder, which generates more sap than any other species of maple.

Three states, all with resounding mottoes, claim the sugar maple as their state tree: Vermont ("Freedom & Unity"), New York ("Ever Upward"), and Wisconsin ("Forward"), while the more modest Rhode Island ("Hope") claims an unspecified general-purpose maple. Historic maple trees abound. The town of Livermore, Maine, boasts the Seven Brothers Maples, a stately assortment of trees planted in the early 1800s by Israel and Martha Washburn, one for each of their seven sons. The seven sons so commemorated all grew up to become startlingly successful: four became congressmen (Cadwallader from Wisconsin, Elihu from Illinois, William from Minnesota, and Israel from the home state of Maine), and two served terms as state governors. During the Civil War, one was a major general in the (Union) army and one a captain in the (Union) navy. One was Secretary of State under Ulysses S. Grant, and two were appointed foreign ministers, to France and Paraguay.

A number of sugar maples survive from the Holy Grove in Coventry, Connecticut, planted in 1812 in front of the Nathan Hale homestead by Nathan's brother, David; three sugar maples survive in the Sacred Grove near Palmyra, New York, where Joseph Smith, the twenty-year-old founder of the Church of Jesus Christ of the Latter-Day Saints, had his first encounter with the angel Moroni. An immense sugar maple at Monticello is one of the five surviving trees on the estate planted by Thomas Jefferson — a sight that would have delighted the heart of that perennially youthful gardener, who wrote wistfully from Washington to his sixteen-year-old granddaughter, Anne Cary Randolph, in 1807: "I never before knew the full value of trees. My house is entirely embosomed in high plain trees, with good grass below, and under them I breakfast, dine, write, read and receive my company. What would I not give that the trees planted nearest round the house at Monticello were full grown."

What first leaps to mind at the word "maple" is the thought of colored leaves — the scarlets, crimsons, oranges, and yellows for which all displaced New Englanders grow homesick in the autumn. The average sugar maple, according to one authority, has about 160,000 leaves; the average apple tree 50,000 to 100,000; and the average oak 700,000. Each of these leaves consists of a *blade* (the broad, flat part, susceptible to chewing by pests), a *petiole* (the tough green stem connecting the leaf to the branch), a *midrib* (the backbone-like extension of the petiole which runs up the center of the blade to the leaf tip), and a number of *veins*, which are leaf-sized versions of the food- and water-carrying xylem and phloem tubes of the trunk and roots.

Since the leaf's purpose in life is to bask in the sun — dendrologist Brayton Wilson compares a tree to "a tower bearing many small solar collectors" — the arrangement of leaves on trees is more than a matter of sheer luck. Trees are intimidatingly mathematical constructs, branches, twigs, and leaves positioned at precise intervals and extended at consistent angles such that the leaves — like sun bunnies at Jones Beach — end up with the greatest possible number of bodies soaking up the highest possible concentration of rays. The cleverly aligned result is called a *leaf mosaic*. Nature, being what she is, has more than one method of accomplishing such a leaf mosaic. Maples, like horse chestnuts, ashes, and dogwoods, favor an opposite arrangement of leaves: symmetrical pairs of leaves grow out at the same height on the twig, exactly opposite each other. Most other trees — among them oaks, elms, apples, poplars, cherries, and beeches — position their leaves in ascending spirals, like the stripes that climb a barber pole. Spiralling leaves emerge in singletons rather than pairs, each positioned a partial turn around the branch from its successor. The precise degree of this partial turn varies with type of tree. Elm leaves spiral up the branch at 180-degree intervals, which means that every other leaf is directly aligned. Oak and apple leaves

49

spiral at 144-degree intervals, which means that every sixth leaf is aligned, or that it takes six leaves to make a complete turn around the branch. The tightly packed holly spirals at 135-degree intervals, which means that it takes eight leaves to make a complete turn.

Leaf shapes, for all the attention paid to them in the tree identification handbooks, are not as varied as one might think. Richard Ketchum in *The Secret Life of the Forest* manages to represent all of the twelve hundred species of North American forest trees with a mere fifty-five leaves. The acknowledged oddest of the bunch is the fan-shaped leaf of the gingko or maidenhair tree (*Gingko biloba*), which, strictly speaking, shouldn't even be in the running since it is not a North American tree but an import from China. Second place on the odd list may be the sassafras (*Sassafras albidum*), which produces three different styles of leaves all on the same tree. All these fifty-five shapes of leaves share a common function: using sunlight, carbon dioxide, and water, the leaves manufacture the sugars used by the tree to pack on its annual three to four tons of wood per acre of forest. The process, called *photosynthesis*, proceeds best at around 70 degrees F., becoming less efficient at higher temperatures. Trees, like people, become lazier in the dog days.

Photosynthesis also slows at cooler temperatures and eventually cuts off altogether in the colder, drier, and shorter days of fall. The primary signal for the appearance of the glorious leaf colors that most of us associate with autumn is *photoperiod*: as day length decreases, trees begin shutting down for the winter. Pre-winter shutdown hits the leaves first. With the decline of daylight, chlorophyll molecules in the leaf blade begin to break down and disperse; with the disappearance of chlorophyll's overwhelming green, previously hidden colors begin to appear. It is these sequestered pigments, stored within the leaf cells in specialized organelles called *plastids*, that allow deciduous foliage to go out with a visual bang rather than a whimper. The yellows and oranges of birches, sycamores, and sugar maples are due to a class of pigments called *carotenoids*, the same cheerful molecules that color carrots, corn, egg yolks, and daffodils. Browns also may result from carotenoids — which after a few days of gaudy spectacle gradually go dull — or from tannins. Crimsons, scarlets, and purples are due to *anthocyanins*, which also color red cabbages, red roses, and purple irises.

The anthocyanins are chemical chameleons, changing color with the pH of the environment. In an acid environment, such as that of the red maple leaf, anthocyanin turns scarlet; in an alkaline environment, such as that of the ash leaf, anthocyanin turns plum-colored. Because of this behavior, anthocyanin-containing red cabbage makes a fine, though sloppy, pH indicator. Grate the cabbage into water to cover and let stand until you have a pinkish solution of cabbage juice. Strain to remove the grated cabbage leaves. Then add an acid — a squirt of lemon juice, for example — and the cabbage juice will turn red; add a base — a spoonful of alkaline baking soda, for example — and the juice will turn purple-blue.

The disappearance of chlorophyll is enforced by the formation of an abscission layer at the base of the petiole, where the leaf is attached to the twig. The abscission layer acts as a tourniquet, shutting off the supply of water and minerals to the leaf blade. Deprived of water, leaf activity grinds to a halt, and chlorophyll — which in the healthy leaf must be continually replenished and re-newed — quickly bites the dust. Chlorophyll destruction and its spectacularly colorful aftereffects attract thousands of leaf lookers to New England each autumn. The color display, which sweeps south at a rate of about forty miles per day, is even visible from outer space as a continental swathe of scarlet and gold.

The show lasts three weeks or so, and then fades. Eventually the abscission layer begins to dry and separate, until the leaf's hold on the parent tree becomes so tenuous that the least wind breaks it. The leaf then falls, along with its 160,000 companions, to the ground. Just below the snap-off point on the twig, a leaf scar forms, a plug of wound cork that seals off the tubes carrying water from the main tree trunk.

While the chemistry of changing fall leaf color seems straight-forward enough, some botanists, unable to leave well enough alone, have wondered why leaves are green in the first place. "It's not love that makes the world go round," writes British plant physiologist Andrew Goldsworthy, "it's photosynthesis." Given this, he continues, for organisms that rely on the absorption of light to fuel their inner workings, plants are shamefully wasteful. Plants look green because their primary pigment, chlorophyll, absorbs light only at the red and blue ends of the spectrum and reflects everything in the middle, which is mostly green. The ideal photosynthetic pigment should be a dismal black, efficiently absorbing all available light and reflecting next to nothing. The closest the natural world comes to the ideal black plant is the deepwater red algae. Red algae contain the pigments *phycocyanin* and *allophycocyanin*, which absorb light in the orange portion of the spectrum, and substantial amounts of a red pigment, *phycoerythrin*, which absorbs green. Due to its submarine distance from sunlight, the red algae need to use what light they get as efficiently as possible. Land plants, which generally get plenty of sunlight, are under no such selective pressure and so have no problems remaining insouciantly green.

But why green in the first place? The answer, according to Goldsworthy, comes from a primitive photosynthetic bacterium, *Halobacterium halobium*, a bizarre denizen of salt lakes, where it survives in salt concentrations up to five times that of seawater. *Halobacterium* carries embedded in its cell membrane a purple pigment called *bacteriorhodopsin*, a close chemical relative of the light-sensing pigment *rhodopsin* that transmits images to the retina of the human eye. The bacteriorhodopsin absorbs light energy from the broad green band in the middle of the spectrum, and *Halobacterium* then uses this energy supply to swim and to ingest food. Such primitive bacteria, wriggling their way through the primeval oceanic stew, had one fatal failing: unlike their green successors, they were unable to fix carbon dioxide — that is, they were unable to use carbon dioxide in the synthesis of essential organic compounds. Instead, they lived by taking up organic molecules from their surroundings, and then spewed out carbon dioxide as a waste product — a situation which, after untold millennia, resulted in a primal soup depleted of organics, an atmosphere enriched in carbon dioxide, and a sea of increasingly hungry purple bacteria.

At this crucial point, scientists hypothesize, as a result of increasing selection pressures, a microbe carrying a new chemical — chlorophyll — appeared on the scene. The new microbes were able to use all this leftover carbon dioxide as a carbon source, and, like deciduous green leaves today, combined carbon dioxide and water in the presence of light energy to yield sugars. Chlorophyll was the pigment of choice for the new green microbes because they developed in underwater sediments, far beneath swimming swarms of purple bacteria. These surface swimmers absorbed all the green light on the way down, leaving, for the submerged ancestors of the marigold, the mariposa lily, and the maple tree, only the red and blue leftovers. In short, leaves are green because long ago the seas were purple.

In the sugar maple each year, well before the first leaves turn green the sap starts running. This early sign of life from the quiescent winter tree is part of the process of breaking dormancy, a series of activities triggered by the longer and warmer days of spring. It's the arboreal equivalent of removing one's winter flannels and restringing the tennis racket. Running sap transports the previous summer's stored photosynthesate toward the cambium and the new leaf buds, all gearing up for their imminent burst of spring growth. The summer's sugars, current theory holds, have spent the winter stored all along the tree trunk, most of them in specialized cells in the xylem. The more usual sugar conduit is the phloem, which ordinarily carries finished photosynthesate from the leaves downward. Sugary nectar, beloved by hummingbirds and honeybees, derives from phloem tissue, and when Titania's fairies flitted off to feast on honeydew, they were enjoying a phloem product.

In early spring, however, the xylem takes over: the specialized storage cells pump their sugary contents into the xylem vessels. The increased sugar concentration then creates an osmotic pressure, which pulls water into the xylem vessels. Soon water pressure soars. The metabolic activity accompanying all this sugar-pumping causes the xylem cells to work up the cellular equivalent of a sweat, releasing a number of waste products, among them carbon dioxide gas. The solubility of carbon dioxide decreases as the temperature rises — which is why warmed soda pop goes flat — such that, with the increasingly balmy days of early March, gas pressure also begins to build up within the bulging xylem tubes. In the unmolested tree, these combined pressures, sometimes reaching an expulsive force of twenty pounds per square inch, force the sap upward toward the leaf buds, outward toward the cambium, and even apparently downward, toward the roots. In the tapped tree, they force the sap out the spout and into the waiting bucket.

Probably one of the first tappers of maple trees was *Sciurus carolinensis*, the gray squirrel, whose unparalleled ability to zero in on food supplies has confounded human observers for centuries. The French botanist André Michaux, a keen observer of maples, wrote in the 1780s: "Wild and domestic animals are inordinately fond of maple juice, and break through their enclosures to sate themselves; and when taken by them in large quantities it has an exhilarating effect upon their spirits." Squirrel tapping technique, crude but effective, involves ripping off young maple twigs at the base or gnawing holes in the bark, then lapping the exuded sap. Since squirrels almost always act exhilarated, it's difficult to tell whether or not these spring doses of maple juice have additional uplifting effects.

If not reproducibly uplifting, maple sap is sweet — containing anywhere from 1 to 12 percent sugar, depending on the tree, with a generally accepted average of 3 percent. It takes somewhere around thirty to forty gallons of sap to make one gallon of maple syrup, which flavorful product at completion approximates 63 percent sugar (62 percent sucrose, 1 percent glucose and fructose), 35 percent water, and 1 percent malic acid. The average maple tree, the John Doe of the sugarbush, yields about twelve gallons of sap (or three pounds of sugar) per season. Maple syrup makers' lore, however, has its share of legendary trees. In the spring of 1806, Captain John Barney of Guilford, Vermont, made seventy-four pounds of sugar and one gallon of "molasses" from his remarkable stand of eleven maples (each putting out three times more sugar than the maple norm). Captain Barney, then seventy-seven, gathered all the sap with his own hands. In the 1860s, a record-breaking grove of one hundred trees in Michigan "yielded one spring 950 lbs. of sugar, at the rate of 9½ lbs. to a tree," and a single overachiever in Ohio produced "34 lbs. of very fine sugar one season. It is thought if all the sap had been carefully saved it would have given 40 pounds." Euell Gibbons, the famed stalker of the wild asparagus, once put six taps in an immense maple, thus collecting ten gallons of sap — for some trees, nearly a season's worth — in a single day.

It must have been immense. A maple is considered tappable — one tap — at ten to twelve inches in diameter, usually reached by thirty-five to sixty years of age. Additional taps can be added for each additional five or six inches in diameter, which means that a six-tap tree is some thirty-six inches in diameter, or about 3¼ yards around.

Indian tapping methods, when first observed by European settlers, seem to have consisted mostly of slashing the bark with a tomahawk, then catching the sap in wooden vessels set beneath the dripping gash. The sugar-making process had been in place among Indian cultures for centuries before the arrival of the whites, who were much struck with it. Robert Beverly, in *The History and Present State of Virginia*, published in London in 1705, devoted an entire chapter to the phenomenal sugar maple:

The Sugar-Tree yields a kind of Sap or Juice, which by boiling is made into Sugar. This Juice is drawn out, by wounding the Trunk of the Tree, and placing a Receiver under the Wound. The Indians make One Pound of Sugar, out of Eight Pounds of the Liquor. Some of this Sugar I examined very carefully. It was bright and moist, with a large full Grain; the Sweetness of it being like that of good Muscovada. Though this Discovery has not been made by the English above Twelve or Fourteen Years; yet it has been known among the Indians, longer than any now living can remember.

Among the more detailed accounts of Indian sugaring is that of James

Smith, in his modestly titled memoir *An Account of the Remarkable Occurrences in the Life and Travels of Col. James Smith*. Smith's sugaring know-how was imparted by a tribe of the Ohio territory, who captured him as a teenager in 1755. He lived with the Indians until 1759, when he managed to escape, going on somewhat ungratefully to become an Indian fighter and attaining coloneldom in the Revolutionary War. In Ohio, Smith wrote, sugaring began in February and was, like so many other tedious tasks, the province of the women. Sap was collected in buckets or pans made of birchbark stitched together with spruce roots. The more affluent squaws, according to Smith, possessed up to fifteen hundred of these vessels. The collected sap was often simply allowed to freeze, and the ice sheets thrown away, leaving behind a concentrated brown sugar syrup. In the alternative and more difficult procedure, the sap — collected and pooled in hundred-gallon mooseskin vats — was boiled down in troughs made of hollowed-out logs, by repeatedly dropping in hot rocks to maintain temperature. Finished syrup was used as a seasoning, a dip, or mixed generously with pulverized corn and bear fat as a main course. The Iroquois of New York used to tote maple syrup along on journeys as trail food, cunningly stored in the shells of quail or duck eggs.

The colonists, quick to pick up on the Indian techniques, promptly made their own modifications. Among these was the idea of boring a hole in the tree with an auger and inserting a wooden spout, variously made from elderwood, sumac, or birch. The Philadelphia Society of Gentlemen sagely remarked in 1790, "Although it has been found that the Sugar Maple tree will bear much hardship and abuse; yet the chopping notches into it, from year to year, should be forborne . . . ." A further improvement was the hanging of buckets from the tree, on metal spikes driven in a few inches below the spout. "Hanging the bucket on the tree is preferable to setting it on the ground," pontificated the *American Agriculturalist* in 1870. "It saves hunting for a block or stone; the bucket is more conveniently emptied; the wind cannot blow the sap away as it drops, nor blow the bucket away; and, what is of most importance, the bucket can be covered." A story from late-nineteenth-century Vermont describes one of the more unique instances of tree-tapping: A farmwife, possessed of a single mammoth maple tree, cut the ends off branches and hung dried gourds beneath them until the tree was "decorated like a Christmas evergreen." From the collected sap, she eventually managed to make fifty pounds of sugar, and the tree "was none the worse for it."

A major advance for syrup makers was the arrival of the metal boiling kettle — though in the earliest days of settlement not every family could boast such state-of-the-art equipment. In the late 1700s, for example, the very first five-pail kettle arrived in Fayston, Vermont, hauled in by Caleb Pitkin, from Montpelier, a good fifteen miles away. The event was notable enough to be recorded for posterity.

Still, with whatever equipment, maple sugar-making soon became, if not precisely big business, at least an economically prominent activity. (Bertha S. Dodge, in her *Tales of Vermont Ways and People*, lists it under "Sources of Income — Largely Legal.") Benjamin Rush, the respected Philadelphia physician known as "The Hippocrates of Pennsylvania," wrote in a letter to Thomas Jefferson in 1791: "In contemplating the present opening prospects in human affairs, I am led to expect that a material part of the general happiness which heaven seems to have prepared for mankind, will be derived from the manufacture and general use of Maple Sugar." He was at least temporarily correct: north of the Mason-Dixon line, maple sugar was the major available sweetener and a common medium of barter well into the nineteenth century. According to Bertha Dodge, records from the 1790s show the forty families of a small Vermont town turning out thirteen thousand pounds of sugar in a single year; the state census of 1870 showed that an industrious town of thirteen hundred produced fifty-four thousand pounds, with twelve hundred gallons of syrup thrown in for good measure. "Make your own sugar and send not to the Indies for it," admonished the *Farmer's Almanac* in 1803. "Feast not on the toil and pain of the wretched."

The longer and hotter the developing maple syrup is boiled, the darker and stronger the finished product becomes. The government has caught on to this, and lists color as a major factor in the grading of commercial maple syrups, which come in four increasingly brown grades: Fancy, A, B, and C. Fancy, according to the United States government, should be of a shade known romantically as "light amber." Helen and Scott Nearing, in their delightful and authoritative *Maple Sugar Book*, compare syrup grades more practically to pale ginger ale (Fancy), Pilsner beer (A), tea (B), and coffee (C). All syrups, especially those stronger-flavored and lower-grade types, owe their increasingly intense flavors to browning reactions —as-yet poorly understood interactions between sap sugars and amino acids which may yield up to a hundred organic reaction products. It's this mysterious mix of organics that makes the syrup on pancakes such a Sunday morning delight. Grade C is the best for cooking (my grandma put it in her baked beans), but is hard to find outside of maple syrup territory. Fancy is the stuff in those little buff-colored plastic jugs, sold to tourists and expensively available in progressive supermarkets.

Continued and determinedly hot boiling concentrates the sugar to the point that it will solidify — crystallize out of solution — upon cooling. The way in which the sugar is cooled largely determines the texture of the product. Slow cooling, with a minimum of stirring — "Let no further agitation be had by stirring," directs a sugar-maker of the 1820s — yields chunkily large sugar crystals, and such un-stirred syrup, poured into pans, will harden into the coarse-grained cakes known to the settlers as "maple loaves." Poured into molds, this also makes the sugar leaves, hearts, and male and female Pilgrims popularly sold as maple candy. The Indians seem to have fallen for this sort of confectionary frivolity too: an account of the mid-nineteenth century details Indian sugar made "into all sorts of shapes, bear's paws, flowers, stars, small animals, and other figures, just like our gingerbread-bakers at fairs."

Judiciously stirred, the sugar crystallizes to form a finer, dry, "grain" sugar, the principal sugar of the Indians, put up in birchbark boxes or baskets called *mokuks*. Rapidly cooled and violently beaten, the sugar coalesces in fine crystals dispersed in a small amount of uncrystallized syrup to form maple "butter," a thick creamy substance suitable for spreading.

The colonists also used their painstakingly collected maple sap to make maple vinegar, a concoction that reportedly was much improved by the addition of a gallon of whiskey to the vinegar barrel. Also prepared was maple beer. Of this tipple, Benjamin Rush, who obviously did not know his fellow man, wrote in 1791, "The sap of the Maple is capable of affording a spirit, but we hope this precious juice will never be prostituted by our citizens to this ignoble purpose." While a citizenry capable of fermenting pumpkin chips, persimmons, turnips, tobacco, and wortleberries was unlikely to balk at maple sap, other considerations may eventually have led to the decline of maple beer in popularity. "Brook-water is my chief drink," announced the Reverend Nathan Perkins in 1789. "The maple cyder is horrible stuff."

> ## MAPLE BEER
>
> **T**o *four gallons of boiling water, add one quart of maple molasses, and a small table spoonful of essence of spruce. When it is about milk warm, add a pint of yeast; and when fermented, bottle it. In three days it is fit for use.*
>
> — The Young Housekeeper's Friend, 1846

A less horrible liquid refreshment may have been the concoction known to our ancestors as rhubarb punch and to modern imitators as a "Vermont Special." The traditional recipe is in verse:

> *One of sour*
> *And one of sweet*
> *Two of strong*
> *And drink it neat.*

Translated, this means one part rhubarb juice, one part maple syrup, and two parts rum. The punch seems to have suited its consumers, since there are no known eighteenth-century complaints about it.

Top maple syrup producer in this country today is the state of Vermont, which turns out around half a million gallons of syrup annually. New York holds second place, and Ohio third. Top world producer of maple syrup lies farther north, in Canada, where the province of Quebec turns out 75 percent of the world's maple syrup supply. The northerly location is what makes maple syrup possible. It's not the tree *per se*; it's the weather — as Thomas Jefferson discovered when he attempted to tap the flourishing (but sapless) sugar maples of Monticello.

The rule of thumb for sap weather is freezing nights and warm(ish) days (with suitable and largely undefined conditions of wind, sun, and precipitation). Hamilton Percival, writing a nostalgic account of maple sugaring for *Scribner's Monthly* in 1904, described the ideal sap weather: "The nights continue sharp and frosty, but the sun comes up with a smiling face and the wind is south and mild." Such weather occurs more or less annually in New England, of which meteorological phenomena Ira Allen, brother of Ethan, wrote brightly, "The climate is friendly to the population and longevity; the air is salubrious, notwithstanding it partakes of heat and cold in high degrees, which gradually make their approaches." The population, regrettably, was often less friendly to the climate. President John Adams wanted to escape it altogether by curling up like a dormouse and sleeping out the winter, and poet Ezra Pound said it for a lot of modern northerners when he wrote "Winter is icummen in. Loud sing goddam." Spring, for which disgruntled residents coined the term "mud season," was not much better. "The people of New England are by nature patient and forbearing," quipped Mark Twain in his famous "Speech on the Weather," "but there are some things which they will not stand. Every year they kill a lot of poets for writing about 'Beautiful Spring.' These are generally casual visitors, who bring their notions of spring from somewhere else, and cannot, of course, know how the natives feel about spring."

The sap does not run reliably every day, like turning on a faucet. Cold snaps intervene, or unseasonable warm spells; sleet falls, or the wind veers evilly to the north. Ordinarily the season proceeds in a series of fits and starts. Old-timers, says Mr. Percival, divide the sugar season into "runs," named, for example, a "robin run" (occurs after the robins arrive), a "frog run" (after the frogs start croaking), or a "bud run" (after the leaf buds begin to swell). Sugar season is generally held to begin in March and continue into April — "when the first crow flies" is the traditional rule of thumb — but lopovers of either side are not uncommon. François — son of the aforementioned André — Michaux' attempt at pinpointing the dates reads cautiously, "The sap begins to be in motion two months before the general revival of vegetation" — a phrase which irresistibly reminds me of E. B. White's equally cautious "The only time not to have a son is eighteen years before a World War." The season lasts anywhere from a few days to several weeks, again depending on the weather. This, according to Mr. Twain, is made in New England not by the professional Almighty, but by a collection of amateurs and apprentices, all preparing for future assignment somewhere else.

Chief worry among sugar makers nowadays, however, is not so much when the sap will run as if. A landmark study conducted since 1965 at the University of Vermont under the direction of Dr. Hubert Vogelmann has shown a recent frightening decline in the sugar maple population. Growth in mature trees — ascertained by taking core samples — has decreased 25 percent over the past twenty years, and infant mortality has skyrocketed. Number of surviving young trees less than one inch in diameter is now down by 85 percent. Concerned researchers tramping the slopes of Vermont's Camel's Hump Mountain in 1965 counted 140,000 hopeful maple saplings per acre. In 1983, the count was down to 21,500. There is a high probability that these horrifying statistics are the result of acid rain.

Acid rain, the substance that is slowly dissolving the Washington Monument and the Statue of Liberty, carries the effluvia of the factories and power plants of the Midwest. These industrial pollutants, largely sulfur and nitrogen dioxides, plus miscellaneous heavy metals and organic carcinogens such as PCBs, are converted to sulfuric and nitric acids once airborne. Concentrated in raindrops, these acids raise the pH of rain from its normally slightly acidic 5.0–5.6 (about the pH of a cabbage) to a markedly more acidic 4.2 (about the pH of a tomato). Cloud water or fog — from which mountainside trees may absorb as much as half their recommended daily water allotment — has become even more acidic, pH 3.7, approaching that of a dill pickle.

Neither is the damage done by acid rain confined to a searing drip from above. Once this polluted precipitation hits the soil, it catalyzes a number of lethal reactions, among them the conversion of ordinarily inert soil aluminum to chemically active form. Aluminum, increasingly recognized as toxic, has been implicated in such brain-damaging syndromes as Alzheimer's disease and has been pinpointed as the cause of death for fish in acid-rain-victimized lakes. Chemical analyses of wood samples from the Camel's Hump maple trees show that aluminum concentrations have tripled since the 1960s. Soil lead concentrations have doubled.

Though the sugar maples, with their immense shallow root systems, are notoriously sensitive to pollution, they are not the only trees affected by atmospheric poisoning. Vogelmann has identified signs of distress among many other tree species: red spruce, beech, birch, ash, aspen, alder, larch, and hemlock. Across the border, similar forest decline is concerning the scientists of Canada, and increasing investigation reveals acid rain as a problem of global scale. Overseas, researchers have identified pollution-related devastation in the evergreen forests of Europe, including Germany's famed Black Forest. Among the earliest of warning signs is the abnormal and untimely destruction of chlorophyll, a yellowing known ominously as *chlorosis*, and a harbinger not of winter, but perhaps of what worried Germans term *Waldsterben*. Forest death.

Sugar maple destruction two hundred years ago was a simpler and more straightforward process, usually deliberately brought about by a calculating farmer wielding a flaming torch. His aim was the production of potash. Woods, when it comes to ash production, are not all created equal. Ash content, depending on the species, varies from 1 to 4 percent of dry weight. Maple, at 4 percent, is a

	Ash content (% dry weight)	Pounds ash/cord
Douglas fir	1.0	25
Pine	2.0	45
Hemlock	2.5	55
Birch	3.0	70
Maple	4.0	140

high yielder. Each cord of torched maple leaves behind 140 pounds of ashes, as opposed to a mere 25 pounds per cord of Douglas fir, and 45 pounds per cord of pine. Typically this ash is a chemical mixed bag, consisting primarily of lime (50–70 percent), potash (5–8 percent), and phosphorus (1–2 percent).

The potash was leached out of the mass of the ashes with water, and the liquid evaporated in large iron kettles or pots — hence potash. The crusted result was an assortment of caustic alkaline salts, largely potassium derivatives. (Elemental potassium, which was formally identified in 1807 by Sir Humphrey Davy, was named for its homely association with potash.) Potash was invaluable in the production of soap, which the textile industries of Great Britain required in massive quantities for processing wool. It was also essential in the manufacture of glass and gunpowder. So important, in fact, was the lowly potash to the British economy that in 1751 the British Parliament passed an "Act for encouraging the making of Pott Ashes and Pearl Ashes in the British Plantations in America." "The Process is easy," wrote the Parliamentarians bracingly, "the Expense small; the Profit certain." Northeastern farmers, understandably drawn by the lure of certain Profit, were soon routinely burning off a few acres of forest annually, to the tune of two tons of saleable potash per acre. Often it was the farmer's only source of cash income. Exported to Europe from Boston and New York, potash was colloquially known as "black gold" before petroleum was known as anything other than an ingredient for patent medicines. By 1800, potash prices were up to $200–$300 per ton.

This profitable situation ended in 1807, with the passage of

Thomas Jefferson's Embargo Act. The Act, intended as a reprisal for the search and seizure of American ships by the warring nations of France and Great Britain, forbade export of goods to either of the guilty countries by sea. "Goods and Merchandise shipped in sleighs" were exempt from this ruling, however; and for a brief period the potash industry went overland, sending its product by legal sleigh north to Montreal. The sleigh loophole was eliminated in 1808, with the enactment of the "Land Embargo," which should by all rights have halted all northbound potash traffic. Instead, the potash makers turned to smuggling, a lucrative activity immortalized today in Vermont's "Smuggler's Notch." A century later, northern New England responded similarly to the strictures of prohibition.

What potash wasn't whisked across the border into Canada found a multitude of uses at home. Applied as fertilizer, it was said to grow astounding vegetables. In the first decade of the nineteenth century, Darius Clark of Dorset Hollow, Vermont, harvested a record-breaking 4½-pound potato, 30-pound cabbage, and 94-pound winter squash from his potash-treated kitchen garden. Filtered and heated to make the more refined pearlash, potash was mixed with cream of tartar to make baking powder, with vinegar to poultice wounds, and with hot water to treat mad dog bites. In combination with alcohol, potash was used to alleviate rheumatism; in combination with rainwater and animal fat, it went to make soft soap. Soft soap, in its turn, not only performed all the standard soap functions, but was smeared on exposed faces and arms to fend off mosquitoes and was dissolved in ale, for the treatment of jaundice.

Which all brings us, in a roundabout way, past the settlers' soap kettles and the factories of Detroit, back to the plight of the maple tree, now succumbing to the technological tragedy of acid rain. "Soap and education," wrote Mark Twain, "are not as sudden as a massacre, but they are more deadly in the long run."

SYCAMORE

In the eighteenth-century alphabet, Z stood not for *zebra* but for *Zaccheus*. "Zaccheus he / Did climb a tree / Our Lord to see," pronounced the *New England Primer*, the leadenly religious textbook that set hundreds of little Puritans on the rocky road to literacy. The tree in question was a sycamore, otherwise known as the sycamore fig or Egyptian fig. The sycamore fig is a medium-sized tree, with a maximum height of about sixty feet, and heart-shaped leaves, which *Hortus III* describes sternly as "ovate to nearly orbicular." The tree itself is said to have grown in the Garden of Eden, and perhaps furnished the ovate to nearly orbicular leaves with which Adam and Eve so hastily draped themselves before being booted out to work for a living. The wood is impressively long-lasting and in ancient times was used for mummy cases.

Scientifically the biblical sycamore is known as *Ficus sycomorus*, a relative of *Ficus carica*, the cultivated fig tree, and it bears figs in its own right. The sycamore fig, a yellowish fruit with black spots, is said to smell like an ordinary fig, but to fall down somewhat in taste. It is, however, perfectly edible, which explains all those biblical references to the gathering of sycamore fruits that are so confusing to readers familiar with the American sycamore tree.

The predominant American sycamore, *Platanus occidentalis*, is the largest — in bulk — of any North American deciduous tree. The largest of the large, according to the American Forestry Association, stands on the banks of the Muskingum River in Ohio, about halfway between Cleveland and Columbus. This behemoth stands

129 feet tall, measures 48 feet around the trunk, and sports a 105-foot crown. It is located, appropriately enough, nearly in the middle of the American sycamore's range, which extends from Maine through Minnesota and Wisconsin, then south to Iowa and eastern Texas. *P. occidentalis* boasts the largest single-bladed leaf in the North American forests, as much as ten inches long, three- to five-lobed, and coarsely toothed. Inconspicuous flowers blossom on the branches in early May: the males in deep-red clusters, the females as greenish balls suspended from slender stems. Both sexes exist amicably on the same tree.

Fertilization results in the development of a dense seed ball — compound fruits which, by October, dangle from the branches like so many dull-colored Christmas ornaments. From these seed balls come the sycamore's descriptive common names, buttonwood and buttonball. The balls deck the tree through the winter and in the spring disperse as individual single-seeded nutlets. Each is hair-tipped, designed like a tiny autogyro to spin in the wind.

The most readily identifiable feature of the American sycamore is its bark. As the tree grows, the inelastic outer bark splits and peels off in large thin plates — like "torn wallpaper," says Eric Sloane — revealing the smooth inner bark beneath, in distinctive patterns of ivory, yellow, or pale mottled green. Among the earliest of European naturalists to describe the spectacle of sycamore bark was young John Lawson, who arrived in the Carolinas in the year 1700, with apparently no greater goal in mind than the satisfaction of personal curiosity. He later described the events leading up to his sojourn in America: some months previously in London, he wrote, having professed a desire "to travel," he "accidentally met a Gentleman who had been abroad and was very well acquainted with the ways of living in both Indies." Upon recommendation of this unnamed Gentleman, Lawson promptly boarded a ship for the New World. He spent the next eight years exploring the Carolinas, the outcome of which was a detailed volume published in 1709, titled *A New Voyage to Carolina, containing the Exact Description and Natural History of the Country, together with the Present State thereof, and a*

Journal of a Thousand Miles Travel'd thro' Several Nations of Indians. Giving a particular Account of their Customs, Manners, etc.

"Tis a great Misfortune," begins this magnum opus, "that most of our travellers who go to this vast Continent in America, are persons of the Meaner sort, and generally of a very slender Education . . . ." The author then proceeds to correct this Misfortune to the best of his considerable ability. Progressing through his chapter on the present State of Carolina, where, according to Lawson, the women are beautiful, the men long-lived, the provisions cheap, and the Indians friendly, he arrives at "The Natural History of Carolina," under which he describes the native "Vegetables," "Timber," and "Beasts." It was through Lawson's book that many less adventurous Londoners became entranced with the opossum and the hummingbird, the "Hony-Suckle-Tree," and the "Sensible Plant," "said to be near the Mountains, which I have not yet seen." His descriptive list of New World trees is impressively complete, including a description of the remarkable exterior of the "Sycamore": "Its Bark is quite different from the English and the most beautiful I ever saw, being mottled and clowded with several Colours, as white, blue, etc."

Lawson returned to England to supervise the publication of *A New Voyage* and stayed long enough to receive the acclaim that accompanied his entry into print. The book inspired enough financial backing for Lawson to make a return trip to America in 1710, with the intention of continuing his researches and writing a sequel. Sadly, shortly after his arrival, he was captured and killed by the Tuscarora Indians. The natural history was never finished.

The American sycamore is a notably long-lived tree, often reaching five hundred years of age. Invariably, however, once a sycamore reaches its middle years — say two or three hundred of them — it's not quite all there. "To be a proper sycamore," writes John G. Mitchell in *Audubon*, "with two or three centuries of life behind you is to be disemboweled . . . ." The hollowness of sycamores can reach truly stunning proportions. Colonial record-makers crammed into sycamore trunks like *Guinness*-bound fraternity brothers packing into telephone booths. Ohio, which seems to have held a monopoly on amazing sycamores, boasted specimens that could hold fifteen men on horseback or forty men off. There are numerous stories of handy sycamores serving as temporary homes for colonial families and, later, once homesteads were established, as stables, silos, pigpens, and barns. Perhaps it was this unromantic beginning that led the Victorians to choose the sycamore to symbolize shelter in their language of flowers.

Alternatively, pioneer families avoided the temptingly hollow trees like the plague. The sycamore, a water-lover, thrives on low, damp ground, areas also favored by the malarial mosquito. In colonial days the mosquito was held blameless as a transmitter of disease; instead, one medical faction blamed malaria on the syca-more tree.

A hollow sycamore, despite its hideously unhealthy appear-ance, is not necessarily about to kick the bucket. All normal mature trees are already largely dead. As a tree grows, the actively repro-ducing cambium continues to generate a new batch of xylem each year. As each new assortment of water-conducting tubules takes over, the previous year's functional tubules are pushed farther toward the center of the tree, there to meet their quietus. Actively functioning xylem, involved in water and mineral transport and food storage, is collectively known as sapwood. Once past its prime, sapwood gradually fills with metabolic wastes and resins, which harden to form the (dead) central core of the tree. Known as heart-wood, this interior chemical dumping ground is the portion of the tree coveted by cabinetmakers. The tree, however, can easily do without it. When the heartwood rots, as frequently happens in the case of the sycamore, the tree can still lead a long and happy life — albeit gapingly hollow.

There are also historical accounts of tapping the sycamore for syrup and sugar, and of using raw sap to make — naturally — a sycamore wine. Euell Gibbons' modern-day fling with sycamore-tapping, however, suggests why sycamore syrup never rivaled maple as a commercial pancake topping. In *Stalking the Wild Asparagus*, Mr. Gibbons wrote, "On reading that certain Indian tribes used the sweet sap of the Sycamore (*Platanus occidentalis*) for making sugar and sirup, I tapped a large, double-trunked sycamore that was growing on a creek bank near my home. It produced a copious flow and, with one tap in each trunk, I soon had the two gallons of sap I wanted for the experiment. But when I boiled it down I discovered that I would have done about as well had I merely dipped up two gallons of water from the nearby creek. It gave off a maple aroma as it boiled, but the entire amount produced little over a tablespoonful of very dark-colored sirup which tasted like a poor grade of blackstrap molasses."

Sycamore wood proved more useful, though it was seldom chosen as a fuel wood since its tightly interlocking grain makes it next to impossible to split. *Grain*, among wood experts, is a technically specific term referring to the alignment of the xylem cells. In the most splittable woods, all the cells lie in the same plane, parallel to the vertical axis of the tree. In less likely woodpile candidates, the xylem cells may be irregularly tilted or arranged in spirals. In the case of the elm and sycamore, both ax-wielders' nightmares, the grain alternates in successive years from a left-handed spiral to a right-handed spiral, eventually producing a tightly clenched interlocked arrangement apparently deter-

SYCAMORE WINE

Boil 2 gallons of the sap half an hour, and then add to it 4 pounds of fine powdered sugar. Beat the whites of 3 eggs to froth, and mix them with the liquor; but take care that it is not too hot, as that will poach the eggs. Skim it well, and boil it half an hour. Then strain it through a hair sieve, and let it stand till next day. Then pour it clean from the sediment, put half a pint of yeast to every twelve gallons, and cover it close up with blankets. Then put it into the barrel, and leave the bung-hole open till it has done working. Then close it up well, and after it has stood 2 months, bottle it. The fifth part of the sugar must be loaf; and if raisins are liked, they will be a great addition to the wine.

— Mackenzie's 5,000 Recipes, 1829

mined to remain in one piece. This very toughness is for many purposes an advantage. Described by one admirer as "lustrous cream," the stubborn sycamore traditionally was used for rolling pins, butter prints, butchers' blocks, saddletrees, shipping crates, and the backs of violins — and, in whole cross-slices, for cart wheels. Sawn timber often reveals an attractive freckled figure on a cream or faintly pink background. Referred to as "lacewood," this is used decoratively in cabinets and desk tops, and, in the days when train travel was a luxury experience, was featured in the interior panelling of Pullman cars. Sycamore also went into the slats of Saratoga trunks. Despite its resistance to splitting, sycamore is susceptible to decay and thus has never been used for such ready-to-rot outdoor items as fence posts and railroad ties.

Even better known than the American sycamore, and often confused with it, is its vigorous hybrid offspring *Platanus acerifolia*, commonly known as the London plane. *P. acerifolia*, less prone to hollowness and bark-peeling than its American parent, and remarkably resistant to air pollution, has been a popular city tree — "urban ornamental," according to horticulturists — since it burst into being sometime in the late seventeenth century. Frederick Law Olmsted ordered dozens of them for the young Central Park, where they flourished; tree-conscious denizens of London recently counted theirs and estimated that well over half of the city's trees today are London planes. The same could be said of many Western cities, among them Philadelphia, whose London plane population hovers around half a million.

The name *plane* derives from the Greek for "broad" — as in plane geometry — and refers to the sycamore's sizeable leaves. The Greek version of the sycamore (or plane) tree was *P. orientalis*, the Oriental plane, which hails from Bulgaria, Yugoslavia, Greece, and points east. The Oriental plane is said to have symbolized genius to the ancient Greeks, because philosophers often held forth beneath its branches — presumably sneezing between syllogisms, since, so goes another story, the ancients blamed the tiny hairs or spicules flaking off the plane tree's leaves and seed balls for a persistent form of bronchial catarrh resembling hay fever.

The historian Herodotus describes an unprecedented passion for a plane tree, conceived by the Persian King Xerxes (519–465 B.C.), who found his chosen tree "so beautiful that he presented it with golden ornaments" and assigned it a personal bodyguard. Eventually it became necessary to force the besotted king away from the arboreal object of his affections. To "ease the pain of parting," Xerxes had a gold medal engraved with the image of his tree, which he wore ever after as an amulet.

Greek mythology also includes a disgraceful story involving a plane tree: that of Marsyas, the flute player, who challenged Apollo to a musical duel, to be judged by the Muses. Apollo won, and promptly tied his opponent to a handy plane tree and skinned him alive. "The Flaying of Marsyas," with prominent plane tree, was a subject artistically appealing enough to be immortalized by both Titian and Tintoretto. Christian moralists have used the story as a cautionary tale, citing the unfortunate Marsyas as a symbol of pride going before a painful fall. A more apt conclusion, however, is that Apollo was deficient in sportsmanship.

P. orientalis and *P. occidentalis* met sometime in the early seventeenth century, possibly in England, where plant enthusiasts had been eagerly importing new species of trees for over a century. (By the calculations of nineteenth-century plantsman J. C. Loudon, 89 new species of trees and shrubs arrived in England in the sixteenth century, 131 in the seventeenth, 445 in the eighteenth, and 699 in the first third of the nineteenth.) It is uncertain where the offspring of this meeting, *P. acerifolia*, first saw the light. One story holds that the landmark cross took place in the exotic garden of the John Tradescants, that avid pair of seventeenth-century explorers and collectors whose fantastic horde formed the nucleus of Oxford University's Ashmolean Collection. Included in the Tradescant cupboards were such irresistibles as:

Divers sorts of Egges from Turkie: one given for a Dragons egge.
Two feathers of the Phoenix tayle.

Penguin, which never flies for want of wings.
Dodar, it is not able to flie being so big.
Divers things cut on Plum-stones.
Flea chains of silver and gold, with three hundred links a piece and
*   yet but an inch long.*
A piece of the Stone of Sarrigo-Castle where Hellen of Greece was born.
Anne of Bullens silke knit-gloves.
Henry 8 hawking-glove, hawks-hood, dogs-collar.
A hat-band made of a sting-ray.
Turkish tooth-brush.
An umbrella.

The Tradescant garden featured an equally entrancing miscellany. Among the rare plants growing there, all introduced to England by the adventurous father and son, were lilac (the "Blew Pipe-tree"), dogwood, goldenrod, gladioli, stock, phlox, scarlet corn poppies, and spiderwort (*Tradescantia virginiana*), which bears their joint name. The London plane, whether from the Tradescant garden or some other serendipitous source, was first officially recognized in the Oxford Botanic Garden in 1670. It quickly spread, by virtue of hybrid vigor and, in later centuries, a complete indifference to asphyxiating daily doses of coal smoke. Today, like the pigeon, it thrives in the inner city, a thoroughly street-smart tree, occasionally heaving up the pavement stones with its questing roots.

While the English plane is all sycamore, the English sycamore is a maple: *Acer pseudoplatanus*, the plane-leaved maple. As robust as its plane namesake, it survives smoke, soot, and stony soil. Golden, variegated, and purple cultivars exist, respectively described by tree expert Alan Mitchell as "rather splendid," "rather blotchy," and "inexcusably dreary." *A. pseudoplatanus* also thrives in Scotland, where it is referred to as a plane tree. The hybrid (London) plane, which is what Americans refer to as a plane tree, but occasionally, due to botanical confusion, as a sycamore, can be distinguished from the American sycamore by its seed balls. While *P. occidentalis* bears single seed balls, *P. acerifolia* produces multiple seed balls strung necklace-like on a single stalk. *A. pseudoplatanus*, being a maple, produces no seed balls, but the winged seeds known in common lingo as maple keys.

It seems likely that the Tolpuddle Martyr's Tree — a so-called sycamore — may have been an elderly specimen of *A. pseudoplatanus*. Tolpuddle, a small village in Dorset, had its moment in the political sun in the 1830s, when local farm workers under the leadership of one George Loveless formed what may have been the first agricultural trade union in England. Their meetings were held under a towering sycamore (or maple) at town center — and ended abruptly with the conviction and transportation of all the prominent union members to Australia. George Loveless, the story goes, prior to boarding ship for the Antipodes, plucked a leaf from the village sycamore (or maple) and pressed it between the pages of his Bible. The tree, which came to be called the Martyr's Tree after the deported laborers, was subsequently lovingly preserved by the Tolpudlians left behind, its rotting trunk stuffed with vermiculite and held together with iron hoops.

Tree leaves traditionally have been used as book markers in Bibles. Called Bibleleaves, such leaves were chosen for their scent and durability — or, like George Loveless' sycamore (or maple) leaf, for their sentimental associations. Particular favorites were leaves of tutsan (*Hypericum androsaemum*), an evergreen shrub of the St.-John's-wort family, and of costmary (*Chrysanthemum balsamita*), an herb also known as alecost or mint geranium. The latter is said to smell like either fresh pipe tobacco or Christmas cake, the former like a cross between lemon and peppermint.

Since the American sycamore is so large and long-lived, sycamores throughout the East have been deemed historic trees in honor of the deeds performed under, near, or around them. Washington and Lafayette met under a massive sycamore in Stanton, Delaware, to plan their strategy for the upcoming Battle of Brandywine (poorly, as it turned out; they were soundly trounced by the British). Washington paused to rest under a sycamore, duly named the General Washington Sycamore, in July 1782, in Hope, New Jersey, while en route from Philadelphia to his military headquarters in Newburgh, New York. The citizens of Newport, Rhode Island, in the rebellious days of 1766, chose a sycamore for their Liberty Tree. Liberty Trees appeared (already full grown) throughout the New England colonies in 1765 and 1766 as symbols of defiance to the despised Stamp Act, a legal measure with which the financially strapped British government hoped to raise enough money to support its military forces in America. The colonists, never willing to part with their cash, united in opposition, rallying under their Liberty Trees. The brouhaha was too much for the British government, which rescinded the hated Act in 1766. It was followed in 1767, however, by the even more hateful Townsend Acts — the British troops were, after all, still garrisoned in the colonies, eating, drinking, and demanding wages. The Townsend Acts slapped a stiff surcharge on such necessaries as lead, glass, paper, paint, and tea, which left the disruptive colonists still meeting under their Liberty Trees, boycotting tea, and drinking in its place a homemade coffee made from raspberry leaves.

Newport's Liberty Tree — the sycamore — was cut down by British soldiers during the Revolutionary War. Another, of unknown species, was planted in its place and lasted until the Civil War; then an oak was planted during the Centennial of 1876, which hardly lasted at all. The present Liberty Tree, a beech, was planted in 1897, and is still going strong.

In twentieth-century history, the sycamore has made it to the moon, the seeds carried aloft by Colonel Stuart Allen Roosa on the Apollo XIV mission in 1971. Germinated by U.S. Forest Service scientists at NASA's Manned Space Center in Houston, the "Moon Sycamores" have now embarked upon their — with luck — five hundred-year-long career on earth. Today one of them stands in Washington Square in Philadelphia, directly facing Independence Hall.

BIRCH

n ancient Rome the birch was a symbol of power and authority. Birch branches were bound around a central ax, positioned with the blade exposed, and these threatening bouquets — called *fasces* — were carried ahead of Roman processions to alert the populace to the approach of a V.I.P. From *fasces* comes the modern *fascist*, still a term symbolic of power and authority, though these days thoroughly pejorative and redolent of tyrannical jackboots. In ancient Scandinavia, the birch was one of the trees held sacred to the thunder-god Thor; a Thor-sanctioned branch attached to the house was said to protect the residents from many tribulations, among them lightning, the Evil Eye, gout, and barrenness.

Other cultures have taken a less macho view of the birch tree. In the Victorian language of flowers, the birch symbolized such un-Thor-like traits as meekness and grace, and American poet James Russell Lowell in his "An Indian Summer Reverie" mentions "the birch, most shy and ladylike of trees." The ladylike birch was chosen as the Mother Tree of America by the American Forestry Association, which in the 1920s worked up some publicity by persuading dutiful sons and daughters to plant trees on Mother's Day in honor of their female parents. The first Mother's Tree — a paper birch — was planted in May 1923, at Lake Antietam in Berks County, Pennsylvania. It was followed by similar Trees planted on the White House grounds (for the mothers of the presidents), in Arlington Cemetery (for the mother of the Unknown Soldier), and on the Capitol grounds (for the mothers of the nation). The birch was one of Eleanor

Roosevelt's favorite trees, which is appropriate since Eleanor was the mother of four. Her other pick was the maple.

For all its association with delicacy, meekness, and traditional femininity, the birch in general is a whippy, tough little number suited to cold climates, high altitudes, and the unseasonable north woods. In the United States, it is the state tree of New Hampshire, whose state motto — "Live Free or Die" — is surely the most threatening in the Union. In the perennial chill of the Scottish Highlands, little else grows but birch. The Highlanders, wrote J. C. Loudon in 1842, "make everything of it; they build their houses, make their beds and chairs, tables, dishes and spoons; construct their mills; make their carts, ploughs, harrows, gates and fences, and even manufacture ropes of it. The branches are employed as fuel in the distillation of whiskey, the spray is used for smoking hams and herrings, for which last purpose it is preferred to every other kind of wood. The bark is used for tanning leather, and sometimes, when dried and twisted into a rope, instead of candles. The spray is used for thatching houses; and, dried in summer, with the leaves on, makes a good bed when heath is scarce." According to English historian Dorothy Hartley, bundles of birch twigs were once placed at the bottom of cooking pots while making soups or stews to prevent the meat from sticking to the bottom and burning, as a sort of vegetable Teflon.

Betulaceae, the Birch family, includes, along with the birches (*Betula*), the related alders (*Alnus*), hornbeams (*Carpinus*), hop-hornbeams (*Ostrya*), and hazels (*Corylus*). The birches are a group of fifty or sixty species of deciduous trees and shrubs scattered across the northerly regions of the Northern Hemisphere. Seven of these are trees native to North America. All have remarkably similar leaves — oval, edged with small sharp teeth — and many have dramatically distinctive barks.

The classic birch, the birch of Christmas cards and *Vermont Life* magazine, is *Betula papyrifera*, variously known as the paper birch, the white birch, and the canoe birch. *B. papyrifera* has an enormous range, from Labrador to Virginia in the East, west through Montana and Washington, north through the Yukon to Alaska, and south to

Nebraska and Ohio. Within this range, botanists have identified six or seven different varieties of paper birch, somewhat difficult to sort out since all have a promiscuous tendency to overlap and interbreed. The northeastern version, due to a snowy pigment called *betulin*, is truly paper-colored: "pure dull whitewash white with small black dots and patches," writes Alan Mitchell. A similarly white-barked northeastern relative is the gray birch, *B. populifolia*, whose leaves narrow to slim long points. Alan Mitchell describes these as "long-tailed," but they actually look more like the long-toed slippers worn by medieval jesters. The unappreciative stigmatize the gray as a "weed tree."

Birch bark peels off in curls and strips as the tree grows, and this versatile substance was used by American Indian tribes for everything from kindling to canoes. Birchbark was used in North America to make plates and baskets, and to waterproof wigwams; the Norwegians shingled their roofs with it; the Laplanders fashioned clothing from it; and the natives of the Kamchatka Peninsula, on the eastern coast of the Soviet Union, ate it. The making of birchbark canoes was an exquisite craft peculiar to the American North. The prime practitioners were the Malecite Indians of Maine and New Brunswick, whose chosen range corresponded to that of the biggest and best of the canoe birches. Their vessels, generally ten to twenty feet long, were sheathed with cedar planks, sealed with spruce pitch, and decorated with porcupine quills. Most canoes were a crazy quilt of bark sheets and pieces, stitched together with spruce roots, since only very rarely could a canoe be fashioned with the bark peeled from a single birch tree. The bark was laid on inside-out, such that the canoes, rather than a glittering white, ranged in color from the buff of summer-peeled bark to the rich red-brown of bark peeled in winter, before the flowing of the sap. Henry David Thoreau — probably "*the* first tourist in the Maine woods," says John McPhee — made two trips in such bark canoes in the years 1853 and 1857. For these vacation idylls, he paid eleven dollars a week (which included canoe rental and an Indian guide). His party lived off smoked beef, coffee, tea, and plum cake, eaten off birchbark plates with forks whittled from alder. Their canoe paddles were made of rock maple, and Thoreau, like many a canoeist before and after him, found the continual use of them onerous. The accepted bent-knee paddling position he described as "torture," and he did his best to get some relief by rigging up a blanket as a sail. The Indians, perhaps for the same reason, often propelled their vessels with sails made from moosehides or flat sheets of bark.

Birchbark canoes were so strong and flexible—and so respected by their makers — that they survived most natural disasters, living out an average lifespan of ten years, which puts them well ahead of many of Detroit's finest. They shot heavy rapids, braved the ocean, and, with the French *voyageurs*, crossed three thousand miles of Canadian waterways to establish fur trade routes to the far Northwest. Canoes also were made with other barks: tribes lacking available birch substituted barks of elm, hickory, spruce, basswood, and chestnut. All, however, had a common failing. They absorbed water, eventually becoming waterlogged and heavy, like soggy sponges, and though serviceable, were markedly less efficient than the slickly waterproof birch.

B. papyrifera, true to both scientific and common name, was also used as paper by some American Indian tribes, for drawing or writing in a pictorial language, using sticks dipped in vegetable inks. Later, the European colonists, chronically short of paper, occasionally resorted to birchbark. Sometimes birchbark was selected deliberately. Thomas Jefferson, admonishing the about-to-depart Lewis and Clark on the importance of daily records, wrote, "Several copies of these should be made at leisure times & put into the care of the most trustworthy of your attendants, to guard by multiplying them, against the accidental losses to which they will be exposed. A further guard would be that one of these copies be written on the paper of the birch, as less liable to injury from damp than common paper." It was a good idea, but Lewis and Clark, who never had much in the way of leisure time, failed to carry it out. The use of birchbark paper was not limited to North America. Sixteenth-century birchbark scrolls — in a "moderately legible state" — have been preserved in

Russia, where such scrolls, because of their durability, were the medium of choice for family records well after the introduction of conventional pulp paper.

The sweet, black, or cherry birch, *B. lenta*, is a more southerly tree, ranging from Maine to Alabama, and west as far as Ohio. Its bark, said to resemble that of a wild cherry tree, is described by Alan Mitchell as "smoky gray-black to dark red, with purplish flakes." Less colorful authors label it "dark brown." Given this descriptive ambiguity, a better distinguishing feature for sweet birch seekers may be the catkins, cheekily erect small fruiting bodies poised at the tips of the branches. These catkins remain on the tree over the winter and are cockily obvious in the spring, when interest in the sweet birch once ran highest. Like the maple, the sweet birch produces a copious spring flow of sap — but somewhat later in the season, since, unlike the maple, the birch becomes active in more clement weather, with nights above freezing and warmer days. The sequence was convenient for colonial sugar-makers, who frequently simply transferred their spiles and buckets from the recently closed-down maples to the next species in line. Birch sap, however, is less than half as sweet as maple sap. It takes ten gallons or more of sap to make a mere pint of birch syrup, which, according to Euell Gibbons, "is good, with a flavor resembling that of sorghum molasses." The sap of the paper birch is even more dilute: transforming it to syrup requires a volume reduction of 150 to 1.

Birch tappers are thus likely to forego birch syrup in favor of birch beer, which was made with sweet birch sap, birch twigs (enough to furnish a quart of twig buds per gallon of sap), and honey. Sanborn Brown in *Wines and Beers of Old New England* describes this preparation as "light and somewhat sweet"; Euell Gibbons says it has a kick like a mule and is "definitely not suitable for children." A simpler equivalent, according to Brown, can be made with the more readily available maple sap (5 gallons), 2½ quarts of honey, and 2 ounces of wintergreen extract — or, lacking even that, you can get the general effect by adding a teaspoonful or so of wintergreen extract to any basic beer recipe prior to fermentation.

The wintergreen essence associated with the sweet birch derives from an essential oil concentrated in the inner bark and young twigs. (If the upright catkins aren't enough to conclusively identify a sweet birch, you can try chewing on a twig — the wintergreen flavor is a dead giveaway.) Chopped sweet birch twigs, steeped in hot birch sap, make a tasty wintergreen-flavored tea. The oil of wintergreen extracted from the sweet birch is identical to that of creeping wintergreen (*Gaultheria procumbens*), also called checkerberry or teaberry. *G. procumbens* was the original source of commercial wintergreen oil, a substance once much in demand for flavoring drugs and candies. It was superseded in the nineteenth century by the sweet birch, a move profitable for the wintergreen-extracting Appalachian mountaineers but nearly disastrous for the species *B. lenta*, since it took one hundred birch saplings to yield a quart of essential oil. The sweet birch was saved in the nick of time by the development of synthetic wintergreen oil, and the mountaineers turned to moonshine.

Best of the birches as a timber tree is the yellow birch, *B. alleghaniensis*. Its pale gray-brown bark, which peels off the tree in scroll-like rolls, is described as faintly tinged with yellow, but the common name derives from the glorious sun-yellow fall leaf display. The yellow birch, an eastern tree, ranges from Newfoundland to Wisconsin and Minnesota, and south through Pennsylvania and along the Appalachian mountain chain to Georgia. The wood is hard and dense; some woodworkers compare it to maple. The colonists used it for ox yokes, sledge frames, and wagon wheel hubs; their modern descendants use it for spools, upholstery frames, and plywood. Some varieties show a curly grain — sometimes marketed as "Canadian silky wood" — prized for cabinets, panelling, and marquetry. *B. papyrifera*, cut for timber, also ends up as spools, as well as clothespins, dowels, Popsicle sticks, tongue depressors, and toothpicks, those lethal little items that, according to the National Safety Council, are the objects most often choked upon by Americans. The wood of the sweet birch is sometimes used in furniture-making. The wood color, initially pale, deepens with time and exposure to air to a rich mahogany color. It is therefore sometimes referred to as "mountain mahogany."

Less useful birches include the water birch, *B. occidentalis*, occasionally called the black birch, a smallish shrubby tree bordering the cold streams of the Rocky Mountains, and the river birch, *B. nigra*, also occasionally called the black birch, whose claim to fame is its taste for warm weather. The most southerly birch in the world, *B. nigra* ranges from Massachusetts to Florida and then west in a wide swathe along the Gulf Coast to Texas, extending north through Kentucky, Tennessee, and Missouri. The Carolina planters once used it to make hoops for their rice casks.

North America now also features an imported birch, the European white, *B. pendula*. Sometimes known as the silver birch, *B. pendula* can be distinguished from the perkier natives by the shape of its crown, within which the slender new twigs dangle limp-wristedly from the rising main branches like tinsel on a Christmas tree. Calvin Coolidge, in a shameful display for a Vermonter born in the heart of *B. papyrifera* country, planted a European white birch on the grounds of the White House.

All birches have a reputation for being springily supple — a trait that generations of rambunctious youngsters have had cause to regret, since flexible birch twigs have traditionally served as schoolmasters' switches. A "birching" has meant a thrashing since the seventeenth century, and to conscientious Puritan parents, "Spare the rod and spoil the child" meant a frequent application of birch. Tradition holds that birch rods were used for the scourging of Jesus — in retaliation for which at least one birch species was dwarfed and doomed to spend its life in the Arctic, never attaining a height over two feet.

Because of its flexibility, the birch has also been used traditionally for broom-making. The birch broom, or besom, is essentially a large whisk-like bundle of twigs bound around a shaped handle — the sort of broom ridden by witches at Halloween — and early believers affirmed that witches' brooms were indeed made of birch. Birch brooms were used in Scotland to sweep the ice in the ancient game of curling. They were the favored broom for sweeping cobblestone yards, and nowadays they are purchased by those gentle souls who sweep, rather than rake, leaves off their lawns. Richard Mabey in *Plantcraft: A Guide to the Everyday Use of Wild Plants* cites their use in modern vinegar refineries. Fermentation vats are lined with birch broom heads to help clarify the liquor. Mabey also claims that a small birch whisk makes an excellent kitchen tool, ideal for the beating of eggs, sauces, and creams, since, unlike its stiffer wire relatives, it bends to conform to the contour of the mixing bowl or pan. However, birch whisks are, he admits, "rather fiddlesome to wash."

An alternative to the bundled besom was the shaved or "splint" broom, whittled from birch, ash, oak, or hickory. Walter Needham in *A Book of Country Things* describes how his grandfather made shaved birch brooms:

To make a shaved broom he would take a white birch probably two inches or more in diameter. He might tie cornhusks around the end for a guide as to how much to shave back. He would start at the bottom and shave up toward the handle end as far as the cornhusk marker, round and round, till he had made enough splints to satisfy him. That would leave a core at the lower end and he would cut it out from among the splinters. Then he would turn the broom around, and start up on the handle, and shave toward the other splints. Of course he wouldn't go far enough to let the upper splints come so close to the lower set that they'd split off. Then he would turn down the second lot of splints — turn them inside out, you might say — and bind them around with braided cornhusks or any other withes he had handy.

Shorter birch lengths were used to make similar small stiff brushes. The splint brooms were meant to be used wet, since frequent dunkings in water kept the splints pliable and prolonged the life of the broom.

The life of the birch is positively fleeting in the time-scale of trees: by sixty, a birch is elderly and by one hundred, Methuselan.

The birch is impressive not for size or age, but for sheer beauty —
and for dogged resilience, as anyone knows who has watched
birches bent over like croquet hoops by winter ice storms struggle
gamely to right themselves again in spring. Such birches were
immortalized by Robert Frost, that cold and crotchety poet, who,
among other things, certainly knew his trees.

Perhaps the worst crime ever perpetrated against a tree by
human beings was performed upon an eleven-foot birch in September 1980 by Jay Gwaltney of Chicago, Illinois. Over an eighty-nine-
hour period, he ate the whole thing.

HICKORY

*H*ickory, if you can get your hands on it, is the stuff to stick in your woodstove. A heavy wood, slow burning and low in smoke production, hickory can yield the same amount of heat per cord as a ton of bituminous coal. Actually all wood, taken pound by pound, puts out about the same amount of heat, generally measured in British Thermal Units (BTU). A BTU is defined as the amount of heat required to raise the temperature of one pound of water one degree Fahrenheit — or, roughly, the amount of heat generated by a single kitchen match. A pound of hardwood thus yields about 8,700 BTU; a pound of softwood, which burns hotter because of its content of resin and pitch, yields about 9,300 BTU. All pounds, however, are not inherently equal, as in the old saw about the pound of feathers and the pound of lead. A cubic foot of light wood, such as poplar, thus puts out a good deal less heat than a cubic foot of heavy wood, such as hickory.

The crucial measure here is density, precisely determined in laboratories by weighing chunks of oven-dried wood of standard size. In these terms, prime candidate for the world's lightest wood is balsa, *Ochroma pyramidale*, a South American weed tree with a wood so soft and spongy that it will decay if left lying on the ground for more than a day or two. The common name *balsa* comes from the Spanish for "raft," originally applied because the South American natives were observed roping the buoyant tree trunks together and using them for that purpose. Balsa density measures 7 pounds/cubic foot, about a ninth that of water (62½ pounds/cubic foot). As light and floatable as balsa is the wood of the African pith-tree, or ambatch (*Aeschynomene elaphroxylon*), from which are made pith helmets and, along the Nile, buoys for hippopotamus harpoons. Heavier than balsa, but still relatively featherweight, is cork, at 13 pounds/cubic foot. On the heavy end of the scale are lignum vitae at 88½ pounds/cubic foot, and ebony, the stuff of piano keys, at 73 pounds/cubic foot, both of which sink in water. Hickory, which floats, weighs in at around 51 pounds/cubic foot, a good dense fireplace log, rivalled on this continent only by black locust and live oak. Oaks, red and white, weigh 48 and 47 pounds/cubic foot, respectively; maples 30–45 pounds/cubic foot, depending on what kind you cut; and pine, the most common wood in present-day home construction, 25–30 pounds/cubic foot.

The amount of heat generated by a given armload of logs is more than a simple function of wood density. Green — or wet — wood, for example, is only about 60 percent as efficient a fuel as seasoned — or dry — wood, primarily because considerable heat energy is frittered away in the unproductive vaporization of moisture. Wet wood can contain up to 65 percent water, depending on the species of tree and the time of year at which the tree is cut. The balmy days of spring, though pleasant for planting the vegetable garden, are the worst of times for felling trees, since the moisture content of the wood increases as the sap begins to run. The yellow birch, for example, doubles its water content in April and May. For this reason, in old China, woodcutting was flatly prohibited in the springtime, and on Calvin Coolidge's farm calendar, the (dry) month of January was prudently devoted to getting in the wood. It has even been suggested that "seasoned" wood may originally have referred to wood cut in the proper season of the year.

Dry, in the woodpile owner's vocabulary, is still slightly damp. Seasoned wood averages 15–30 percent moisture. Firewood reaches this condition after several months to a year of exposure to air, during which the average cord rids itself of one thousand pounds of water. Split wood dries faster than whole logs, because more surface area is made available to the air. Similarly, pieces of split wood, formally known as "sticks" despite their often hefty size, burn better than round logs, since more surface area is available to react with the oxidative processes of the fire.

HEAT FROM FIREWOOD

Species	Weight (Pounds/Cord)	Heat Generated Per Cord (Million BTU)
Hickory	3,900	27
Locust	3,900	27
White oak	3,900	27
Sugar maple	3,800	26
Pecan	3,800	26
Red oak	3,600	24
Walnut	3,400	23
Soft maple	3,200	19
Elm	3,000	20
Magnolia	2,900	20
Sassafras	2,900	20
Sycamore	2,900	20
Chestnut	2,500	18
Redwood	2,200	11
White pine	2,100	13
Poplar	2,100	15
Spruce	2,100	16
Willow	2,100	14

Wood splitting, at least by ax, is viewed by some as a Zen-like occupation romantically redolent of communion with nature. Splitting thus is defined as finding and exploiting the cleavage planes present within the about-to-be-bifurcated log — a natural separation, as opposed to cutting, which implies brute force with overtones of the Texas chainsaw massacre. For this reason, says David Tresemer, author of a whole volume on the art entitled *Splitting Firewood*, atoms are split rather than cut, which indicates that nuclear physicists perform their subatomic manipulations along natural lines. Less spiritual wood-splitters cleave their firewood with gasoline-powered hydraulic rams, which, along with logs, split ears — or equally violent, but cheaper, screw-like devices that can be rigged up to the back wheel of a pickup truck. Not all woods are equally splittable: notably resistant are those with interlocking grains such as sycamore, elm, and hemlock. Others, though easy to split, are hardly worth the effort (see table on page 86). An example is the aforementioned poplar, of which David Tresemer relates an old country tale of firewood barter:

There is a story which describes a cobbler who agreed to trade a pair of boots for a pile of firewood. The woodsplitter delivered poplar (also called "popple"). A month later the boots began to come apart at the seams, and the woodsplitter returned to the cobbler to complain. The cobbler had been waiting with this reply: "What do you expect from popple boots?"

Wood, cut and split, is conventionally delivered and paid for by the cord, a "neat stack" four feet high, four feet wide, and eight feet long, totalling 128 cubic feet. In practice, the actual volume of solid burnable wood in a cord, as determined by forestry researchers clutching calipers, varies from fifty-eight to one hundred cubic feet, depending on stick size, shape, and stacking method. A cord of split wood generally has a greater solid content than a cord of round logs. The name *cord* probably derives from the rope or cord with which these vaguely variable stacks were traditionally measured. In eighteenth- and nineteenth-century England, stones, similarly irregular, were also sold by the cord.

The present-day combination of reduced wood consumption and increased wood prices has led to the evil invention of the "face cord" — a measure of wood four feet high and eight feet long, thus presenting to the world a cord-like face, but a mere one to two feet deep. In recent decades unscrupulous Massachusetts wood dealers, true descendants of the Yankee wooden nutmeg peddlers, became so given to the selling of face cords for full cord prices that the state attempted to do away with the slippery term "cord" altogether. In its place, Massachusetts instated the word "unit," defined as a sternly precise 128 cubic feet. It doesn't seem to have caught on yet, at least in rural newspaper advertisements.

The early American cord, in theory the same size as the modern cord, cost considerably less. Abigail Adams, in an appalled letter from New York to her sister Mary in Massachusetts in 1789, mentioned firewood as her greatest household expense: walnut, in the newly independent Big Apple, was running seven dollars a cord. William Cobbett, that cantankerously astute observer of rural America in the 1820s, shelled out "2 dollars a cord for Hickory," which was more like it. As late as the 1920s, it was still possible to buy a cord of firewood for $3.50, while a modern cord, seasoned, often costs upwards of $100. (In California, $175.) On the other hand, in these days of insulation and airtight woodstoves, we need less wood to ride out the winter. The average colonial New England farmhouse, equipped with two fireplaces, consumed twenty to thirty cords of wood annually, and stayed chilly. Thomas Jefferson's many-fire-placed Monticello, in temperate Virginia, used a seasonal fifty cords — his kitchen alone, one cold February, burned a cord every five days. His wood, "green hiccory" and pine, was free, cut right on the home property, and he sold firewood to his neighbors on a cut-and-carry basis at $5 per winter's supply.

This excessive wood consumption was at least in part the fault of the inefficient colonial fireplace. The crackling open hearth is a shameful heat sink, with an attributed efficiency of 10 percent — which means that of the heat available in any given cord of wood, 10 percent goes to heat the house and 90 percent is dissipated up the chimney. This sad state of affairs took a turn for the better in the early 1700s with the introduction of the woodstove. The first of these were of German origin, installed by the comfortable Pennsylvania Dutch. Early models were "six-plate" stoves, essentially six-sided cast-iron boxes on legs. The plates, in fancier versions, were ornamented with biblical scenes.

Benjamin Franklin's scientifically designed stove became

available in the 1740s, personally promoted by Franklin in a propaganda pamphlet titled "An Account of the New-Invented Pennsylvania Fire Places: Wherein their Construction & manner of Operation is particularly explained; their Advantages above every other Method of warming Rooms demonstrated; and any Objections that have been raised against the Use of them answered & obviated.&c." The Pennsylvania Fire Place, soon nationally known as the Franklin stove, featured a number of cunningly fashioned vents and drafts which directed heat into the room rather than up the chimney. By the 1790s Thomas Jefferson had purchased stoves for Monticello, thus doubling heat production and halving wood use. Jefferson was so pleased with the results that he wrote to his son-in-law Thomas Mann Randolph, "I believe I shall adopt the general use of the stove against the next winter."

As well as suitable for the warming of skating socks, backsides, and whole living rooms, hickory, a tough but surprisingly elastic and bendable wood, was used for tool handles, barn door hinges, barrel and bucket hoops, and the backs of Windsor chairs. Hickory ramrods accompanied the early muzzleloaders; hickory splints were woven into baskets, chair seats, and sieves. The sumpter beam in colonial barns and houses was often cut from a single hickory trunk. This was the major horizontal beam, bearing the burden of the entire building. The name comes from the old English sumpter or pack-horse — the term later applied to any sturdy burden-bearing beast, as in sumpter mule, sumpter ass, sumpter camel, and even *sumpter* canoe and sumpter car. (In the mush-mouthed American colonies, the word degenerated, which is why the burden-bearing beam in many old dwellings is referred to as the "summer beam.") John Dos Passos in *The Big Money* claimed that the Wright brothers' famous airplane that flew for a heart-stopping twelve seconds across the beach at Kitty Hawk was "whittled out of hickory sticks," but soberer aeronautical literature claims ash and spruce. Today hickory is still valued for its stubbornness, shock resistance, and staying power. It is found in modern ax and hammer handles, ladder rungs, golf club shafts, deep-sea fishing rods, and drumsticks.

The traditional toughness of hickory led to at least one presidential nickname. Andrew Jackson, during the War of 1812, headed a rowdy troop of Tennessee mountaineers, frontiersmen, and backwoods plug-uglies with an unprecedented reputation for strength, endurance, and true grit. Jackson somehow managed to outclass them all, displaying so much stamina and energy that his admiring men dubbed him "Old Hickory." The "Old" seems debatable — Jackson was forty-five at the time — but the name stuck. Sixteen years later, during the presidential campaign of 1828, Jackson supporters all over the country promoted their candidate by erecting symbolic hickory poles.

The modern word *hickory* comes from the Indian *pohickery* or *pawhiccorri.* Botanical letters home from seventeenth-century Virginia routinely referred to "pohickery trees." The "po" seems to have been dropped by the end of the century, leaving *hiquery, hickery, hiccory,* and *hackerry,* which all eventually solidified into the contemporary name. William Penn in a "Letter to the Committee of the Free Society of Traders of that Province residing in London," written in 1683, mentioned the "Hickery" as one of Pennsylvania's "Trees of most note." The observant John Lawson, diligently exploring the Carolinas in the first decade of the eighteenth century, described three kinds of hickories: "Hiccory . . . is of the Walnut-kind, and bears a Nut as they do, of which there are found three sorts. The first is . . . the common white Hiccory . . . not a durable Wood . . . another sort . . . we call Hiccory, the Heart thereof being very Red, firm and durable; of which Walking-Sticks, Morters, Pestils, and several other fine Turnery-wares are made. The third is call'd Flying bark'd Hiccory, from its brittle and scaly Bark . . . of this Wood, Coggs for Mills are made, etc. The Leaves smell very fragrant."

Hickories are indeed of the Walnut-kind, members of the family *Juglandaceae* and relatives of the true walnuts. According to *Hortus III,* they comprise a smallish group of deciduous trees, most of them native to the eastern United States. One or two are natives of Mexico and Central America and another couple are Chinese. There is also a so-called Australian hickory, which is really an acacia and as such undeserving of further mention. The true hickories produce compound — *pinnate* — leaves with stalks that may be over two feet long. A pinnate leaf, from the Latin *pinna*, or feather, is defined as one constructed like a feather, the leaflets arranged on opposite sides of a central axis or rachis. Leaflet number varies from species to species. The shagbark hickory leaf, for example, usually consists of five leaflets (two pairs plus an enlarged singlet at the terminus); the mockernut leaf consists of seven to nine leaflets; and the pecan leaf eleven to seventeen.

Hickory nuts, once ripened, range in edibility from the abominable bitternut to the pleasing pecan, with varying degrees of gustatory appeal in between. Lowest of the low in terms of toothsomeness is *Carya cordiformis*, the aptly named bitternut. *C. cordiformis* is the hardiest of the hickories, thriving as far north as Quebec and south to Louisiana. It is distinguished by a light gray or brown bark — the palest of any hickory — and slim sulfur-yellow terminal buds visible in winter and early spring. Below the buds appear the scars left on the twigs after the demise and fall of the previous year's leaves. Each scar represents a leaf stem in cross-section, patterned with tiny dots where the xylem and phloem tubes were snapped off and sealed shut. Each species bears its own distinctive leaf scar, which scars often, to the observant and imaginative, resemble bizarre human faces. Of these, natural historian Rutherford Platt writes:

Hickories bear some of the most vivid and ludicrous faces. Take the mockernut . . . which has large scars that you can see easily with the naked eye. The head is wide at the top and curves to an elongated chin. Often this is pushed to one side and the features show an agonizing expression like a cartoon of a prize fighter who has just received a terrible wallop. The bitternut hickory . . . has a long oval face with little beady eyes and a nose-wide mustache. The effect of a little sulphur-colored bud is like an undersized hat sitting on top of this face, and this makes it all the more whimsical. You will see camels and monkeys when you look at the walnuts. The butternut

. . . is a remarkable animal with a long chin and a pad like a forelock across the top of its forehead. Poplars have pompous and scholarly visages. Their leaf scars form wide solemn faces, surmounted by tall hats, exactly like brownies who have grown very serious and intellectual. In contrast, the elm has a frivolous and dissipated expression. It has a wide oval face as though it were squashed and sometimes one eye is smaller than the other, making it wink.

The loathsome *C. cordiformis* nuts are round with a sharply pointed end, a sort of bulbous heart shape. From this derives the scientific *cordiformis*, which in fact means "heart-shaped." The meats, despite their Valentine-like packaging, are so mouth-puckeringly bitter that only squirrels habitually eat them, which means that they have a better chance than their tastier relatives of sprouting and developing into trees. The pioneers collected the nuts and pressed them for oil, which was both burned in lamps and swallowed as a cure for rheumatism.

The pignut, *C. glabra*, with a somewhat more southerly range, only makes it as far north as Massachusetts, Connecticut, and Pennsylvania. It is often, but not always, sweeter than the bitternut, and the common name honors its most devoted consumer. Definitely sweet, but largely unget-at-able, are the fruits of *C. tomentosa*, the mockernut. The scientific name comes from the Latin for "hairy" and refers to the furry surface of the leaf stalks, twigs, and undersides of the leaflets. The common name, according to one source, comes from the Dutch for "heavy hammer," indicative of the rock-like thickness of the nutshell and the necessarily serious measures taken to crack it. Alternatively, the name may mean just exactly what it says: with its thick shell and miniature meat, the mockernut is a maddening mockery of a nut. The leaves of the mockernut are fragrant: crushed, they are variously described as smelling of paint, soap, and new-mown grass.

In the eighteenth century, mockernut bark enjoyed a brief popularity as a dyestuff. Recipes survive for using the bark to produce various yellows — yellow-tan, yellow-brown, yellow-green, brass, and gold — in woollen goods. Mockernut yellow looked hopeful enough that Edward Bancroft, the British physician who so effectively exploited quercitron, took out a patent on it. The patent turned out to be a waste of time, and Bancroft never managed to make a penny off his hickory bark. The hickory-derived yellows, at closer inspection, proved duller and less attractive than those of other commercially available dyes, and the bark, possessed of its share of the legendary hickory toughness, was hard to grind and concentrate.

Most distinctive of American hickories is almost certainly the shagbark, *C. ovata*. The shagbark is named for its unmistakable bark, a shaggy and tattered production peeling off the tree in long unkempt vertical strips. This, clearly, is John Lawson's "Flying bark'd Hiccory." Its nuts are borne within four-sided egg-shaped husks which split apart spontaneously upon ripening. This preliminary split, unfortunately, is as far as nature goes, leaving the eager consumer with a harvest of sweet pecan-like nuts, all notoriously difficult to crack. Similarly shaggy-barked is the shellbark hickory, *C. laciniosa*. Shellbark nuts, flavorfully sweet, have the thickest husks and shells of any hickory, which is no idle boast. Experts suggest extracting the meats from the recalcitrant shell by placing the nut seam-side up on some solid surface — some suggest clamping it in a vise — and whacking it with a hammer until it cracks. The nut can then be pried out of the inner chambers with a nutpick, or, if you lack formal nut equipment, a jackknife.

The American Indians made a milk from sweet hickory nuts, by a process described in plant collector William Bartram's *Travels in North America*:

They pound [the nuts] to pieces and then cast them into boiling water, which, after passing through fine strainers, preserves the most oily part of the liquid; this they call by a name which signifies hiccory milk; it is as sweet and rich as fresh cream, and is an ingredient in most of their cookery, especially hominy and corn cakes.

Euell Gibbons in *Stalking the Wild Asparagus* attempted to duplicate this dish, producing a pale-brown broth dotted with floating nut-meats, about the consistency of bean soup. He ate a bowlful, with crackers, and gave it a lukewarm review: "While it wasn't the best soup I ever ate," wrote Mr. Gibbons, "it was pretty good, and it must be very nourishing."

Both Indians and settlers ate hickory nuts, cracked and raw, by the handful; colonial ladies served them, shelled, with pastries at fancy teas; and the better dinners ended with dishes of hickory nuts, fruit, and wine. Hickory nuts are even better baked or roasted, in cakes, breads, muffins, and cookies. A yellowed newspaper clipping in a recipe scrapbook belonging, once upon a time, to my next-door neighbor's Great-aunt Dorothy turned up the following:

Mrs. Thomas A. Edison, wife of the famous inventor, possesses creative ability.

Her genius lies in the field of culinary art and the recipe she contributed to the New Bedford Times *recipe contest is proof of her ability. Her recipe for hickory nut cake follows:*

1½ cups sugar, 1 cup butter, scant, 1 cup milk, 3 cups flour, 2 teaspoons baking powder, whites of 6 eggs beaten stiff, 1 teaspoon vanilla, sugar and beat until it gets cold. Flavor to taste.

King of the edible hickories — "the Cadillac of the nut trees," writes one professional grower — is *C. illinoensis,* the pecan, the only hickory commonly cultivated for nuts. The pecan is a pointedly warm-weather tree. Notoriously tender — food historian Waverley Root describes its growth habits as "crotchety" — it requires a long hot summer for proper nut development. Its range is accordingly southerly, extending down the Mississippi River Valley and west-ward into Texas. One hypothesis holds that the pecan actually originated in Texas. The scientific *illinoensis* may simply indicate that classification-minded explorers — probably French missionaries — first bumped into the pecan in Illinois. The first European mention of the pecan, however, dates to 1541, when Hernando de Soto, slogging through Arkansas in a fruitless search for gold, came upon a plain full of "walnut" trees. De Soto's walnuts, however, bore thin-shelled nuts — which certainly no native walnut ever did — so modern historians hold that the Spaniards had stumbled upon the pecan.

The pecan was promoted on the east coast by Thomas Jefferson, an indefatigable supporter of hickories, who planted specimens of nearly all the major American species at Monticello. Jefferson imported his "paccans" from the Mississippi Valley and shared the nuts with various friends, among them George Washington. Washington planted his in the Botanical Garden at Mount Vernon, referring to them in his plantation records as "Illinois nuts" and "Mississippi nuts." Two of the oldest surviving original trees on the grounds of Mount Vernon today are pecans. Once his trees were established, one story goes, Washington always carried pecans in his pocket — though perhaps not for personal consumption, since Washington lost his last remaining natural tooth in 1789, the year he became president. From then on he was dependent on the awkwardly fitting hippopotamus-ivory dentures so irreverently immortalized on canvas by Gilbert Stuart. Washington cleaned these exotic teeth by soaking them overnight in beer.

C. illinoensis is the largest tree of the hickory genus. Appropriately it is the state tree of size-conscious Texas, whose state motto ("Friendship") presumably precludes jealousy of Mississippi, which possesses the present American pecan champion. The champion, according to the American Forestry Association, flourishes in Warren County, Mississippi, measuring 130 feet tall and 23 feet, 10 inches, in girth, with a 90-foot crown spread. Like the rest of the hickories, pecans bear both male and female flowers on the same tree. Such a tidy juxtaposition of the sexes — often male and female blooms develop shoulder-to-shoulder, from the same compound bud — should ensure that the self-sufficient pecan has all the equipment in place for prompt fertilization and nut production. This is not, however, generally the case: most pecans require a mate to generate offspring. The reason for this is faulty timing. Each male flower — catkin — consists of a slender stalk of one hundred or more tiny florets, each capable of producing some eight thousand grains of pollen. The wind transports this pollen to the clusters of pale-green female — or pistillate — flowers. If primed for fertilization, the stigma, the smokestack-like tip of the pistil, has undergone a chemical change that renders it sticky, such that passing pollen grains adhere to its surface. On a given pecan tree, male and female flowers usually mature at different times — that is, pollen shedding by the catkins and stigma receptivity in the pistillate flowers overlap either very briefly or not at all. This condition is known to botanists as *dichogamy*, from the Greek meaning "double marriage," and is Mother Nature's way of simultaneously promoting cross-fertilization and preventing self-fertilization, with its potential Jukes-like consequences. Self-pollinated pecans tend to produce inferior nuts.

Dichogamy varies from cultivar to cultivar. In some, dubbed *protandrous*, or "male first," the catkins mature before the pistillate flowers. In other more chivalrous varieties, stigma receptivity in the female flowers precedes pollen-shedding by the males. These are known as *protogynous* ("female first") pecans. Oddly, sexual precedence may vary with geographical location. The Barton pecan, for example, is protandrous in the United States, but protogynous in Brazil, which leaves one with the impression that everything goes topsy-turvy south of the equator, in the same manner in which water suddenly starts swirling in the opposite direction as it goes down the drain. Not true, however: the Western pecan proved protandrous in New Mexico and Texas, protogynous in Oklahoma, and monogamous, or synchronous, in Brazil, where pollen-shedding and stigma receptivity occur at the same time.

None of this sexual maneuvering applies to the young pecan, however; after a long and chaste adolescence, the pecan may only begin to bear nuts at the ripe old age of twenty or so. Once mature, healthy trees produce anywhere from one hundred to six hundred pounds of nuts per year. The states of Georgia and Texas are the top pecan growers in this country; Georgia accounts for about a third of the American crop, which totals over one hundred million pounds of nuts each year. Texas, home of chili and barbecue, is America's top pecan consumer. Nearly all this country's butter pecan ice cream is eaten by Texans, leading one puzzled food analyst to remark of the Lone Star State, "Texans will buy anything with pecans in it." One Texas doctor, according to the National Nut Growers Association, advises his patients to eat twelve pecans a day as a remedy for arthritis.

Prominent among historic pecans is the Hogg Pecan of Austin, Texas — an immense tree planted in lieu of the conventional marble tombstone on the grave of former governor James Stephen Hogg. The nuts of this tree, according to a proviso in the governor's will, were to be distributed to the populace in order to make Texas a "land of trees." The nuts have been handed out since 1926, most of them initially planted and reared to the sapling stage on the grounds of Texas A&M University in College Station. The project seems to have succeeded, since Texas, at last rough count, possessed at least seventy million nut-bearing pecan trees. Governor Hogg, who dominated the Texas political scene from 1891 to 1895, is generally remembered less for his pecans than for his daughter, the melliflu-ously named Ima.

Today there are somewhere between three hundred and one thousand named varieties of pecans, the number varying with the chutzpah of the reference source. *Hortus III*, which treads a conser-vative middle line, claims five hundred. The first of these, called 'Centennial', was developed in 1846 on Oak Alley Plantation in St. James Parish, Louisiana, by a slave gardener known only as Antoine. Most modern cultivars issue from the USDA's Pecan Field Station in Brownwood, Texas, and are fetchingly named after Indian tribes: hence Cherokee, Cheyenne, Chickasaw, Kiowa, Mohawk, Pawnee, Shawnee, Shoshoni, and the like. This is wholly appropriate since the natives of pecan territory were ardent supporters of the oil-rich nuts, grinding them into meal, incorporating them in succotashes, and roasting them whole to carry on hunting trips, as the original trail mix. The word *pecan* itself is an Indian term, derived from the Algonquian *pakan* or *pagann*.

Many present-day pecan cultivars are thin- or "paper"- shelled, a trait which allows ordinary human nut eaters to get at them without resort to vise and hammer. Others are (relatively) cold-hardy. The southern pecans, which like a long hot summer, require a 270- to 290-day growing season for nut development. Northern pecans are speedier, ripening a crop in 170 to 200 days. "Northern," as applied to pecans, is still somewhat loosely defined — hardy cultivars seem to do well through Illinois and Iowa; bearing, but struggling, trees have been coddled along in Pennsylvania, Minnesota, and southern Canada. At the limits of their range, however, nut quality suffers. Nut shells may be only partly filled with shrivelled kernels, the result of the harried tree's decision to cut its losses and mature as quickly as possible before the growing season draws to a close.

Another possibility for pecan lovers who lack the proper pecan climate is the hican, a hickory x pecan hybrid that is generally hardier than the delicate pecan and thinner shelled than the impenetrable hickory. Many northern growers, however, have found these disappointing. The nut crops tend to be small and kernels partially empty. "It has taken several years to prove it directly," wrote a disillusioned expert from Ontario, Canada, in the 1987 *Annual Report of the Northern Nut Growers Association*, "but most of the well known hican cultivars are essentially worthless."

Our chief contender for the pecan, hican, or hickory harvest is the squirrel, a fuzzily attractive rodent whose cleverness at nabbing nuts is near legendary. (Witness the number of extant patents for "squirrel-proof" bird feeders.) Ernest Thompson Seton, naturalist extraordinaire, estimated the squirrel population of the eastern hardwood forests at something over a thriving billion when the Pilgrims landed. Each squirrel, at Seton's highly informed guess, accounts for something between one and ten thousand nuts each autumn, which, multiplied out, totalled a truly staggering amount of arboreal plunder. The squirrels and the early settlers squared off almost immediately, recognizing an insoluble interest conflict. Many colonial governments soon offered bounties on squirrels. In the mid-1700s, Pennsylvania paid off on a yearly 640,000 gray squirrels at threepence apiece. The total outlay exhausted the state treasury, and eventually it became necessary to levy a special tax for the purpose of raising squirrel-bounty money. In 1808, the squirrel-infested Ohio Territory turned about and made squirrel-hunting mandatory: a three-dollar fine was levied against anyone failing to bring in the annual quota of one hundred squirrel scalps.

The squirrel population has fallen off in these urban days, but remains substantial and invasive enough that nut growers refer to them snarlingly as major pests. It is uncertain how many cultivated nuts are caged annually by squirrels. "All if allowed," growled John Davidson in a 1943 status report to the Northern Nut Growers Association (NNGA) — which almost unanimously anti-squirrel organization passed a formal anti-squirrel resolution in 1958. Annual losses of ten million pounds of pecans are attributed to squirrels, with perhaps twice that amount travelling down the gullets of other nut predators, such as crows, jays, possums, and deer. Squirrels, for a one-third share in the pickings, seem to come in for more than their share of resentment — perhaps because they are so cheerfully blatant about their nut-snatching behavior. Donald M. Christisen, Senior Wildlife Biologist at the Missouri Department of Conservation in Columbia, recently submitted a report to the NNGA titled "The Second Crop for Nut Growers." It begins:

Tree squirrels, by nature, are nut eaters (and planters) at cross purposes with nut growers. Traditionally, the response to squirrel depredation of nut crops has been trapping and/or poisoning squirrels which creates a negative public image for the nut grower.

Mr. Christisen seeks to reverse this negative public image by putting the squirrel campaign on a sporting basis: he urges the opening of nut orchards to hunters. Pecan-fed squirrels — Mr. Christisen refers to them as "nut by-products" — in analogy to peanut-fed hogs, make excellent eating. Under the Christisen program, the feckless squirrels, rather than falling victim to senseless slaughter with its accompanying negative public image, would go to round out the human dinner menu. The nut orchard would thus double, profitably, as a sort of arboreal butcher shop.

While not everyone is attracted to the idea of blithely harvesting squirrels with a .22, squirrels historically have played a feature role in American cooking. Squirrel was the original star ingredient of Brunswick stew, a savory mix of corn, onions, tomatoes, and lima beans, with a dash of cayenne pepper, said to have been invented in 1828 by "Uncle Jimmy" Matthews of Brunswick County, Virginia. Opposing claims for stew inventorship have been filed by Brunswick County, North Carolina, and the town of Brunswick, Georgia. Brunswick stew, a traditional staple of southern political rallies, potluck suppers, and the Kentucky Derby, is related to *burgoo*, originally a grain porridge and standard fare for the long-suffering eighteenth-century seaman. On land, burgoo evolved into a spicy grain stew, often based on squirrel. Jerry Mack Johnson recommends squirrel in a kettle over the campfire, simmered with rice and ketchup; a gourmet-minded Louisiana recipe proffers squirrel ravioli, the pasta stuffed with minced squirrel, garlic, and watercress.

Mr. Christisen likes his squirrels fried, and followed, in poetic culinary justice, with pecan pie.

WALNUT

*W*alnuts, accompanied by Stilton cheese and port wine, formed the traditional last course at the upper-class Victorian meal — all three enjoyed in chauvinist leisure by the gentlemen after the ladies had tactfully retired elsewhere. The walnuts so consumed were English walnuts, *Juglans regia*, also known as Persian walnuts, French walnuts, or Madeira nuts, the last from their frequent pairing with Madeira wine — in the same fine spirit today, seasoned peanuts are frequently known as beer nuts.

The English walnut may indeed have originated in or near Persia. Though a few stubborn souls hold out for China, the majority of reference sources cite the Middle East as the walnut's primal breeding ground. *J. regia* arrived in Europe in prehistoric times. Battered remnants of walnut shells have been retrieved from the garbage dumps of Swiss Lake dwellings, and dated to seven thousand years ago. The first formal mention of the not-yet-English walnut occurs in records from ancient Babylon, where the trees were under cultivation. The Greeks knew it as the "Persian nut"; the Romans knew it as "Jupiter's acorn" — in Latin, *Jovis glans*, hence the contracted genus name *Juglans* — and ate it for dessert. Petrified walnuts were found on the table at the Temple of Isis in Pompeii, abandoned on the fatal 24th of August A.D. 74. The Romans may have introduced the walnut to Great Britain — or may not, since some evidence indicates that walnuts were already flourishing on the island when the legions arrived. At some point, however, the British natives certainly viewed the walnut as an alien life form — the Old

English *walh-hnuta*, according to the *Oxford English Dictionary*, means strange or foreign nut.

The walnut, once Anglicized, was co-opted for a large number of culinary and medicinal purposes. According to the medieval Doctrine of Signatures, which ascribed therapeutic properties to plants based on their resemblance to specific parts of the human body, the walnut with its skull-like shell and brain-like kernel was a likely treatment for ailments of the head. Ground walnut shell was thus prescribed for head wounds, and walnut meats for headaches and mental illnesses. Somewhat less logically, walnuts were said to ward off lightning, witchcraft, and epileptic fits. The head-like aspect of the walnut led to the nineteenth-century use of the word "nut" to mean head and the accompanying "off one's nut," to mean crazy; and to the twentieth-century phrase "to use one's nut," which meant to think, "nuts," which meant cuckoo, and the associated "nut-case," who more often than not ended up in a "nut-house."

Charlemagne ordered walnuts planted in his extensive orchards, and walnuts were a prominent enough item of trade in medieval Europe to require an official "measurer of walnuts" to protect consumers from fraud. The Persian walnut, among the Persians, was frequently used like the almond to make a thick paste as a base for sauces. This culinary custom was brought home by appreciative Crusaders and enthusiastically adopted by the cooks of western Europe. Among the earliest known of English recipes is a walnut sauce intended as a topping for fish, dating from 1430: "Take curnyles of walnotys and clovys of garllek and piper bred and salt and cast in a morter and grynd it smal and tempre it with some of the broth that the fysshe was sode in, and serve forth."

Walnuts are featured in an even earlier French cookbook titled *Le Menagier de Paris*, a tome written in 1392 by an elderly Parisian lawyer for the edification of his fifteen-year-old bride. It includes instructions for salvaging scorched stew (break up walnut meats and boil them in the kettle along with the rest of the burned ingredients) and directions for a "monumental conserve" of green walnuts, prepared with mustard, horseradish, spices, honey, and "red roots," which are known in this day and age as carrots. Elinor Fettiplace's seventeenth-century *Receipt Book*, along with enchantingly descriptive recipes such as "To Make Sirrop of Violetts," "To Bake a Rabbet," and "To Make Apricocke Wine," includes instructions for preserving green walnuts in rosewater, and suggests an external application of walnut oil as a treatment for eczema.

The Persian walnut came to the New World from England with the English colonists, who accordingly referred to their transplanted saplings as "English walnuts" to distinguish them from the already-established American species. Nearly all of the walnuts now grown commercially in the United States are English walnuts and over 98 percent of them come from California. These are the walnuts commonly available in supermarket nut bins.

Despite our overwhelming dependence on the English walnut, North Americans have six walnut species of our very own. Best known of these is the black walnut, *Juglans nigra*, which ranges from Canada to eastern Texas. John Lawson observed *J. nigra* in his exploration of the Carolinas, and wrote of it, "The Walnut-Tree of America is call'd Black Walnut to distinguish it from the Hiccories, it having a blacker Bark . . . . The Wood is very firm and durable, of which Tables and Chests of Drawers are made . . . to bottom Vessels for the Sea withal; and they say, that it is never eaten by the Worm. The Nuts have a large Kernel, which is very oily, except laid by, a long time to mellow. The Shell is very thick, as all the native Nuts of America are . . . ." Mr. Lawson, as usual, spoke true. The black walnut is distinguished by its ridged dark brown bark — one tree lover compares it to alligator hide — which often deepens with age to black. It is also, like its other walnut relatives, distinguished from the hickories by a chambered pith. A walnut twig, sliced lengthwise, reveals a series of hollows separated by cross plates, spaced at about twenty to the inch. Similarly sliced hickory twigs have solid centers. Walnut leaves, like those of the hickories, are compound, composed of fifteen to twenty-one "lancehead-shaped" leaflets, all in pairs except the singleton at the terminus. Also like the hickories, the walnuts are *monoecious* and incompletely *dichogamous* — which means that though most are at least partially self-fertile, to ensure a good nut crop, two walnuts are better than one. The nuts develop embedded in a round green fleshy fruit and as such are not true nuts, but drupe stones, like the stones of peaches and plums. The nut meats are a pair of greatly enlarged fleshy *cotyledons*, or modified "leaves," designed to store enough protein to fuel the developing embryo. Walnuts are highly proteinaceous, though less so than the pecan or the ubiquitous peanut. Modern walnut promoters have touted them as higher in protein than milk or meat. This is certainly true in the former case — cow's milk contains 3.5 percent protein; human milk even less — and debatably true in the latter. Walnuts, at 21 percent protein, top pork (12) percent), lamb (16 percent), beef (18 percent), turkey (20 percent), and fish (20 percent), but are outclassed by the nutritious chicken (30 percent).

NUTRITIONAL COMPOSITION OF SOME EDIBLE NUTS
(Percent)

	Protein	Fat	Carbohydrate	Water
Acorn	8	5	68	14
Chestnut	3	2	42	52
Hickory	13	69	13	3
Peanut	26	48	19	6
Pecan	9	71	15	3
Black walnut	21	59	15	3
English walnut	15	64	16	4

Native Americans, who lacked chickens, exploited walnuts from pre-Columbian times. Cracked walnut shells from prehistoric feasts have been excavated from two-thousand-year-old campsites in the Great Lakes region. Equally old black walnut shells, delicately carved in the shape of birds and pierced for earrings, were found among the treasure hoards of the Mound Builders of Ohio and Indiana, along with caches of river pearls, mica disks, and copper breastplates. Settlers observed the Indians eating black walnuts, raw and roasted, and pounding them like hickory nuts to make "milk."

The settlers themselves were disillusioned with the native walnuts. Robert Beverly in *The History and Present State of Virginia* (published by R. Parker at the Unicorn under the Piazzas of the Royal Exchange in 1705) damned them as "rank and oily." Public opinion supported him for some decades thereafter, the native nuts being universally viewed as coarser and less appealing than the homestyle European variety. By the late eighteenth century, however, the tide had turned. George Washington and Thomas Jefferson grew both English and American walnuts on their respective estates, and Jefferson was proud enough of his black walnuts to write home in 1786 from his diplomatic post in Paris for half a bushel, to be distributed among European friends as seeds. Early American recipes using walnuts include walnut ratafia, a feminine alcoholic beverage heavy in sugar, cloves, and cinnamon; walnut cakes and breads; and pickled walnuts, made with unripe nuts gathered in early summer. Martha Washington's *Booke of Cookery* includes a recipe for such preserved walnuts, beginning, "Take wallnuts between whitsontide & midsumer when they are a little bigger than nutmeggs." Whitsuntide traditionally is the seventh Sunday after Easter, which means that potential picklers should start collecting their nuts in mid-June. In a good year, one historian suggests, pickleable walnuts may even be available in May, which in turn could explain that peculiar nursery-rhyme reference to "gathering nuts in May." The Washington *Booke of Cookery* also features a medicinal preparation of "Wallnut Water," "good against winde & other illnesses," and a recipe for a walnut-containing "Restorative Marmalet" which must date from Elizabethan times. Along with the ounce or two of walnut meats, the Marmalet calls for green ginger, red nettle seeds, the back and belly of a skink, oil of cinnamon, and "6 leavs of gold & 2 drams of prepared perles." Simpler, cheaper, and probably equally Restorative was an 1829 recipe for Walnut Mead Wine, which required only water, three and a half pounds of honey, twenty walnut leaves, and a spoonful of yeast. It was reportedly drinkable after aging for three months.

Walnut mead, moreover, could be prepared without cracking

any nuts, a task of such magnitude that the NNGA advertises a specially designed black walnut nutcracker made of cast-iron and carbon steel. The extraordinary toughness of the black walnut shell is the major reason it has not had the commercial success of its English cousin. Walnut husks, unlike those of the more cooperative hickories, do not spontaneously split apart upon ripening. Instead the entire fruit plummets heavily to the ground "with a sound like horses galloping." Black walnut consumers recommend a number of rough-and-ready methods for separating nuts from the enveloping husks. Euell Gibbons suggests stomping on the nuts in heavy boots, using for this purpose, in lieu of the up-and-down prance of grape treading, a vicious grinding crush delivered from the heel. Other black walnut growers rely on their pickup trucks, which are apparently worth maintaining if for no other purpose than for driving slowly back and forth over posi-tioned rows of fresh nuts. The USDA, less excitingly, recommends a corn sheller. Once liberated from their husks, the nuts must be picked out of the debris and spread out to dry for several weeks in some dry well-ventilated place before cracking.

It is preferable, if not essential, to wear rubber gloves while pawing through crushed walnut husks, since walnut juice stains all that it contacts a deep and permanent brown. This phenomenon was

---

PICKLED WALNUTS

Gather the green nuts when they are full-sized but soft enough that an ice pick can be thrust straight through the entire fruit. Dunk in boiling water and rub off the fuzz on the outside of the husks. Put the nuts in a large kettle, cover with water, and boil until the water turns brown. Pour off the discolored water, add fresh water, and boil again. Repeat until the water remains clear.

Pack the boiled nuts in sterile quart jars. To each jar add one dill flower, 3 walnut leaflets, 1 heaping teaspoon pickling spices, and ¼ teaspoon alum. Fill the jars with boiling cider vinegar and seal.

The pickles will be ready to eat in four weeks.

described in the mid-eighteenth century by the Swiss naturalist Peter Kalm. Kalm, Linnaeus' prize pupil, spent three years, from 1748 to 1751, exploring and plant-collecting in the American colonies. The three years were scientifically and personally profitable. Kalm canoed up the Hudson, caught poison ivy, visited Niagara Falls, balked at eating unripe persimmons, made friends with Ben Franklin — who loaned him a "Pennsylvania Fire Place" — and got married. He was particularly observant of American trees, noting of the black walnut that it dropped its nuts in October. "The green peel which enclosed them," wrote Kalm, "if frequently handled, would yield a black color which could not be got off the fingers in two or three weeks time, though the hands were washed ever so much. It was therefore not advisable to carry these nuts with their green shells in any cloth, for it would then be spoiled." In this day and age, if the stain is fresh, it can be removed with household bleach; once set, however, there's nothing for it but patience. The bogus Indians of the Boston Tea Party, who, for greater verisimilitude, stained their hands and faces with walnut juice must have remained revealingly brown for weeks thereafter. Colonial housewives used the bark and hulls of the black walnut for dyeing wool brown and occasionally as an under-dye, in preparation for dyeing black. The English walnut releases a similar brown dye, used by the Romans. The English walnut is responsible for what is perhaps the longest-lasting walnut-juice stain in history, still visible, according to Waverley Root, on the cliffs of La Barre near Le Malene in France. The cliffs were dyed by the oily smoke from a walnut-crammed warehouse that was burned down by enraged peasants during the French Revolution.

The walnut, even in the absence of edible nuts, would still be a highly valued tree. The wood, a lustrous dark brown with occasional streaks of purple, has been in demand for centuries for interior panelling and cabinetwork. Boston diarist Samuel Sewall ordered for his daughter Judith, upon the occasion of her marriage in 1720, a vast assortment of household furnishings, among them "A Duzen of good Black Walnut Chairs fine Cane with a Couch." There were also "A Duzen Cane Chairs of a Different Figure and a Great Chair for a Chamber; all black Walnut," and "A true Looking Glass of Black Walnut Frame of the Newest Fashion, if," he added prudently, "the Fashion be good" and the price no more than five or six pounds. The woodwork of the Daniel Boone house in Defiance, Missouri, completed after seven years' labor in 1810, is entirely of black walnut, handcarved by Daniel himself.

Besides being beautiful, walnut is harder than oak and extremely stable once seasoned, for which reason it was the wood of choice for gunstocks, in which even minor warping could discombobulate the barrel and sights of the weapon. English walnut was first used for this purpose, but gunsmiths later turned to American black walnut, equally stable and more available in long straight lengths. The Brown Bess muskets that figured so lethally in the Revolutionary War had walnut stocks, as did the Winchester repeating rifles that slaughtered the buffalo and won the American West. By the 1820s "to shoulder walnut" meant to enlist as a soldier. Militarily, black walnut kept up with the times: in World War I, it was used for airplane propellers.

The butternut or white walnut, *J. cinerea*, is a more northerly ranging walnut, found from Quebec to Minnesota and south to Missouri and Tennessee. "Our black walnuts rarely grow beyond ye 41 or 42 degree northward," wrote John Bartram, the Pennsylvania farmer who became the eighteenth century's premier American naturalist and, eventually, King's Botanist, "but the white walnut or butternut grows much further north." There it attains heights of up to one hundred feet and bears two-foot-long compound leaves, furred on the underside with dense soft hairs. This is most likely the tree under which Henry David Thoreau lounged when he penned:

> *Here while I lie beneath this walnut bough,*
> *What care I for the Greeks or for Troy town . . .*

The poem, which echoes many summer-student sentiments, is titled "My Books I'd Fain Cast Off."

The Indians occasionally tapped the tree for sugar, though

inefficiently, four times more butternut sap than maple being required to produce a quart of syrup. They also used the bark in a medicinal tea renowned for its laxative properties. This tea was adopted by internally distressed pioneers, and butternut bark, notably that stripped from the tree roots, was officially registered in the *United States Pharmacopoeia* from 1820 to 1905.

The nuts are packaged like stubborn Russian dolls in sticky elliptical husks surrounding pointy-ended roughly ridged shells that are, if possible, even more difficult to crack than those of the black walnut. The meats, once obtained, are delicious, tasting, says one discerning butternut fan, "like a mild black walnut with a hint of banana." Delicious, and fattening: the name *butternut* derives from the kernels' high oil content, which may at peak ripeness total 60 percent. The Iroquois Indians routinely extracted this oil and used it in cooking or as a hair-dressing pomade. Richard Mabey recommends using individual oily nut kernels to polish furniture. The nuts impart a lovely satiny finish but are, admits Mabey, "rather fiddle-some to hold" and the polisher ends up frequently stubbing finger-tips on the wood surface. As a rule of thumb, a single nut kernel is sufficient to thoroughly oil one walking stick, and a walnut walking-stave, walnut-polished in this fashion, would be, says Mabey, "a prize indeed, as elegantly self-contained a delicacy as squids cooked in their own ink."

Like black walnut, butternut is a valued furniture wood, favored in colonial days for carriages and church altars. Also like the black walnut, the butternut yields a permanent brown dye. Butternut brown was known to the colonists as early as 1669 when Governor Winthrop of Connecticut submitted some dyed fiber samples to the Royal Society of London, accompanied by the legend, "Shreds of stuff made by the English planters of cotton and wool, put up to shew the colour, which was only dyed with the bark of a kind of walnut-tree, called by the planters the butter-nut-tree, the kernels of that sort of walnut being very oily, whence they are called butter-nuts. They dyed it only with the decoction of that bark, without alum or copperas, as they said." This last sentence refers to the fact that the walnut pigment is a substantive dye, which means that it binds directly to the fiber without the assistance of a mordant, or intermediary chemical cross-linking agent. The use of various mordants will, however, give a greater range of color variations — butternut hulls with an alum mordant, for example, yield a greenish tan color; with an alum mordant plus a bit of ferrous sulfate (Governor Winthrop's "copperas") yield gray. Butternut bark boiled in an iron kettle, announced a dye manual of 1811, will eventually dissolve away enough of the iron to yield a "tolerable black," much exploited in the coloring of early American stockings. The browns of the overshot coverlets turned out by home weavers during the eighteenth and nineteenth centuries often came from the walnut tree, though other homegrown browns were derived from the barks of alders, hemlock, or red maple, or, occasionally, tobacco leaves. It was butternut bark and nut hulls that colored the uniforms of Confederate soldiers a tan closely akin to the modern khaki. The prevalence of this color among the Southern forces led the Yankees to nickname both butternut-clad troops and Southern civilians "butternuts." A similar brown, made from the nut hulls of the shrubby little Arizona walnut, *J. major*, was used by the Navajo weavers of the Southwest.

The brown pigment found in walnut twigs, leaves, bark, roots, and nut hulls is *juglone*, a cyclic compound known to chemists as *5-hydroxy-1, 4-napthoquinone*. Its primary function as regards the walnut tree is aggressive. Exuded into the environment, juglone is toxic to neighboring plants. This chemically murderous method of maintaining personal space is known to botanists as *allelopathy*. The earliest written reference to walnut toxicity is believed to date to ancient Greece, when Pliny the Elder wrote in his *Historia Naturalis*: "The shadow of walnut trees is poison to all plants within its compass, and it kills whatever it touches." John Evelyn, in a famed seventeenth-century treatise on trees titled *Sylva*, stated of the walnut that "the very husks and leaves, being macerated in warm Water, and that Liquor poured on the Carpet of Walks, and Bowling-greens, does infallibly kill the Worms, without endangering the grass . . . ." Early American farmers, observing the lethal activities of walnut trees, believed they possessed insecticidal properties and planted them around their barns to ward off flies.

Juglone exists within the walnut primarily in the form of *hydrojuglone*, a colorless, non-toxic compound. Hydrojuglone remains benign until exposed to air or to oxidizing substances produced by the roots of encroaching plants. Oxidizing agents, like blood spurring on a shark, convert hydrojuglone to attack form. Juglone has proved toxic to microorganisms, fungi, insects, fish, and an occasional mammal, though its effects are best recognized on associated plants. Sensitive species attempting to snuggle up to the walnut tree are soon afflicted by "walnut wilt," an ominous condition of browning and wilting, eventually ending in death. Legendarily sensitive to walnut wilt are tomatoes; also among the affected are alfalfa, apples, asparagus, chrysanthemums, honeysuckle, peonies, potatoes, rhododendrons, and roses. Not all plants, however, fall before the walnut's chemical assault. Among the resistant, according to a 1986 *Horticulture* article by gardener Frank Robinson, are hollyhocks, bellflowers, bee balm, Jerusalem artichokes, snowdrops, grape hyacinths, weeping forsythia, Virginia creeper, begonias, marigolds, and pansies. Some grasses are also impervious: John Evelyn's wormkilling walnut extract spared the grass on his "Bowling-green." Blackberries and raspberries, which prefer partial shade, are said to positively flourish under walnut trees.

Walnuts, though perhaps the best known, are not the only species to exhibit allelopathy. Many herbaceous plants produce chemical weaponry damaging to tree seedlings. Asters and goldenrod are toxic to yellow poplar and Virginia pine; ragweed, hawkweed, timothy, and the tall buttercup inhibit growth and development of sugar maples. Giant foxtail has proved toxic to loblolly pines; broomsedge, crownvetch, and wild carrots all poison black locusts. Broomsedge is a weedy grass, noted for its ability to thrive on miserable soil. A 1972 report in the *American Journal of Botany* hypothesized that broomsedge's success in the horticultural slums may be due to its chemical ability to inhibit the growth of *Rhizobium* and *Azotobacter*, important nitrogen-fixing bacteria which colonize nodules on the roots of legumes. By wiping these admirable micro-organisms off its turf, the self-sufficient broomsedge blocks the growth of all species with higher nitrogen requirements. Broomsedge, perhaps in retaliation for all those walnut-wilted roses and tomatoes, is also toxic to walnut seedlings, as are asters, goldenrods, and tall fescue.

Barring insidious attack by broomsedge, a healthy walnut may stand for two or three centuries. An immense walnut in Alabama, known as the Colbert Ferry Walnut, marks the site of the ferry that once connected the Natchez Trace with the Tennessee River. The ferry, in the early years of the nineteenth century, was operated by George Colbert, one-time chief of the Chickasaws, who turned this prestigious-sounding post over to his brother in order to become a ferryman. The walnut shaded the ferry landing where, one day in 1812, Andrew Jackson and his men gathered on their victorious way home from the Battle of New Orleans. The story goes that they arrived at Colbert's boat dock penniless, having spent all their money on riotous living in New Orleans, and Colbert prudently refused to ferry any of them across until Jackson sent runners to Nashville for some cold cash.

The Colbert Ferry Walnut measures 14½ feet in girth and 78 feet in height and is the largest walnut in Alabama. The largest walnut in the country, a black walnut growing in northern California, is some sixty feet taller. Both seem to have attained these heights through natural verve, despite the ancient jingle implying a necessity for violent human intervention:

> *A woman, a dog, and a walnut-tree,*
> *The more you beat 'em, the better they be.*

This has been proved flatly false in the case of women and dogs, and is of doubtful virtue in the case of walnut-trees.

APPLE

*A*pples, like women and snakes, have a nasty reputation dating back to the Book of Genesis. Unlike women and snakes, however — whose hypothetical past activities have been largely forgiven and forgotten — the apple's part in the fiasco in the Garden of Eden has been immortalized in scientific Latin. The generic name of the modern apple is *Malus*, from the Latin for bad, as in malicious, malevolent, and malcontent. It seems unfair that the apple should have been saddled with this moral stigma, since biblical scholars now agree that the fatal fruit probably wasn't an apple at all. Modern votes have gone to the date, the fig, the apricot, the orange, the banana, and, the current favorite, the pomegranate.

Some of this uncertainty may have arisen from the early catch-all use of the word *apple* to mean any unfamiliar roundish fruit or vegetable — which definition, according to the *Oxford English Dictionary*, may have preceded *apple* as the specific fruit of trees of the genus *Malus*. Thus we have the love apple (tomato), earth apple (potato), Persian apple (eggplant), Median apple (lemon), golden apple (orange), velvet apple (mangosteen), and pineapple (pineapple). Other biblical "apples" have similarly been called in question: when the lover in Solomon's Song of Songs demanded to be comforted with apples, she was speaking of apricots. Medieval Europeans, however, remained stubbornly convinced that Adam ate an apple (*Malus*). The most popular of the eleventh-century miracle plays, known as the Paradise Play, featured Adam, Eve, and a fir tree temptingly hung with forbidden apples. It was this apple-decked stage tree, according to Anthony Mercatante in *The Magic Garden*, that eventually evolved into the modern Christmas tree.

The apple is and was, by all accounts, a temperate fruit, requiring a three-month dormant period while mobilizing its forces to set fruit in the spring. Since the apple so obviously needs winter, food historian Waverley Root hypothesizes that the apple originated in northern Europe, possibly in the Baltic countries. Others shift the ancestral apple to the east, believing it arose in the Caucasus Mountains of Asia or perhaps in Anatolia. The apple is a member of the vast Rose family, which comprises some one hundred genera and over two thousand species of herbaceous plants, shrubs, and trees. Apple relatives thus include not only the true rose, but the pear, plum, peach, cherry, blackberry, raspberry, and strawberry, as well as spiraea, the graceful white-flowered shrub commonly called bridal-wreath, and flowering quince, cocklebur, hawthorn, mountain ash, and a small California evergreen dismally known as mountain-misery.

The apple genus itself, after some three thousand years of human meddling, is a confusing network of incestuous interrelationships, defeating even the authoritative *Hortus III*, which states helplessly: "The taxonomy of the cultivated apple is obscured by centuries of breeding and selection by man . . . ." Cultivated apples today are generally assumed to be descendants of *Malus pumila*, the aforementioned Caucasian or Anatolian apple, or of hybrids between *M. pumila* and *M. sylvestris*, the European crab apple. Crab apples, on the other hand, are thought to be descended from *M. baccata*, the Siberian crab, or, more recently, from hybrids of *M. ioensis*, the American wild or prairie crab, with various of the cultivated apples. From such ancestral stock, the apple, fruitfully multiplying, has generated over sixty-five hundred registered horticultural varieties and now accounts for over 50 percent of the world's deciduous fruit tree production.

The pharoahs of Egypt had apples planted along the Nile delta by the thirteenth century B.C.; the Greeks had them by the seventh century B.C. Apples figured heavily in Greek mythology, though the famed golden apples of the Hesperides which distracted Atalanta from winning her race are now said to have been oranges. It may have been a real apple, however, that Paris handed over to Aphrodite, thus judging her the fairest of them all and setting the wheels in motion for the Trojan War. Greek apples were rare and expensive at first — a bride and groom, by formal decree, were limited to one apple between them at their marriage ceremony — but by the fourth century B.C., according to the playwright Aristophanes, they were common enough to be tossed to favored clients by dancing girls at houses of ill repute. "Tossing apples," in ancient Greek, soon became the popular euphemism for sexual intercourse, and perhaps it was Grecian slang that led to the lingering northern European superstition that eating apples could make one pregnant.

The Romans, by the time of Pliny the Elder (A.D. 23–79), had thirty or forty different varieties of cultivated apples — among them the Pomme d'Api, considered the most ancient apple still grown today. The Pomme d'Api, known in this country as the Lady or Christmas apple, is a small, flattish fruit, creamy yellow to crimson in color, depending on its exposure to the sun. The name *Api* is said to refer to Apicius, the Roman cookbook author who left us the recipes for camels' heels and larks' tongues, and who reportedly propagated these apples by grafting. Historically it was one of the favorites of Louis XIV, and the ladies of his court were said to carry Api apples in their pockets because of their sweet scent. In early America, Pomme d'Api was popular as a dessert fruit at Christmastime — hence the nickname Christmas apple — and this is the apple that commonly appears in della Robbia wreaths. The Romans may have brought the Pomme d'Api to England, where, legend has it, the first apple trees were planted by order of Julius Caesar, who numbered botany among his many obsessions. (Or the apples may already have been there: an alternative account claims that the invading legions found apple trees firmly established and the natives drinking cider.)

Whichever, the post-Roman English apple flourished, interbreeding to yield such prized and largely vanished varieties as

Pearmain, Bittersweet, Pomewater, Costard, Apple-John, Gold Pippin, Marigold, Cornish Gilliflower, Catshead, Geneting, Sugar Apple — "so called of the sweetnesse" — Sops in Wine, Pot Apple — "a plaine Country apple" — Rosemary Russet, Gravenstein, which came to England from Denmark in 1669, and Irish Peach, which was appropriately green. John Gerard, whose definitive *Herball or General Historie of Plants* was published in 1597, classes his apples as sweet, sour, or "harsh or austere, being unripe," this last class strictly forbidden for human consumption on the grounds that it caused colic. He mentions, among others, the Pearmain ("Summer" and "Winter"), the Pomewater, and the Queening. Gerard's apples, as well as edible, were medicinal: apple pulp, whipped to a froth in water and drunk by the quart, was said to ameliorate the symptoms of gonorrhea; raw apples distilled with camphor and buttermilk, to remove smallpox scars. There was also an ointment of apple pulp, "Swines grease," and rosewater, recommended for beautifying the complexion. This preparation, sold in the shops as Pomatum, is the source of the modern "pomade," which nowadays refers to an Elvis-Presley-like dressing for the hair.

While Gerard sticks to *Malus* in naming his apples, John Parkinson, Apothecary, and eventually First Botanist to Charles I, proposes the kinder *Poma* — from Pomona, the Roman goddess of fruit trees — in his herbal of 1629. Parkinson, who was farsighted in the matter of apples, claims the number of varieties is "infinite." He then lists sixty, among them the great and summer "pearmaines," the Sops in Wine, "so named both of the pleasantness of the fruit, and the beautie of the apple," and the Kentish Codlin, a "faire great greenish apple, very good to eate when it is ripe; but the best to coddle of all other apples." Parkinson's heart is with the culinary, rather than the medicinal, apple. He recommends apples baked in pies, stewed with rosewater and sugar, or coddled — roasted, then dropped into warmed wine, beer, or ale. The best eating apples he proposes should be proudly produced as the last course at dinner, "in most mens houses of account, where, if there grow any rare or excellent fruit, it is then set forth to be seene and tasted."

The Pearmain is the first named apple for which there was a written English reference, around the year 1200; the Bittersweet was immortalized in verse by Chaucer; the Pomewater — in *Love's Labour's Lost* — by Shakespeare. The Costard apple, first mentioned in an account book of 1292 from the household of Edward I, was a large, ribbed apple, sometimes described as "five-sided." John Parkinson describes it as "gray"; later authors mention white and red forms. It was in its day a popular apple, with both tasty eating and good winterkeeping qualities, commonly sold in the city streets from carts by "costard-mongers." The "costard-monger," a seller of apples, eventually evolved into "costermonger," a seller of practically anything from a street barrow, still a useful, if unappreciated, term today. It was a Costard apple, historians hypothesize, plummeting from a tree in the Woolsthorpe orchard one fine day in 1666 that inspired the young Isaac Newton to come up with the theory of gravitation.

Most famous of the early keeping apples was probably the apple-John, also called the Two-Years Apple: ship's stores for Richard Hakluyt's voyages in the late sixteenth century included "the apple John, that dureth two yeeres." The apple-John, by all accounts, was a hefty deep green apple blushed with crimson, which, with age, gradually turned yellow and pale orange. Toward the end of its Methuselan shelf-life, even the apple-John withered and wrinkled; hence Falstaff's wail in *Henry IV, Part II*: "Why my skin hangs about me like an old lady's loose gown: I am wither'd like an old apple-John."

These — Pearmain, Pomewater, Costard, apple-John — were the apples the English settlers brought with them to America. The first cultivated apples in the new land, according to most accounts, were planted on Beacon Hill in Boston by an Episcopalian minister named William Blaxton or Blackstone. William Blaxton arrived in Boston Harbor in 1623 along with several boxes of books and packets of apple seeds, as spiritual leader to a group of colonists sponsored by Ferdinando Gorges. Gorges, who cherished hopes of the royal governorship of all New England, intended his enclave of Episcopalians to prevent the anti-establishment Puritans from dominating the Massachusetts Bay Colony. The Episcopalians, less hardy than the Puritans, barely lasted a year before cutting out for home. Blaxton remained behind, the sole survivor, comfortably settled in his cabin on Beacon Hill — so-called from its designation by Gorges as the place to light beacon fires in the event of Indian attack — surrounded by books and an infant orchard of newly planted apple trees. He remained there, solitary, for seven years, reading, and developing the New World's first named apple variety, Blaxton's Yellow Sweeting. This horticultural idyll lasted until 1630, when seventeen shiploads of Puritans sailed into Boston Harbor, led by John Winthrop. Blaxton, by then an old hand at survival in Massachusetts Bay and doubtless eager for English-speaking company, was prepared to welcome the latest settlers to the New World. His overtures were rejected, however, by Winthrop's saintly flock, and Blaxton was summarily banished to more liberal Rhode Island — where, the story goes, he entered the city of Providence riding on a bull which he had trained to the saddle.

The Puritans, who took over Beacon Hill and Blaxton's abandoned apple orchard, furthered apple cultivation in America by importing English honeybees. The English bees pollinated the English apple blossoms — large, showy, and exquisitely fragrant, the quintessential insect flowers — and the apple crop, previously sparse, multiplied astronomically. Winthrop, perhaps feeling guilty, dispatched a hive of honeybees to Blaxton in Rhode Island, along with all of his books; Blaxton started another apple orchard and passed seeds on to Roger Williams in Providence and to the neighboring Indian tribes.

By the 1640s, orchards were well established. Nearly all landowners planted apple trees, among them Peregrine White — the first child born to English parents in, or at least near, New England, since the happy event took place on board the *Mayflower* on November 20, 1620 — who planted an orchard on his twenty-first birthday on his farm in Marshfield. By 1709, John Lawson recorded a sizeable list of apples observed growing in the Carolinas — Golden Russet, Pearmain, Harvey, Winter Queening, Leathercoat, Juneting, Codlin,

Redstreak, Longstalk, and Ladyfinger — and by the 1740s, American apples were being profitably exported to the West Indies.

The Old World apple rapidly became Americanized in the New World, crossing and backcrossing with the native crab apples to produce vast numbers of new varieties. Of the twenty-five or thirty species of apples in existence worldwide, perhaps six are native to North America. Of these, the most familiar is probably *M. coronaria*, the sweet, sweet-scented, or American crab apple, which ranges roughly from New York and Illinois south through Arkansas and Georgia. *M. coronaria* is a somewhat fluid species, consisting, according to Alan Mitchell, of some five distinct forms which off and on have been granted species status of their own. The trees reach twenty-five feet in height at maturity, and in the spring are covered with delicate pale-pink flowers. The flowers are usually described as rose-scented, but Peter Kalm, who found them "very pleasant," thought they smelled of raspberries. Sweetest-smelling of all is a double-flowered variety known as 'Charlotte,' whose lush blooms cluster in bunches of six, resembling less the wild crab than the famous Japanese cherries that line the tidal basin in Washington, D.C. Slightly taller is the midwestern prairie crab apple, *M. ioensis*, which ranges from Minnesota and Wisconsin south to Oklahoma and Missouri. The favored horticultural prairie crab is a variety known as 'Plena,' from its plentiful output of overendowed blossoms — all generously double, with thirty petals or more apiece. (The usual crab apple boasts a mere five or six.) Both *M. coronaria* and *M. ioensis* bear squat one- to two-inch greenish fruits, too sour to eat right off the tree, but fine in jelly. Peter Kalm deemed them "unfit for anything but vinegar." The Indians reportedly gathered crab apples in the fall, stashed them over the winter in birchbark containers buried in the ground, which treatment sweetened them up a bit; then used them in the spring to make syrup and cider.

The far western version of the crab apple, *M. fuscus,* is the only apple to display bright colors — scarlet and orange — in the fall. This seasonally gaudy tree, sometimes called the Oregon crab, is found from the Kenai Peninsula of Alaska down the coast to northern

California. It produces half-inch-long purply-black fruits shaped like olives.

The native-crab/foreign-cultivated-apple collaboration produced the landmark apples of the seventeenth, eighteenth, and nineteenth centuries, many of them only available today — if at all — from preservation societies and historically minded nurseries. These, collectively, are the apples that made apple pie an American symbol on par with the Flag, Mom, and Uncle Sam. Regrettably, no state has adopted the apple tree as its state tree. Instead, Arkansas and Michigan both selected the apple blossom as their state flower, while Washington, which grows the lion's share of the nation's apples, opted for the rhododendron.

Among the first of these all-American apples to make its mark in colonial society was the Rhode Island Greening. Though green in color — one expert describes it as "grass green with a light cinnamon blush" — the apple was named for a Mr. Green, the tavern-keeper near Newport in whose orchard the famed apple originated. Mr. Green distributed the fruit of his find among the guests at his tavern, impressed customers requested scionwood, and the new variety slowly spread throughout the East. Though tasty, the desirable Rhode Island Greening had its drawbacks: it was a slow producer — the hopeful orchardist could wait fourteen years for his trees to bear apples — and a biennial bearer, which means that the trees put out a substantial crop only in alternate years. It was accordingly replaced in the next century by the Newtown Pippin, which first saw the light near the French Huguenot settlement of Flushing, New York. A smallish greeny-yellow apple with what has been described as a "piney" flavor, the Newtown Pippin was a favorite of Governor Jonathan Belcher, who ruled the colonies of Massachusetts and New Jersey in the 1750s. (It is after the apple-loving Governor Belcher that Belchertown, Massachusetts, is so euphoniously named.) Thomas Jefferson grew "Newtown pippings" at Monticello; George Washington cultivated them at Mount Vernon. Benjamin Franklin, also fond of them, brought samples to London, where their general scrumptiousness soon won over the British public and led to a brisk transatlantic apple trade. Newtown Pippins were still being exported from Virginia in the mid-nineteenth century for the delectation of Queen Victoria.

The term *pippin* is of uncertain origin. There is some evidence that it originally indicated an apple grown from seeds — the pips or pippins — as opposed to a *reinette*, an apple propagated by grafting. Early pippins were therefore the equivalent of what nineteenth-century American farmers referred to as "common apples" — low-quality, seed-grown fruits used for livestock feed or cider-making. In all probability, superior pippins were identified and, since apples do not breed true from seed, propagated by grafting to preserve their desirable qualities. For this reason — unreliable offspring — American nurseries no longer sell apple seeds today, though in the 1880s it was possible to buy them by the quart from the W. Atlee Burpee Company for the bargain price of ten dollars. "Pippin" thus became incorporated in the varietal names of several prominent apples — a reminder of humble origins — as in Twenty Ounce Pippin, a mammoth green-and-red striped fruit developed in the 1850s; Ribston Pippin, a seventeenth-century English dessert apple and progenitor of the famous Cox's Orange Pippin; and St. Edmunds Pippin, a flattish russet-colored apple that tastes like a crunchy Seckel pear.

Other apple names are simpler to trace. The Baldwin apple, for example, a crisp, classically bright-red fruit and Number One apple of the late nineteenth century, is named for its chief promoter, a Colonel Loammi Baldwin of Woburn, Massachusetts. By all rights, according to *The Apples of New York*, a two-volume magnum opus on apples published by the New York State Department of Agriculture in 1905, the Baldwin should have been called the Ball:

Soon after 1740, the Baldwin came up as a chance seedling on the farm of Mr. John Ball, Wilmington, near Lowell, Mass., and for about 40 years thereafter its cultivation was confined to that immediate neighborhood. The farm eventually came into the possession of a Mr. Butters, who gave the name Woodpecker to the apple because the tree was frequented by woodpeckers. The apple was long known locally as the Woodpecker or Pecker. It was also called the Butters. Deacon Samuel Thompson, a surveyor of Woburn, brought it to the attention of Col. Baldwin of the same town, by whom it was propagated and more widely introduced in Eastern Massachusetts as early as 1784.

Other accounts, which leave out Ball, Butters, and Thompson altogether, retaining only Col. Baldwin and the woodpeckers, report that Baldwin happened upon the unusual bird-infested tree while out surveying in 1784. Impressed with the apples, he took scions and grafted them onto rootstock in his own orchard. Col. Baldwin was subsequently elected to the post of High Sheriff, a position that entailed much travelling about the country to attend local courts, during which travels he distributed scions of his fabulous apple. The ticklish question of a name seems to have been settled at a dinner party of unspecified date, at which Baldwin served his apples — baked — as the last course. Asked by an admiring guest what name the delectable apples were known by, the Colonel modestly replied, "By no name in particular. Call them, if you please, Baldwin apples."

The McIntosh apple, conversely, was really discovered by a McIntosh (John), in the province of Ontario on the banks of the St. Lawrence River sometime in the 1870s. There was also an actual Granny Smith (Maria Ana), who came upon the now-famous grass-green apples sprouting from her rubbish pile in New South Wales, Australia, in the 1850s — their source a mystery, since all Ms. Smith recalled was at some point throwing out in that area a batch of French crab apples grown in Tasmania. The Delicious apple that so dominates the market today appeared in the 1860s, as a freak in the orchard of an Iowa farmer named Hiatt, who seems not to have hankered after horticultural immortality. And the red-and-yellow striped Northern Spy, which was first identified in an orchard near East Bloomfield, New York, around the turn of the eighteenth century, may or may not have had anything to do with spies. One suggestion holds that the name refers to the clandestine activities of the Underground Railroad, which, with its freight of fugitive slaves, passed through East Bloomfield in the days preceding the Civil War.

The apple, like the native pumpkin and corn, played a dominant role in early American cuisine. The first recipe for that all-American favorite, apple pie, appeared in the first American cookbook, published in 1796 by the enterprising Miss Amelia Simmons. The First Pie, not all that much altered by two hundred years of culinary improvement, contained stewed apples flavored with grated lemon peel, cinnamon, mace, rosewater, and sugar, all baked in a "paste." New Haven tradition holds that Yale students were served apple pie for supper every night for an unbroken one hundred years, and New Englanders ate it for breakfast, with cheese. Martha Washington's *Booke of Cookery* includes recipes for apple tarts, "puffs," fritters, and "tansies" — early herb-flavored omelets — six recipes for apple preserves, three for jellies, one for "pippin marmalet," and instructions for making a "greene paste" of apples which corresponds to the modern fruit leather. Dried-apple pie, the crust rolled out on the wagon seat, was a favorite dessert of the wagon trains — though not everybody's favorite; one disgruntled pie-fed poet left behind an anti-pie verse beginning "I loathe, abhor, detest, despise/ Abominate dried-apple pies." The Pennsylvania Dutch, who liked dried-apple pies, were known for their dried sliced apples — strings of *schnitz* decked the first American Christmas trees.

The prime use for the early American apple, however, was for cider. The term *cider* derives from the Hebrew *shekar*, meaning intoxicating drink, and in English, the unmodified term meant apple cider. Ciders were made from other fruits: there was a peach cider, called peachy; a pear cider, perry; and a rarer cherry cider, but apple cider was by far the most common. Alice Morse Earle in *Customs and Fashions in Old New England* cites a town of forty families that turned out three thousand barrels of cider in 1721, which, if all for personal use, put them well above the estimated per capita consumption some fifty years later, of 1.14 barrels. This was none of your lily-livered sweet cider, either, which blameless brew was generally considered undrinkable in colonial times. The usual farmhouse cider barrel held fermented, or "hard," cider, containing about 8 percent alcohol. This circumstance was doubtless responsible for the old saying "Cider smiles in your face and cuts your throat" and for traditional recommendations of cider as a cure for "melancholy." It was also touted as a promoter of longevity: witness John Adams, who routinely started his day with a pitcher of hard cider, and lived to be ninety-one. There is also an ancient and much-repeated English story of a famous morris dance performed in 1609 by twelve still-sprightly oldsters, cider drinkers all, whose ages totalled twelve hundred years.

For many, hard cider was not quite hard enough, which led to the production of "cider oil" or applejack — a potent beverage obtained by a process of fractional crystallization via freezing. Removal of water, as ice, eventually converted hard cider to a liquid said by its advocates to taste just like Madeira wine. Final potency depended on the weather — the colder the temperature, the higher proof the applejack. A really frigid season, with temperatures down to -30 degrees F., could produce a truly phenomenal applejack, with an alcohol content of up to 30 percent. Overindulgence in this beverage led to a state of intoxication known as "apple palsy." Most "applejack" sold today is actually apple brandy, distilled from hard cider and still sold in this country by descendants of its first American maker, William Laird. Laird, a displaced Scotsman, established his distillery in New Jersey in 1698 — for the purpose, Waverley Root suggests, of finding a substitute for Scotch whiskey — and its alcoholic output was soon known as "Jersey lightning."

"Royal cider," an equivalently lightning-like potion, was made by adding a quantity of hard liquor to hard cider, ostensibly to improve its keeping qualities. Harvard College students, who were routinely served cider with their meals, received such royal treatment during the presidency of a Mr. Holyoke, who governed Harvard from 1743 to 1759. His duties included adding "spirits" to the cider in the college cellars to give it "greater authority." Other colonial drinks called for cider in combination with other harder liquors. Ethan Allen's favorite, the stonewall — so-called because its effect was that of running into one — consisted of half rum and half hard cider, and was rumored at least partly responsible for the Green Mountain Boys' heroic capture of Fort Ticonderoga during the early days of the Revolutionary War. A traditional Christmas wassail mixture was a hot punch of hard cider and gin flavored with nutmeg and sugar.

Cider was so much the drink of the common man that in 1840 it earned itself a place as a presidential campaign symbol. An early publicity agent for William Henry Harrison and John Tyler decided to capitalize on the voting public's soft spot for the man of humble origins. Harrison, who really was born in a log cabin, thus ran on the "log cabin and cider" ticket, with a homely barrel of cider prominent at political rallies. Whether through political savvy or potent refreshments, Harrison won by a landslide (234 electoral votes to 60).

Cider was also reputedly good, if regularly drunk, for rheumatism, gout, and bladder stones, and was said to alleviate fevers. It demonstrably prevented scurvy, which, through the seventeenth and eighteenth centuries, was a major medical problem. Scurvy killed off more sailors during this period than did enemy bullets, and often less attractively: victims of scurvy suffered weakness, swollen gums and loosened teeth, ulcerations, infections, anemia, and hemorrhages. The cause of the disease puzzled observers for centuries. It was first described in the sixteenth century, and initially blamed on the notorious moral laxity of seamen. It was next attributed to cold and foggy climates, and eventually, and correctly, to a diet deficient in fresh fruits and vegetables. The molecular root of all evil — a lack of vitamin C — only came to light in 1925, when a Hungarian biochemist, Albert Szent-Gyorgyi, first isolated the crucial vitamin from paprika peppers. He called it "ignosic acid," since the scientific community was as yet ignorant of its precise structure and function. The name was soon dropped, however, in favor of the humorless but more accurate *ascorbic acid, ascorbic* being a contraction of *antiscorbutic.*

Luckily, effective cures for scurvy had been discovered in a hit-or-miss fashion two centuries earlier. Various ships had escaped the scourge by carrying supplies of peppers, potatoes, or sauerkraut — and in the 1750s, under the direction of Scottish physician James

Lind, citrus fruits. The lime ration for British seamen went into effect around 1800, simultaneously generating the nickname "limey" and putting the quietus to the scurvy problem. An equally effective early cure — though considered by some inferior to rum and lemon juice — was hard cider. References to the efficacy of cider as an antiscorbutic appear throughout the medical literature of the seventeenth and eighteenth centuries. Sir Francis Bacon deemed it a "notable beverage for sea voyages" and a Dr. John Huxham (himself a cidermaker) recommended in 1747 that sailors put down a pint of cider a day to prevent what was dismally known as the "reigning British Disease." Ships' logs undeniably show that the cider cure worked. For example, a Dr. Edmund Ives, on board the *Yarmouth* in 1740, pulled some five hundred seamen through the disease with several hogsheads of "best South Hams cyder." By all modern rights, however, it shouldn't have. Apples are hardly touted as a source of vitamin C. The vegetarian cookbook *Laurel's Kitchen*, in a long list of vitamin-C-containing fruits from the medium-sized guava (240 mg) to the medium-sized banana (12 mg), ignores the hapless apple, and present-day cider is generally considered C-less. According to science historian Roger French, who insists upon spelling his "cyder" with a *y*, precise measurements have shown that while modern cider contains only a trace amount of vitamin C — 3.3 mg per liter — old-fashioned unpasteurized cider contains ten times that amount. Cider of the sort stored in Dr. Ives' hogsheads probably totalled 30–35 mg of vitamin C per quart. A bit of cider-drinking thus should have kept the average eighteenth-century sailor in fighting trim. While the most commonly recommended daily allowance of vitamin C is about 45 mg per day, a mere 10 mg is enough to hold the symptoms of scurvy at bay.

Old-fashioned cider, of the high vitamin C type, was made by mashing whole apples to make *pomace*, a coarse applesauce-like mush of apple pulp, skins, cores, and seeds. The mashing was at first done by hand — two men wielding long-handled wooden hammers over a wooden trough could account for twenty to thirty bushels of apples per day — but soon progressed to the horse-driven "edge-runner" mill of the sort used since antiquity to grind olives, linseed, woad, sugarcane, and later charcoal, for gunpowder. The pomace was then left to stand overnight to darken, a process brought about by an enzyme called *polyphenyloxidase*, the same biochemical entity behind the browning of half-eaten apples and cut apple slices. (The enzyme is sensitive to acids; a squirt of citric-acid-containing lemon juice will prevent browning of the apple chunks in your Waldorf salad.) The pomace was then layered into the cider press, packed between layers of straw and slatted pressboards to form a sort of apple-mash Dagwood sandwich commonly referred to as a "cheese." Pressing, by means of a giant wood screw, forced the cider out the sides of the press and into a waiting trough. The cider was poured into barrels or kegs, carefully vented so as to prevent explosions, and stored in the cellar to ferment — or "work" — slowly at a cool temperature, preferably between 40 and 50 degrees F. The final product was "palatable," according to Vrest Orton, author of *The American Cider Book*, in half a year, but most early cider makers probably didn't have the heart to hold off that long.

The now-ciderless pressed pomace was then discarded — usually fed to the family pigs — or was thriftily mixed with water and pressed again to yield "small cider" or "ciderkin." Seventeenth- and eighteenth-century English day laborers were often paid in this weakened cider — two gallons a day for men, a quart a day for women and children. While small cider did not keep as well as the stronger stuff, canny employers rapidly figured out that workers performed more industriously on it than on the "best beer."

The pressing process left the apple seeds intact, and it was from the debris of commercial cider mills that John Chapman — known to generations of schoolchildren as Johnny Appleseed — collected his raw material. John Chapman, that grand old man of American apples, was born in a cabin in Leominster, Massachusetts, in 1774, a generation too late to participate in the stirring events of the Revolutionary decade. The gap was more than filled, however, by his father, Nathaniel, who served as one of the original Minutemen, fought at the Battle of Bunker Hill, and spent a bitter winter with

General Washington at Valley Forge.

Young Johnny seems to have left Leominster at the age of eighteen and started meandering west. Historical rumor has it that he spent several years in Pennsylvania, where he may have planted his first apple trees along Big Brokenstraw Creek near the town of Warren. By 1801, he was in Ohio distributing appleseeds, at the beginning of a long career of gentle and generous oddity. He was renowned for his kindness to living things — he refused to eat meat or ride horseback and would douse his campfire if mosquitoes fell into it — and for his bizarre wardrobe, which included the tin pan hats of the picture books and often an old coffee sack worn as a shirt, with holes cut for arms and neck. And, of course, for his life's work, summed up in his own words in a will written in the 1830s: "I, John Chapman (by occupation a gatherer and planter of appleseeds). . . ." The appleseeds were planted in small nurseries scattered across Ohio and Indiana, which Johnny periodically visited and tended, and from which he passed on established apple seedlings to newly arrived settlers. The apples must have been a mixed bag, since Johnny spurned the practice of grafting as abusive and painful to the tree, and apples, as previously mentioned, do not breed true from seed. (Johnny's own favorite apple, sternly propagated back east by grafts, is said to have been the Rambo — which name, despite its modern cinematic associations with machine guns and mayhem, probably derives innocently from the French *rambour,* which in turn comes from the town of Rambures, where these apples were originally grown.)

John Chapman was certainly not the first to bring apples to the Midwest — the French had introduced them to the Great Lakes region and upper Mississippi over a century previously — but, according to historian Edward Hoagland, he had the enviable demographic knack of anticipating the pattern of frontier settlement. Johnny's apple trees were always in the right place at the right time. When the first homesteaders pulled in, Johnny was already there, a horticultural Kilroy, ready with transplantable saplings. As well as apple trees, Johnny planted and distributed medicinal herbs, among them pennyroyal, catnip, horehound, rattlesnake root, wintergreen, and the evil-smelling mayweed, which spoiled the taste of milk if eaten by cows. Johnny believed — erroneously — that it prevented malaria and urged that it be planted in every cabin dooryard. In his honor, families along the new frontier referred to this odoriferous offering as "Johnnyweed."

It remains unknown why John Chapman devoted his life to his self-appointed apple mission. If anyone ever asked him, the answer was not passed along. One over-romantic nineteenth-century biographer suggested that it was because appleblossoms tapped at the window when he was born (doubtful, since Johnny came into the world in late September). Flatly unromantic contemporary gossip claimed it had something to do with being kicked in the head by a horse in childhood. Whatever the reason, his obsession made him, next to Adam and Eve and their talking snake, the greatest of apple legends. He died in Indiana in 1845, of pneumonia acquired on a fifteen-mile hike through the chill of mid-March to repair one of his apple nursery fences, which had been broken down by hungry cattle.

John Chapman never carried his beloved apples any further west than Illinois. It was thus left to the British to bring the apple to the Pacific Coast, which they did, according to the *Encyclopedia of Practical Horticulture*, in the 1820s:

At a lunch party in London, about the year 1825, given in honor of some young gentlemen who were about to embark for Fort Vancouver in the employ of the Hudson Bay Company, seeds of fruit, eaten at the party were slipped by some young ladies into the waistcoat pockets of the young men who, upon their arrival at their destination, gave them to Bruce, the gardener at the fort.

Waverley Root identifies one apple-eating party-goer as a Captain Aemilius Simpson, who planted the seeds with his own hands at Fort Vancouver in 1824. At least one of these survived long enough to bear fruit, though no one, according to Root, paid enough attention to it to identify the variety. Another version of the story holds that substantial numbers of the seeds developed into trees, one of which still survives. According to the American Forestry Association's *Famous and Historic Trees*, the seeds were brought from London by Sir George Simpson, a governor of the Hudson's Bay Company. (Sadly, there is no mention of the staid Sir George having obtained said seeds at the hands of obstreperous young ladies.) The seeds were planted at Fort Vancouver by gardener James Bruce in 1826. A positive orchard developed from the seeds, but nearly all of it has since fallen to natural causes or chainsaws. The sole survivor, designated "The First Apple Tree in the Northwest," is now lovingly protected behind a chain-and-concrete-post fence. The apples are said to taste good, but nobody knows what kind they are.

Wherever the Vancouver apples came from, it is generally agreed that the great northwestern apple industry originated not as botanical souvenirs of wild life in old London, but as a considered business investment on the part of a pair of sober Iowans, solidly named Henderson Luelling and William Meek. Luelling started lumbering west in 1847 with a covered wagon filled, in lieu of the usual pioneer paraphernalia, with Iowa earth and apple saplings. The heavy load rendered the Luelling wagon too slow to travel with the conventional wagon train, so the apples and their caretaker made the long and risky journey essentially on their own. They arrived intact, just in time for the Gold Rush, during which financially hysterical period Washington apples sold to the miners of California for $125 a bushel.

Nowadays Washington is the top apple-producing state in the country, followed by Oregon and New York. Top world producer of the fruit we so fondly view as all-American is the U.S.S.R., which turns out some seventy-two hundred metric tons annually, as opposed to our own thirty-seven hundred. The dominant apple all across the board is the Red Delicious, generally described as the "generic red apple" and condemned by members of the North American Fruit Explorers Association (NAFEX) as the (bo)Red Delicious. Second place in this country goes to the McIntosh; then the Winesap, Jonathan, Rome Beauty, and Stayman. Since 1980, however, the Granny Smith has been moving toward the top of the charts, along with the recently introduced Gala — a plump little red-and-yellow number from New Zealand — and the Criterion, a yellow offshoot of the ubiquitous Red Delicious.

The value of apples as fruit has precluded much use of apple as wood. In colonial New England, in fact, many states flatly forbade the cutting down of apple trees. The wood, when available, is a fine-textured pinkish buff, similar to pearwood. Traditionally it was favored for rocking-chair rockers and for flutes. One story goes that at one time all the toll-bridge keepers in Connecticut played apple-wood flutes, supplied by one enterprising peddler in exchange for free bridge passage. As firewood, apple wood gives a fragrant smoke, though garden writer Richardson Wright finds it "not distinctive," preferring magnolia, cottonwood, birch, or bamboo.

Americans, on the average, eat eighteen pounds of apples per year, which comes nowhere near an apple a day. The average Italian, at fifty-six pounds, does better; and the average Dutchman, at one hundred pounds a year, may well be keeping the doctor away. The efficacy of the daily apple was recently confirmed by a study of students at the University of Michigan: the apple-a-day kids, statistics showed, had fewer colds and paid fewer visits to the college infirmary than did the apple-deprived control group.

The apple has had such an impact on American life that our vocabulary, past and present, has become heavy in apple phrases. "To upset the applecart" has meant to make a general mess of things since 1796; "apple pie order" has meant neat and tidy since 1813. Rosy-cheeked children have been "apple-cheeked" since the mid-nineteenth century; and "go climb a sour apple tree," as of the turn of the century, was a polite way of telling somebody to go to hell. "Sure as God made little green apples" meant absolutely certain by 1909; by the 1920s, "apple" was a slang term for the baseball, thrown about the "apple orchard" by "apple hawks." Gross exaggerations or flat-out lies were collectively referred to as "applesauce" by 1910, as in "Politics is applesauce" — which phrase Will Rogers used to demolish all those apple-polishing smart apples in Washington, D.C.

CHERRY

George Washington, no matter what the history books say, never chopped down his daddy's cherry tree. The cherry tree tale, with accompanying high-minded dialogue, was made up out of whole cloth by Mason Locke ("Parson") Weems, whose *Life of George Washington; With Curious Anecdotes, Equally Honorable to Himself and Exemplary to His Young Countrymen* hit the stands in 1806. Weems, who also gave us that nice bit about Washington throwing the silver dollar across the Delaware River, won a certain immortality with his decimated cherry tree — even persisting across the Atlantic in the British "cherry-tree class" battleships of the 1930s. The ships reportedly were reduced in tonnage by the Treaty of Washington (D.C.) — that is, like the cherry tree, "cut down by Washington."

If young George *had* chopped down a cherry tree, it would most likely have been a European tree, since cultivated cherries in the American colonies were of imported stock. The ancestral cherry probably originated in northeastern Asia, in the fertile bloc that once was to newly developing species what Nashville now is to country music. The Japanese cultivated them, prizing them as ornamentals. Japanese springtimes are still celebrated with formal cherry-blossom viewings, cherry-blossom festivals, and parades, complete with a traditional children's song:

Cherry blossoms, cherry blossoms
bloom in the March sky

CHERRY

as far as the eye can reach
like a mist or floating cloud
filling the air with fragrance.
Come, oh come,
let's go and see them.

The samurai warriors traditionally regarded the cherry blossoms, which fall at the peak of their beauty, as a symbol of their way of life. Their wives immortalized the blooms in exquisite silken embroidery. The Japanese cherry most familiar to Americans is *Prunus yedoensis*, the flowering cherry that rims the Tidal Basin in Washington, D.C. The trees were first presented to this country by the Tokyo Municipal Council in 1909, as a token of friendship, but the initial presentation backfired: the trees were found to be infected with fungus and were subsequently destroyed. A second shipment in 1912 proved cleaner, and the trees were planted with much fanfare, the first sapling lowered into the ground by Mrs. William Howard Taft. Unfortunately, these cherries also proved a mixed blessing. It later became evident that they harbored the Oriental fruit moth, which, once established, proved itself a pest of the first magnitude, highly destructive to the American peach crop.

The ancient Greeks and Romans also grew cherries, and the Roman city of Pompeii before its spectacular volcanic demise in A.D. 74 was famed for its cherries. The early English positively doted on cherries. Geoffrey Chaucer, apparently appalled to discover the omission of cherries from the delectable orchard described in the thirteenth-century French poem "Romaunt de la Rose," promptly inserted them into his English translation: "Cheryse, of which many on fayne is" ("Cherries, of which many a one is fond") were slipped in after the original text's medlars, plums, pears, and chestnuts. Cherries symbolized love and beauty in literature. Helena's lips in Shakespeare's *A Midsummer Night's Dream* were lusciously described as "kissing cherries" and Robert Herrick's poetic lovelies were all cherry-lipped with teeth like pearls. In European religious paintings, cherries routinely represented the sweetness of life, as opposed to the fatal apple, which represented mankind's inevitable disasters; in Chinese art, cherries symbolized female beauty and sexual power. Appropriately, Henry VIII, whose eye for a likely lady wreaked so much political havoc, had a passion for cherries, and grew imported Dutch cherry trees in his palace gardens.

The English celebrated their cherry harvest with rural festivities known as "Cherry Fairs," with attendant markets, dancing bears, jugglers, and other trappings of medieval revelry. These seasonal party weekends soon came to represent the end-all of life's delights, irresistibly sweet but regrettably short. By 1393, John Gower, a friend of Chaucer, had coined the phrase "For al is but a cherry faire," a sentiment that survives today as "Life is just a bowl of cherries." To dream of cherries, on the other hand, was not an anticipation of good times coming, but an indication that ill fortune was on the way; and in Germany cherries carried a certain gustatory risk: traditional dogma held it "unadvisable to eat cherries with potentates" for fear that an evil-minded monarch might use the pits to gouge out your eyes. Cherry pits were employed more benignly by the youth of Shakespeare's day, in a game known as "Cherry-pit," which seems to have been a seventeenth-century version of pitching pennies. Under the Bard's direction, Sir Toby Belch mentions the pastime in *Twelfth Night*: "What man, 'tis not for gravity to play at cherrie-pit with Satan."

Cherry, presumably also from its short-lived lusciousness, entered English as a slang term for "young girl" sometime around 1850. Similarly defined were *cherry-pie* and *cherry-ripe*, the latter also cooperatively used to mean a footman dressed in red plush. From cherry, young girl, came cherry, virginity, and cherry, the hymen, and — inevitably — the practice, designated as "low and raffish" by Eric Partridge, of cherry-popping.

The morally impeccable fruit-type cherry belongs to the genus *Prunus*, along with the peach, plum, apricot, almond, and nectarine. There are at a guess some hundred species of cherries, but only ten or twelve of these are commonly found in Europe and North America. The cultivated European cherry, over which the Elizabethans waxed so enthusiastic, fell into two basic categories: the sweet and the sour. Sweet cherries are the progeny of *Prunus avium*, sometimes called the bird cherry. Run wild, they are known as *mazzards* or *geans*. Sweet cherries in their various manifestations ripen bright-red to black — hence some nineteenth-century play on the phrase "cherry-colored," which arguably meant either red or black, thus providing endless opportunities for verbal cheating at cards. Best known of the sweet cherries today is probably the Bing, a rich mahogany-red fruit bred in the nineteenth century by the Llewellyn brothers of Oregon and named for their Chinese house-boy. The Llewellyns also developed the Lambert cherry, today's number two commercial cherry after the Bing, similarly dark red and vaguely heart-shaped. Heart cherries, so named for their distinctive shape, date to the earliest cherry orchards. John Parkinson in 1629 describes "Lesser and Greater Hart Cherries" as "full above, and a little pointing downward, after the fashion of an heart, as it is usually painted." Washington and Jefferson grew Black Heart cherries on their respective estates. They also grew White Hearts and Carnations — both white sweet cherries, which as a general rule are a rosy-cheeked yellow rather than snow-colored, with pale flesh and colorless juice.

Among the oldest of known cherries is a white — or at least non-red — variety sold today as the Yellow Spanish. Believed to have been described in the first century by Pliny, the Yellow Spanish was introduced to America in 1802 by the Prince Nurseries of Long Island, New York. The crimson-cheeked Yellow Spanish closely resembles the blush-yellow Royal Anne or Napoleon, a typical "white" cherry used today to make the maraschino cherries that top banana splits, hot fudge sundaes, and Manhattans. The original maraschino, which dates back several hundred years, was an Italian liqueur, traditionally distilled from the marasca cherry — a small black sweet cherry also used, according to both William Makepeace Thackeray and the *Oxford English Dictionary*, to make maraschino jelly. The modern maraschino is a different proposition altogether: the pitted "white" cherries are bleached, then soaked in sugar syrup with red food coloring — until recently the notorious Red Dye No. 2 — and flavorings.

Sweet cherries have traditionally been eaten ripely raw — in fresh-picked handfuls by the common folk, in more elaborate versions by their betters. A conceit of aristocratic socialites in the seventeenth and eighteenth centuries was to serve up fruit at the end of banquets, elaborately piled into towering pyramids, the construction of which was an art in itself. A confectionery cookbook of 1692 describes the finicky process of building a cherry pyramid, using a series of metal molds: "One must have pyramidal tin funnels, of various sizes, to fit the porcelain dishes on which you will place them. You put a cherry at the bottom for the point . . . on the second layer you put three, on the third, four or five, and thus to the end, crisscrossing the stems to the middle, which you will fill up with some chopped worthless leaves, because your fruits will only be around the edges." This unstable-sounding arrangement was made even more so by the stacking of the cherry-laden porcelain dishes — sometimes as many as twenty high — to make a positive skyscraper of fruit and crockery. One obviously delighted banquet-goer described a party in which the after-dinner fruit display toppled over en route to the table, "the noise of which silenced the violins, oboes, and trumpets." Cagier cooks stabilized their creations by dribbling caramel over the stacked fruit or by adding water and freezing solid. In none of these arrangements, unfortunately, was the stacked fruit readily accessible to the hopeful eater, and in retrospect it seems a shameful waste of cherries.

On a lesser scale, cherry growers sought to preserve their much too seasonal fruit by drying, preserving, and pickling. Elinor Fettiplace preserved her cherries in sugar and the "Juice of Respice" (raspberries); Martha Washington's *Booke of Cookery* includes four recipes for cherry preserves: one for drying cherries in a barrel of hay such that "you may have them for tarts at Christmass"; one for "Red Paste" of cherries; and one for "Black Cherry Water," a brew recommended for such ailments as convulsions and "ye winde." Pickled cherries also were made with sweet cherries. Euell Gibbons suggests "Cherry

Olives," made with (wild) Napoleon cherries:

Just wash firm, umblemished cherries in cold water, then pack them fresh into half-pint jars. To each jar add ¼ teaspoon of salt and 1½ tablespoons of cider vinegar. Fill the jars with cold water and seal. Allow at least three weeks before using them.

They taste nothing like olives, but are served similarly, in salads or on relish trays.

The best cooking cherry, colloquially known as the sour or pie cherry, is of the species *Prunus cerasus. P. cerasus* is a smaller and tougher tree than its sweet cousin, flourishing and setting fruit as far north as Manitoba, Canada. The trees average a mere fifteen feet in height, in contrast to the sweet cherry's thirty-five. The "sour" appellation is usually softened to "tart" in the nursery catalogs, and Waverley Root prefers the term "acid." Whichever, there's generally a little too much of it for enjoyment of sour cherries in the raw. These are the cherries recommended in 1597 by John Gerard: "Many excellent Tarts and other pleasant meets are made with Cherries, sugar and other delicate spices." The most popular sour cherry grown nowadays is the Montmorency, a classic bright-red cherry with colorless juice, believed to have originated in France in the latter half of the seventeenth century.

The colorless juice classifies the Montmorency cherry as an *amarelle*, the name possibly from the Italian *amarella*, "bitter." Sour cherries with colored juice are known as *morellos*, a name that may come from the same linguistic root or may just possibly, the *Oxford English Dictionary* hints weakly, derive from the Italian *morella*, "dark-colored." Morellos are famed for their use in a cherry brandy known familiarly as cherry bounce, a beverage reportedly enjoyed by Queen Victoria. Morellos are thus behind the time-honored term "cherry merry," which means riotously drunk, a condition apparently never attained by the queen. Unlike most cherries, the English morello is self-fertile, which makes it the cherry of choice for growers who have space for only a single tree. And not a bad choice either:

John Parkinson described it as having a "fine sharpe or sower taste very delectable," which still applies.

A cross between sweet and sour cherries, grown by both Washington and Jefferson, is the Duke cherry. The scientific name, according to *Hortus III*, is *Prunus x effusus*: basically it looks like *P. avium*, but tastes like *P. cerasus*. The Germans, with a fine respect for legitimate bloodlines, refer to these as *Bastardkirschen*.

Wild cherry trees were observed with delight by the early explorers in North America. William Wood in his *New Englands Prospect* (1634) composed a long poem about native North American trees, including a paean to the "ruddie Cherrie." The fruit of the ruddie Cherrie, subsequently tasted, proved a painful and unpoetic disappointment. American cherries, wrote a chastened Wood, "so furre the mouth that the tongue will cleave to the roof." Wood's cherry was *Prunus virginiana*, the chokecherry, so named for its ability to shrivel the human palate. Despite its southern species name, the chokecherry ranges from Newfoundland to Georgia, and west into Texas and Nebraska. Flowers and the bitter pea-sized fruit develop from long racemes dripping from the ends of the branches. Perhaps it was this to which John Josselyn referred in *New England Rarities Discovered* (1672), when he wrote of the wild cherry: "They grow in clusters like Grapes, of the same bigness, blackish, red when ripe, and of a harsh taste." Josselyn reports them good for the treatment of "Fluxes." Almost as sour was the native bird or pin cherry, *P. pennsylvanica*, which despite its northern species name, is found from Labrador south to North Carolina, and west to British Columbia and Colorado. Paler than the chokecherry — the fruits ripen to a light clear red — the pin cherry is generally considered worthless, though a few stubborn souls use the fruit to make jelly.

Best of the native cherries, from a cherry-eater's point of view, is doubtless the American sweet black cherry or rum cherry, *P. serotina*. *P. serotina* ranges from Nova Scotia to the Dakotas, and south to Florida and Mexico. Its bark is described as "dark purplish gray"; leaves are about five inches long, elliptical in shape, and turn bright yellow in fall. The fruits are glossy black when ripe and up to half an inch in diameter, almost a respectable size for a cherry. The American Indians ate these fresh or dried, and in New England boiled them down into a wild cherry jam, sweetened with maple sugar. They competed for these cherries with the local bears, which congregated at cherry-ripening time to participate in the harvest. Cherry-bound bears, old and young, tended to be singlemindedly determined; in later pioneer lingo a "cherry bear" was considered particularly feisty and best left alone.

Cherries also figured prominently in *pemmican*, an early version of the modern hiker's gorp. This Indian energy food consisted of lean dried meat, pulverized and mixed with berries in melted fat. Berry content varied from region to region: the Crees of Montana favored wild cherries, the Plains Indians buffalo berries, and the tribes of Massachusetts cranberries. The berries were an essential ingredient, providing a balance of vitamins to the proteins and fats. Cherries, for example, are an excellent source of vitamin A. The only better fruit choices — apricots and peaches — were unavailable to the American natives. Both were European imports.

NUTRITIONAL CONTENT OF VARIOUS FRUITS
(Per 100 g of edible fruit)

Fruit	Water (%)	Protein (g)	Fat (g)	Carbohydrate (g)	Vitamin A (IU)*	Vitamin C (mg)
Apple	84	0.2	0.6	15	90	4
Apricot	85	1.0	0.2	13	2700	10
Blackberry	85	1.2	0.9	13	200	21
Blueberry	83	0.7	0.5	15	100	14
Cherry	84	1.2	0.3	14	1000	10
Cranberry	88	0.4	0.7	11	40	11
Peach	89	0.6	0.1	10	1330	7
Pear	83	0.7	0.4	15	20	4
Plum	81	0.5	trace	18	300	–
Raspberry	84	1.2	0.5	14	130	25
Strawberry	90	0.7	0.5	8	60	59

International Units

The colonists used the rum (or whiskey) cherry to make their own version of cherry bounce. The general view remained, however, that the cultivated European cherries were superior, and by the eighteenth and nineteenth centuries, recipes routinely called for imports. Peter Kalm, touring the East in 1749, mentions — after a brief discussion of the fondness of snakes for wild strawberries — the prevalence of cultivated cherry trees: "Cherry trees were planted in great quantities before the farmhouses and along the highroads, from Philadelphia to New Brunswick; but beyond that place they became very scarce. On coming to Staten Island, in the province of New York, I found them very common again, near the gardens. Here are not so many varieties of cherries as there are found in Pennsylvania. I seldom saw any of the black sweet cherries [black heart cherries] in New York, but commonly the sour red ones. All travellers are allowed to pluck ripe fruit in any garden which they pass by, provided they do not break any branches; and not even the most covetous farmer hindered them from so doing. It was a common custom, and any countryman knew that if the farmer tried to prevent it, he would be abused in return."

Kalm also had a few words to say about the Cornelian cherry, by which he probably meant *Cornus sericea*, the red or American dogwood. Eighteenth-century Canadians crushed and ground Cor-

CHERRY BOUNCE

Mix together six pounds of ripe morellas and six pounds of large black heart cherries. Put them into a wooden bowl or tub, and with a pestle or mallet mash them so as to crack all the stones. Mix with the cherries three pounds of loaf-sugar, or of sugar candy broken up, and put them into a demijohn, or into a large stone jar. Pour on two gallons of the best double rectified whiskey. Stop the vessel closely, and let it stand for three months, shaking it every day during the first month. At the end of three months you may strain the liquor and bottle it off. It improves with age.

— Miss Leslie's Complete Cookery, 1839

nelian cherry bark and mixed it with their tobacco to weaken it, the local tobacco being too strong to smoke undiluted. The French, wrote Kalm, refer to this tree as *bois rouge* and know of no other use for it. The true Cornelian cherry, *Cornus mas*, is native to central Europe and Asia. It bears small dark-red oblong fruits — distinctly cherry-like; hence the name. Cornelian cherry wood, tradition holds, was used to build the Trojan horse.

Most cultivated cherries in this country now come from Michigan, where, in May of 1976, the World's Largest Cherry Pie was baked, on the grounds of the Medusa Cement Corporation in Charlevoix. The pie was fourteen feet, four inches, in diameter, weighed seven tons, and contained 4,950 pounds of cherries. The cherries were probably Montmorencys, the quintessential sour pie cherry. Northerly Michigan, whose climate demands some toughness from its trees, is sour — not sweet — cherry country. The (sour) Cherry Capital of the United States, according to local promoters, is Traverse City, on the northern end of Michigan's lower peninsula.

Historically the cherry has been used for more high-minded purposes than the seven-ton pie. The American Indians used the bark medicinally. Cherokee women were given cherry-bark tea to alleviate the pain of childbirth. The Chippewas poulticed the stumps of amputated limbs with pounded wild black cherry bark. The Mohegans fermented wild black cherries and strained off the juice, which was drunk as a remedy for dysentery. The settlers and their descendants used wild cherry bark in home remedies as a specific against coughs and colds. Cherry bark's effectiveness as a cough suppressant is attributed to its content of cyanogens. Biochemically these are inactive sugar-cyanide complexes that, when contacted by the proper enzyme, are cleaved to release hydrocyanic (prussic) acid. This compound, a favorite of murder-mystery authors, is a powerful poison which in lethal doses paralyzes the respiratory system. Cyanogens are found in the seeds of edible members of the Rose family — apples, pears, peaches, apricots, plums, and almonds — as well as in lima and kidney beans, yams, sweet potatoes, and bamboo shoots.

Ordinarily this does not pose much threat to human life. Some lima beans, however, primarily the colored varieties cultivated in South America, do contain potentially hazardous cyanogen levels, up to thirty times the amount present in the all-white limas grown in the United States. There have also been scattered incidences of curious gastronomes toasting batches of apple seeds and dying of cyanide poisoning. Peach pits, which nobody so far seems to have made a concerted effort to eat, contain enough hydrocyanic acid to have once served as a commercial source for cyanide. The poison, luckily, confines itself strictly to the pit and does not leak out into the surrounding fruit. The fruit pulp may in fact contain some line of enzymatic defense. One study showed that peach seeds from stones that had split open within the fruit were cyanogen-free. Bark and leaves of cherry trees also contain hydrocyanic acid. Overindulgence in cherry leaves has occasionally proved fatal to livestock, and scraped cherry twigs give off the distinctive "bitter almond" odor so tellingly identified in Agatha Christie's teacups. In cough syrups, the small amounts of hydrocyanic acid present in the bark extract has a mild sedative effect on the respiratory nerves, which suppresses coughing. Hydrocyanic acid content is highest in the autumn, which is when medicinal bark was traditionally collected.

A touch of cyanide is also flavorful in beverages. The German liqueur known as *kirsch* or *kirschwasser* ("cherry water") is distilled from crushed cherries, stones and all, which process imparts a tasty touch of poison to the final product. Miss Leslie's nineteenth-century recipe for cherry bounce (see page 140) similarly instructed cherry-crushers to crack the cherry stones before fermentation. The spiced and sweetened ratafias favored by ladies of the eighteenth and nineteenth centuries were often steeped with the bruised stones of cherries, peaches, or apricots for flavoring.

While the native American cherry was a disappointment to cooks, it was far otherwise to cabinetmakers. The wood of the cultivated cherry tree, like that of the apple, is rarely found in usable quantities: biologically, orchard trees concentrate on the production of fruit, not lumber. *P. serotina*, the wild black cherry, however, with less energy expended on fruit-growing, spends its time developing into a sizeable tree. Black cherries average eighty feet in height, and can reach one hundred feet, with trunks five feet in diameter. Today *P. serotina* is the second most popular hardwood in the United States, outranked only by the ubiquitous oak. Early American cabinetmakers referred to the black cherry as "American mahogany" and deliberately stained it to imitate the same, a process that George Grotz, author of *The Furniture Doctor*, compared to gilding a lily with mud. Un-muddied black cherry is an exquisite wood, which polishes — depending on the tree, the technique, and the eye of the beholder — to a "deep glowing red," "beautiful reddish brown," or "translucent warm amber-orange."

The aesthetic appeal of cherry is due not only to the color, but also to the structure of the wood itself. Cherry is what botanists classify as a *diffuse-porous* hardwood. Diffuse-porous woods typically possess tube-like transport vessels forty to sixty microns in diameter scattered evenly throughout. The usual example is maple: flatsawn maple displays thin bands of fibrous tissue — for support — bordering each annual ring, plus an even dispersal of minuscule pores. In the average maple, this construction makes for a rather bland wood. Maples in general, barring those lucky few that possess distinctive grain patterns, lack what wood expert Jon Arno refers to as "real character." Similarly damned are the diffuse-porous birch, basswood, and yellow poplar. All are pale, tight-grained, rather featureless woods, which in written descriptions sound rather like a lignified version of American cheese.

Cherry, though officially diffuse-porous, manages to rise above its anatomy. The most attractive woods tend to be non-uniform in texture — notably the *ring-porous* hardwoods, such as the oak. Oak features a ring of very large pores, or transport vessels, at the beginning of each annual ring. Most are over three hundred microns in diameter, which makes them visible to the discerning naked human eye. A few smaller pores are scattered through the latter portions of the ring. In cherry, the pores, slightly larger than those of the maple, form at the beginning of the growing season, and thus line up around the inner edge of the annual ring. Cherry is thus only semi-diffuse-porous, tending toward a ring pattern — which peculiarity gives the wood that extra little something that makes for a beautiful figure.

Colonial cabinetmakers used cherry for highboys, tables, candlestands, and chairs. The wood is extremely stable in response to changes in humidity — a cherry front door, for example, shouldn't start sticking in the summer — and for this reason it was favored for clocks, weighing apparatus, and for typesetting blocks in the days of poured-lead type. For this reason also, it was a wood of choice for coffins. Daniel Boone, in the course of his long and exciting lifetime, is said to have made several wild-cherry coffins for himself — keeping each current model under his bed, where it could be periodically hauled out and tried on for size. He gave all of them away except the last.

E L M

*A*n ancient travellers' tale from Ethiopia, recounted by the Greek author Philostratus, tells of a talking elm. Two philosophers, the story goes, were arguing beneath its boughs, when the tree, to the amazement of all concerned, suddenly put in its two cents, speaking in a "high, shrill voice, like a woman's." Annoyingly, no record exists of the ensuing conversation. Perhaps it was lost; perhaps the rambling philosophers thought it enough to report that the elm talked, period. The latter seems slighting to the elm, along the lines of Samuel Johnson's wholly insulting "A woman's preaching is like a dog's walking on his hinder legs. It is not done well; but you are surprised to find it done at all." Unfortunately, the Ethiopian elm's philosophical performance can no longer be evaluated. The talkative tree seems to have vanished from modern taxonomy, along with the mysterious Caribbean tree that reputedly bore oysters, the Moluccan tree whose falling leaves turned into butterflies, and the barnacle tree of medieval lore, which was said to produce barnacle geese.

There are eighteen species of elms worldwide according to *Hortus III*, though more open-handed botanists up the ante as high as forty-five. The Elm family (*Ulmaceae*) is a member of the nettle order, along with the sinful *Cannabiaceae*, which includes marijuana and hops, and the respectable *Moraceae*, which includes mulberries, figs, and osage oranges. Elms range through northern and central Eurasia, eastern North America, and Central America south to Panama. Six (or so) species are native to the United States, where the prize specimen is *Ulmus americana*, the white or American elm, found from Nova Scotia south to Florida and Texas. *U. americana* is the classical vase-shaped tree — some authors liken it to a fountain or a wine glass — that dominated so many village greens, town squares, and Main Streets in the happy days before Dutch elm disease. It can attain heights of 120 feet or more at maturity, which, though no great shakes for a redwood, is awesome for an elm, most of which are small to middling-sized trees. Similarly large is *U. procera*, the English elm, which according to *Hortus III* averages heights of 90 feet, but according to boastful British botanists can reach 150 feet under "ideal" growing conditions.

A major distinguishing characteristic of the elm is its lopsided leaf. Elm leaves are generally oval, with serrated edges, and are markedly asymmetrical, with one side of the leaf blade extending farther down the stalk than the other. Held by the tip, the elm leaf has the look of a shrugging shoulder. Most elms blossom in the spring, before these nonchalant leaves appear, bearing reddish purple perfect flowers. The "perfect" designation is not mere elmish conceit, but, in the scientific sense, indicates that both male and female sexual organs are found within the same blossom. The small blossoms are borne in bunches on drooping stalks, vaguely reminiscent of miniature string mops. Perversely, the (female) stigmas mature and wither before the (male) anthers ripen, preventing self-fertilization. Seeds, necessarily the offspring of friendly pairs of neighboring elms, are samaras, winged single-seeded versions of the double maple key.

Familiarity with the English elm prepared the early American colonists for the lurking evils of the attractive American elm. The narrow crotches that form the acclaimed vase shape make for weak branches with a tendency to separate from the tree and crash down on objects and persons below. Such arboreal mishaps occur not only in windstorms, but unpredictably in dead still weather. Understandably, such behavior led to considerable distrust of the lordly elm and, among English country dwellers, to the ominous traditional saying "The Ellum hateth man and waiteth." The French phrase "I'll meet you under the elm" reflected a similar attitude on the Continent: it's the equivalent of "when hell freezes over" and means never, presumably because nobody of sound mind would linger under an elm. John Wesley, on the other hand, in the fervent early days of Methodism, was given to outdoor preaching under elm trees, thus demonstrating his unshakeable faith in God.

Elm wood is possessed of a twisted, interlocking grain, which renders it difficult, if not flatly impossible, to split. While most woodcutters therefore view elm with an understandably cold eye, the twisted grain does bestow certain advantages on the wood. Elm has a marked ability to hold nails — unlike the eminently splittable maple, which tends to sullenly spit its nails back out again — and is highly resistant to shock. As such, elm functions well in ships' keels and chair seats.

Perhaps the most famous recipients of elm seats were the Windsor chairs, those graceful hoop-backed wooden chairs with vertical spindles that have become symbolic of eighteenth-century America. The origin of the Windsor chair is unknown. One story describes a Cinderella-like leap from obscurity, claiming that King George III came across it while sheltering from an unexpected rainstorm in a cottage near Windsor. Impressed by its comfortable design, he ordered a batch of "Windsor" chairs for the royal palace. The chairs were soon the standard seats for inns and taverns, and, painted green, graced innumerable summerhouses and gazebos. Scholars snoozed in them: a journal of the 1760s described the introduction of Windsor chairs "admirably calculated for ornament and repose" into Oxford's Bodleian Library. The chairs were exported to America, where they were enthusiastically adopted in time for the delegates to the Constitutional Convention to sit in them. Philadelphia became the center of Windsor chair production in early America, where the chairs, among the natives, were insularly known as Philadelphia chairs. Genuine examples nowadays may sell for upwards of $10,000.

The shock resisted so ably by elm chair seats is not that exerted by the firmly planted human bottom, but that administered in the attachment of the chair legs. Traditionally, the English Windsor chairs were a joint effort, assembled by an assortment of specialists: the bodgers, itinerant craftsmen of the beech woods, who turned out the legs; the bottomers, who cut the elm seats, shaving them into behind-fitting saddle shapes; and the framers, who assembled the finished parts into a coherent whole. Legs were whacked into the bottom of the chair seats with a wooden mallet, an operation likely to crack and split lesser woods. The shock resistance of elm also led to the long tenure of elm stumps as the traditional pedestals for black-smiths' anvils.

John Evelyn in *Sylva* mentions elm used for "Trunks and boxes to be covered with leather and Dressers, and Shovelboard Tables" — these last, also called shuffleboards, date from the fifteenth century and were used to play a popular parlor game called "shove h'a penny." Shakespeare's characters played at it in *The Merry Wives of Windsor.* Elm was also popular for wagon and carriage wheel hubs; some sources indicate that elm went into the chariots of ancient Egypt. More prosaically, it was used for rat traps, and the American farmer found it invaluable for harrows and ox yokes. The Romans used it for door hinges. Among its earliest uses was bowmaking. The oldest-known elm artifacts in Europe are a number of Danish flatbows dated by radiocarbon analysis to 2820 B.C. In the England of Robin Hood and the Sheriff of Nottingham, elm was considered the next-best wood after yew for the shaping of longbows. The elm bow enjoyed a brief and bizarre renaissance during World War II. Following the German occupation of Denmark and the accompanying confiscation of firearms, the irrepressible Danes armed themselves with homemade elm bows.

A second arresting feature of elm wood is its water resistance. Elm survives for centuries underwater. The wood was traditionally used for bucket pumps, an early engineering triumph of elm pipes and leather clacks capable of raising water some twenty feet out of the farmyard well. Seventeenth-century London received its water through a system of underground elm pipes — a system which was bedevilled by the illicit practice of driving smaller wooden pipes ("quills") into the public mains to siphon off free water. Many of these pipes, laid in 1613, were unearthed in 1930, still sound. Elm, in its underwater capacity, was also used for the keels of ships, bridge pilings, harbor works, and canal-lock gates. Despite its longevity when wet, elm is classed as a "non–durable" wood, since, if exposed to alternating wet and dry conditions, it rots rapidly. Elm thus makes a lousy fence post and is generally unacceptable for exterior carpentry. It can be used in interior panelling, where, in sawn elm boards, the crossed and twisted grain reveals an attractive pattern known as "partridge breast."

Sawing, in the early days of elm use, was a tedious business. Logs were laid over a sawpit, generally about twelve feet long and five feet deep, and attacked by a pair of sawyers, one above and one below, each wielding one end of a double-handled ripsaw. The sawyers were noted even in the hard-drinking colonial days for their excessive alcohol consumption: the unlucky man in the pit, beset by a continual deluge of sawdust, required frequent refreshment breaks. The average pair of sawyers, refreshment breaks and all, could turn out about a hundred board feet of lumber per working day. The average sawmill, on the other hand, could turn out a hundred board feet an hour, which explain why sawmills were erected so rapidly in the new settlements. Massachusetts Bay had one within four years of the *Mayflower* landing in 1620, and by 1700, there were at least sixty operating along the Maine–New Hampshire coast.

Sawn elm boards were used for dough troughs, chopping blocks, ammunition boxes, and frequently for coffins. While the rich went to their reward in oak lined with swansdown, the poor, of which there were many, settled for elm and calico. Anne Boleyn is said to have ended her brief royal career in elm: after her beheading in 1536, the executioners placed her remains in an elm box once used to store arrow sheaves.

Portions of the elm are edible. The leaves once served as livestock feed. "Cattel," according to John Evelyn, preferred elm leaves to oats — and the inner bark, in times of desperation, could be made into a form of flour. Elm flour formed part of the Laplander's meagre diet well into the nineteenth century. The American Indians ate the mucilaginous inner bark of the slippery elm, *U. rubra*. These glutinous tissues — primarily phloem — were also dried and used medicinally. Prince Maximilian von Wied Neuwied, an aristocratic traveller to America in the early 1800s, commented upon the remedial elm: "A kind of bark, which is now used, is that of the Slippery Elm (*Ulmus rubra*); if chewed or softened for a moment in water, it dissolves into a viscous slime, and is found very useful in dressing wounds, as it is cooling, and allays the inflammation. It is said to have been applied with success in cholera, and is now sold, in powder, in all the apothecaries' shops." A tea was also made of slippery elm bark and used, supposedly successfully, to treat sore throats and gastric disorders. Leaves of English elm (*U. procera*), not to be outdone, were claimed by John Evelyn to heal wounds, mend fractured limbs, and alleviate gout, and a decoction of the bark, generally mixed with aqua vitae, was recommended as an "admirable remedy" for hip pain.

Despite these obvious positive points, practical woodspersons have few kind words for the elms. "They are the most useless piece of vegetation in our forests," wrote one elm opponent. "They cannot be used for firewood because they cannot be split. The wood cannot be burned because it is full of water. It cannot be used for posts because it rots in a short time. It can be sawed into lumber but it warps and twists into corkscrews, and gives the building where it is used an unpleasant odor for years." The "unpleasant odor" — caused by an unfortunate mix of volatile oils — was that of urine; disgruntled colonists referred to the tree as "piss elm."

Elm appreciation, unsurprisingly, thus derives largely from observation of the untouched growing elm. Thoreau considered elms superior to people; Walt Whitman, walking under elms, was inspired with "large and melodious thoughts." John Constable, famed for his enchanting nineteenth-century English landscape paintings, was particularly noted for his portrayals of elms. Even a portrait of an elm was enough for some: George Crabbe (1754–1832), a writer who has managed to remain obscure despite the designation "first poet of the landscape," produced an effusion titled "On a Drawing of the Elm Tree, under which the Duke of Wellington stood Several Times during the Battle of Waterloo."

"If you want to be recalled for something that you do," wrote Donald Culross Peattie, "you will be well advised to do it under an Elm." In the 1940s, when Peattie offered his advice to the future famous, historic elms outnumbered historic oaks in the United States by a ratio of 2 to 1. William Penn's treaty with the Indians — a document distinguished by its unprecedented honesty and fairness — was signed beneath an ancient elm. The event was commemorated by Benjamin West in his famous painting "Penn's Treaty With the Indians," which depicts a plump and pleasant-looking Penn under an attractive, but botanically inaccurate, elm tree. George Washington is said to have formally taken command of the Continental Army beneath an elm on July 3, 1775. Boston's original Liberty Tree was a monstrous elm, chopped down and burned by General Gage's soldiers in 1776, probably in much the same spirit in which rival football teams steal each other's mascots. Daniel Boone meted out justice to his fellow citizens beneath the Judgement Elm, which towered next to his stone house (with third-story ballroom) in Defiance, Missouri. Both John Quincy Adams and Woodrow Wilson planted elms on the grounds of the White House. Ebenezer Webster, whose son Daniel so soundly defeated the Devil with his verbal pyrotechnics, planted an elm on the grounds of the family homestead in Franklin, New Hampshire. The Osage Indian tribe in Oklahoma sold off the oil leases on their reservation under a tree that became known as the Million-Dollar Elm. In 1943, physicists at the University of Chicago met beneath a campus elm to discuss the experiments paving the way to the first atomic bomb. The site of their conference became known as the Scientists' Council Tree. Two states, both with notably long-winded state mottoes, claim the elm (*U. americana*) as their state tree: North Dakota ("Liberty & Union, Now & Forever, One & Inseparable") and Massachusetts ("By the Sword We Seek Peace, But Peace Only Under Liberty").

"What makes a first-class elm?" wrote Oliver Wendell Holmes in *The Autocrat of the Breakfast-Table*. "Why, size, in the first place, chiefly. Anything over twenty feet of clear girth, five feet above the ground, and with a spread of branches a hundred feet across, may claim that title, according to my scale." By Holmes' criteria, there were only six first-class elms in New England — but, by the latter half of the nineteenth century, there were innumerable second- and third-class elms planted up and down the sidewalks and streets of the East and Midwest. The number one American elm today is undeniably first-class. Located outside of Louisville, Kentucky, the grand champion, according to the National Register of Big Trees, stands 99 feet tall, measures 23 feet 2 inches in girth, and has a crown spread of 133 feet.

In this country, the planting of elms as shade trees peaked in the decades following the Civil War. The elms were eminently suitable as town trees. They flourished in relatively poor soil and, at maturity and in full leaf, formed green cathedral-like arches that gave an atmosphere of elegance to even the most plebeian of town streets and squares. In England, the elm was second only to the oak as a common park tree, and many of the great country estates boasted mile-long avenues of elms leading up to their aristocratic front doors.

The general public was passionately pro-elm. In 1851, when the spectacular iron-and-glass Crystal Palace was being erected in London's Hyde Park to display the mechanical marvels of the day at Victoria and Albert's Great Exhibition, a number of elm trees on the construction site were tagged for elimination. Several of the elms bit the dust before outraged reaction in the popular press brought the project to a halt. *Punch* ran a cartoon portraying Prince Albert, ax in hand, advancing upon the elms, and followed it up with a poem, ostensibly written by one of the elms, which began:

> *My sisters live to see the show*
> *From mine and forge and loom,*
> *But o'er my place the turf will grow*
> *Feet will be on my tomb.*

The combined efforts of poets and protesters eventually did the trick. The Crystal Palace was redesigned to accommodate the (three) remaining elms, which were enclosed under a soaring glass arch inserted at the front of the building. The solution was not a wholly happy one for the exhibitors, since with the elms came their substantial population of resident sparrows. The birds promptly made themselves at home throughout the Palace, defacing the exhibits with their inevitable splatterings and proving an annoyance to all. A resentful Duke of Wellington — he who Stood under an Elm Several Times during the Battle of Waterloo — urged Queen Victoria to down the avian malefactors with sparrowhawks.

The days of the shady and sparrow-harboring elm, however, were already numbered. The disease that has come — unfairly — to be known as Dutch elm disease was first officially identified in France in 1918. It sprang up shortly thereafter in Holland, Belgium, and Germany, and reached England by 1927, where the first case was discovered on a golf course in Totteridge, Hertfordshire. Initially the disease was blamed on the war. The fumes from tons of exploding gunpowder, it was hypothesized, had poisoned sensitive elm trees. The gunpowder idea was soon scotched by Dutch botanists, whose researches revealed the true cause of the elm disease: a pathogenic fungus (*Ceratocystis ulmi*) carried by the elm bark beetle.

There are at least two species of fungus-carrying beetles: the smaller (*Scolytus multistriatus*) measures 2–3 mm in length; the larger (*S. scolytus*) is twice that size, or somewhat shorter than the average human thumbnail. Both are determined little creatures, capable in a pinch of flying eighteen miles in search of a likely tree. Once such a tree is identified, the beetles bore into the bark, chewing out nuptial chambers in which mating takes place. The satisfied female then tunnels on into the tree, boring out a channel between bark and sapwood, in which she lays approximately seventy round white eggs, alternating from right to left sides of the tunnel. The eggs hatch to release voracious larvae which tunnel off at right angles from the egg chamber, steadily eating and, in the process, growing to ten times their original size and shedding their skins five times. All this tunnelling leaves a radiating fan-like pattern on the inner surface bark, which gives *S. scolytus* and relatives the common name "engraver beetle." The beetle larvae, once adequately fed, then pupate, eventually emerging through a precisely circular hole as adult beetles, ready and eager to begin the search for their own elm trees. The peppering of exit holes that they leave behind has generated a second nickname: "shotgun beetle."

The beetles on their own, though undesirable, can usually be shrugged off by the healthy elm as one of life's inevitable little misfortunes. (The elm is often described by horticulturists as a "weed tree," which means that it's tough.) The beetles' microbial baggage, however, is another story. The warm humid atmosphere of the egg chamber and larval tunnels provides an ideal environment for the propagation of beetle-borne fungus. *C. ulmi*, thus nurtured, multiplies and spreads throughout the tree, carried in the sap stream within the transport vessels. The walls of the sap-carrying vessels respond to fungal invasion by producing gum-filled enlargements called *tyloses* — in effect, biological stoppers intended to seal off infection at its source. *C. ulmi* infection, unfortunately, is usually so widespread that the tree seals off entire systems of vessels, thus shutting off its supply of nutrients and eventually starving itself to death.

The first sign of *C. ulmi* infection is usually a single yellowed dead branch, known as a "flag." The disease then spreads throughout the tree, branch by branch, like some lingering Oriental torture. Oriental may be an appropriate word: botanists believe that the disease may have originated in Asia, where the resident elms — notably *U. parvifolia*, the Chinese or lacebark elm, and *U. pumila*, the Siberian elm — are resistant to the lethal fungus. The disease reached the United States from Europe in 1930, first identified in Ohio, which state had been the unlucky recipient of a shipment of infected elm logs intended for use in veneer. The logs initially landed in New York and were transported to the Midwest by railroad, in open cars, blithely scattering beetles and fungus along the way. By the 1940s, Dutch elm disease was rampant from Kentucky to

Quebec, and by the 1950s was devastating elms as far west as Kansas. Worse, in America the fungus developed a new and more virulent form, which, passed back to Europe in lumber exports, produced a second wave of elm killing in the 1960s. Since the introduction of the disease in the days of the Depression, an estimated one hundred million American elms have breathed their last.

Efforts to combat the disease sprang up almost simultaneously with its diagnosis. Unfortunately, initial cures actually made matters worse. WPA workers were directed to pile up dead logs or to kill infected elms with copper sulfate and leave them standing, under the misguided assumption that the disease could be isolated or contained by creating a firebreak-like barrier of dead trees. Such a supply of dead timber was simply gravy to the bark beetles, which, for ease of bark-boring, prefer their elms on the unhealthy side. Ensconced in this ideal breeding ground, the beetles with attendant fungus multiplied astronomically.

The next anti-elm-disease weapon was the twentieth century's ultimate insecticide, *dichloro-diphenyl-trichloroethane*, or DDT. DDT was developed in the 1930s by Swiss biochemist Paul Muller and first used in 1939 in Switzerland to tackle the Colorado potato beetle. By mid-century, DDT was touted by the federal government as a cure-all for pests. Accordingly, in the 1950s elm trees across the nation were drenched in a solution of 2 percent DDT in fuel oil. A notable hold-out was the city of Syracuse, New York, whose citizens battled their elm disease with a program of strict sanitation: prompt removal and destruction of all dead or dying elms. The sanitation program, under the direction of Howard C. Miller, entomologist at Syracuse's state forestry college, was highly effective: elm loss rate in the Syracuse area plummeted from one thousand trees per year to less than ten. Despite Dr. Miller's success, the Syracuse sanitation program was discontinued due to lack of funds, and inevitably the remaining Syracuse elms fell.

Anti-beetle activity in these more scientifically advanced days still tends toward the chemically diabolical, though now stops short of the environmentally catastrophic DDT. Elm experts recommend dousing terminal trees with cacodylic acid — an herbicide — followed by multilure, a synthetic pheromone, or sex hormone. Multilure, as its erotic name implies, is irresistibly attractive to beetles. Aroused beetles flock to the treated tree in droves, and, finding nothing to eat but herbicide-laden bark, die of starvation. This technique is known as "tree-trapping."

Sanitation remains a viable solution to Dutch elm disease. Most of the elms in Holland have been preserved by such a program, which involves a national population keeping a sharp eye on the state of the native elms. Less dedicated and cooperative countries have been less successful. In the United States, many researchers have concentrated their efforts on breeding a disease-resistant elm. The first such success along these lines came from elm-conscious Holland, where a resistant variety of the European smooth-leaved elm (*U. carpinifolia*) designated 'Christine Buisman' was introduced in 1939. *U. carpinifolia* is a smallish roundish tree, bearing little resemblance to the towering trees described by Oliver Wendell Holmes as "a great green cloud swelling on the horizon." Though relatively successful in Holland, a country understandably partial to things small, 'Christine Buisman' never satisfied Americans.

Neither have disease-resistant Asian imports — the aforementioned Chinese and Siberian elms — quite filled the bill. The Chinese or lacebark elm, though a mere forty-five feet tall at maturity and thus an unsatisfactory substitute for *U. americana*, is nonetheless a lovely tree in its own right. The common name — lacebark — describes its silver-gray bark, which flakes off to reveal colorful mosaics of pale green, olive, orange-gold, and cinnamon brown. The Chinese refer to this tree as *kwang kwang yu shu*, or "lustrous elm." The Siberian elm has less to recommend it, and some horticulturists have flatly damned it as "inferior." It is generally described as a weak and weedy tree with a marked susceptibility to the elm leaf beetle. It is, however, an elm made for winter, capable of toughing out temperatures down to -45 degrees F. As such, it has found some adherents among tree planters in the blizzard-prone Midwest.

Both lacebark and Siberian elms have figured prominently in

the genetic composition of currently available disease-resistant elm varieties. The USDA Nursery Crops Research Laboratory in Delaware, Ohio, has developed several complex hybrids of Siberian and European elms, all with solid early American names such as 'Homestead' and 'Pioneer'. Though hardy and attractive trees, specimens to date are closer in shape to the red maple than to the classical fountaining elm. Other plant scientists, conscious of this deficiency, have concentrated on *U. americana* itself. Eugene Smalley at the University of Wisconsin has developed a number of relatively disease-resistant American elms, culminating in the 'American Liberty' elm, which looks like an elm. This patriotic plant has won the approval of the Elm Research Institute of Harrisville, New Hampshire, an organization founded in 1964 by Connecticut businessman John Hansel, after his own elms succumbed miserably to Dutch elm disease. The stated aim of the Institute is to restore the elm to its former glory. To this end, it hopes for annual plantings of one hundred thousand 'American Liberty' trees.

Another approach to the fungal devastation of the elm tree has been to fight microbial fire with microbial fire. Certain bacteria — notably strains of *Pseudomonas syringae* — have been found to produce an antifungal chemical capable of killing the invasive *C. ulmi*. When injected into trees, these helpful bacteria have successfully protected the elms from subsequent fungal infection. Unfortunately, this tidy solution has lately acquired an Andromeda-strain-like image in the public eye. In 1987 Gary Strobel and co-workers at Montana State University in Bozeman published the preliminary results of their work on a new form of fungus-zapping bacteria: a genetically modified *P. syringae* with enhanced antimycotic (antifungal) activity. Experiments with elm saplings in pots in the University greenhouse looked hopeful — injections of the new bacterium protected the young trees from infection with *C. ulmi* — and Dr. Strobel made plans to transfer his technology to the outer world. In 1988 he injected fourteen fifteen-year-old elms on the university campus with the antimycotic-producing bacteria, and followed up with an application of fungus. The experiment was performed, however, without the sanction of the Environmental Protection Agency, whose avowed mission includes preventing potentially irresponsible scientists from loosing genetic horrors upon the unsuspecting world. Dr. Strobel's *Pseudomonas*, according to EPA spokespersons, was the first deliberate release of a genetically altered organism without governmental approval. (The first officially approved release occurred in 1987, when Dr. Steven Lindow of the University of California at Davis, after considerable legislative struggle, was allowed to test his ice-minus bacteria in a California strawberry field. The ice-minus bacteria are also a genetically altered strain of *P. syringae*, which, due to the structure of their surface coats, are able to prevent ice crystals from forming on plants. They have great potential for minimizing or preventing frost damage to crops.)

Strobel's *Pseudomonas*, similarly, has great potential for minimizing or preventing death by fungus in disease-sensitive elms. For the moment, however, the project is on hold. Strobel, in the wake of all the public brouhaha, made the dramatic final gesture himself. On September 3, 1987, he sliced down all his experimental elms, a scientific ultimatum that has been dubbed the Bozeman Chainsaw Massacre.

SASSAFRAS

𝒯ravel these days is a pursuit democratically open to all. Even the most wimpish of tourists can now get from coast to coast in cushioned comfort, toting nothing heftier than an overnight bag and facing only such twentieth-century hazards as hijackers, hotel strikes, and the devalued dollar.

Nineteenth-century travel, in contrast, was not a pursuit for the faint-hearted. Lord Byron compared it in riskiness to gambling and battle — a view reinforced by contemporary volumes of travel advice, which dealt with such exigencies as snakebite ("explode gunpowder in the wound"), lack of water in the desert ("the supply to be found in the stomach of the camel should not be overlooked"), attack by mobs (jab them in the ribs with your umbrella), and sudden death (make your will before leaving home). Essential equipment for those brave enough to take to the road included all one's own bedding, towels, tablecloths, napkins, and cutlery, mosquito netting, a portable medicine chest with thermometer, a bottle of Essential Oil of Lavender for the dispersal of vermin, a teapot — and, for the more Byronesque sightseer, a brace of pistols, a swordstick, a sketchbook, opera glasses, and brandy.

In such an atmosphere, in 1827, Frances Milton Trollope embarked buoyantly on the ship *Edward*, en route to make the family fortunes in the United States of America. Frances, in this first year of overseas adventure, was forty-seven years old, the mother of six — including the future Victorian novelist, Anthony — and wife of a disagreeable and chronically insolvent barrister referred to tersely in her journal as "Mr. T." Her American endeavour, financially, proved disastrous. The plan had been to erect and stock a "fancy-goods bazaar" — a forerunner of the modern shopping mall — in the bustling frontier town of Cincinnati. Cincinnati, however, — "by no means a city of striking appearance," wrote Frances grimly — was not yet ready for such blessings of European civilization. By 1830, the fancy-goods bazaar — dubbed "Trollope's Folly" by the natives — was still only partially finished and Frances was flat broke. She decided to cut her losses and write a travel book.

The result, titled *Domestic Manners of the Americans*, chronicled — in slightly purple prose — Frances' vast disillusionment with all persons and things stateside. Included in her long list of objectionable Americanisms were the "incessant remorseless" tobacco spitting (by males), the lack of enlightened conversation (by females), the lack of dinner parties, the "violent intimacy" with which perfect strangers addressed her as "honey," the "indescribably disagreeable" female fashion of powdering the face with pulverized starch, the writings of Thomas Jefferson ("a mighty mass of mischief"), watermelon ("vile"), and the obnoxious habit of serving chipped beef for tea. The book made Frances £1,000 in royalties the first year — no mean profit at a time when £100 was considered an adequate annual income — and variously enraged or delighted avid readers on both sides of the Atlantic. Americans eager to get a bit of their own back were forced to wait until 1869, when Mark Twain in *The Innocents Abroad* deplored the European lack of reading lamps, soap, porterhouse steak, and flapjacks, the superfluity of beggars, and the peculiarity of foreign spelling. Frances, in the meantime, turned to novel-writing, and lived to a ripe and cheerful old age, dying in Italy in 1855.

Notably, one of the few American sights that Frances found pleasing to the eye was the sassafras tree. "The sassafras is a beautiful shrub," wrote Frances, "and I cannot imagine why it has not been naturalized in England, for it has every appearance of being extremely hardy. The leaves grow in tufts, and every tuft contains leaves of five or six different forms. The fruit is singularly beautiful; it resembles in form a small acorn, and is jet black; the cup and stem looking as if they were made of red coral." The tree that so entranced the redoubtable Mrs. Trollope was *Sassafras albidum,* a member of the family *Lauraceae* and relative of the similarly aromatic cinnamon and camphor trees, the sweet bay, the true laurel, and the spicebush.

The genus *Sassafras* is an estimated one hundred million years old, and today consists of three known species: the aforementioned *S. albidum,* which ranges throughout the eastern United States from Maine to Florida and west into Michigan and Texas; and two Asian species, *S. Tzumu* and *S. vandaicuse,* natives respectively of mainland China and Taiwan. The sassafras thus is one of the better examples of a phenomenon known as *dysjunction,* a term used to describe plants with natural habitats in widely separated areas of the globe and nowhere in between.

Dysjunction was first remarked upon scientifically by Harvard botanist Asa Gray (1810–1888), from whom Charles Darwin acquired information on the geographical distribution of plants to be used in his bombshell book of 1859, *The Origin of Species.* There are now at least fifty-six genera of flowering plants blooming dysjunctly in the eastern United States and eastern Asia — a bizarre pair of locations referred to by scientists as "the Eastern Connection." Among such widely separated bloomers, along with the sassafras, are the witch hazel, the magnolia, the tulip tree, and ginseng. Plant dysjunction, scientists now believe, supports the theory that we were all once members of one massive supercontinent, dubbed *Pangaea.* Pangaea, some two hundred million years ago, consisted of two major chunks: *Laurasia,* which contained present-day Europe, Asia, and North America; and *Gondwanaland,* made up of Africa, South America, and Australia. The dysjunct plants of the Eastern Connection all once flourished together in the united land of Laurasia, in the days of the dinosaurs.

Thoreau on his solitary winter walks liked to break off and smell a green sassafras twig: "I am always exhilarated, as were the early voyagers, by the sight of it, and I am startled to find it as fragrant as in summer. It is an importation of all the spices of Oriental summer

161

into our New England winters, very foreign to the snow and the oak leaves. The green leaves bruised have the fragrance of lemons and a thousand spices." Descriptions of the aromatic bouquet of sassafras by various sniffers mention oranges, vanilla, and rootbeer. Whatever, this distinctive aromaticity was almost certainly responsible for the spectacular, if unfounded, reputation of sassafras as a cure-all.

The medieval Europeans were fervent believers in the medical efficacy of strong smells: doctors, during the devastating years of the Black Plague, wore nosebeaks stuffed with odoriferous spices to ward off disease. Similarly the odoriferous tobacco was first introduced to Europe as a medicinal drug, eventually touted as a cure for every respiratory ailment from the common cold to tuberculosis. (Notably not fooled was King James I of England, who wrote perceptively of tobacco smoking: "A custome lothsome to the eye, hatefull to the nose, harmefulle to the braine, dangerous to the Lungs, and in the blacke stinking fume thereof, neerest resembling the horrible Stigian smoke of the pit that is bottomelesse.")

The first word of the impressively scented sassafras reached Europe in 1574, from the West Indies, in an optimistic treatise titled *Joyfull Newes Out of the Newe Founde Worlde. Joyfull Newes* was a product of the pen of Spanish physician Nicolas Bautista de Monardes, who wrote: "From the Florida, which is the firme Lande of our Occidental Indies, liying in xxv degrees, thei bryng a woodd and roote of a tree that groweth in those partes, of greate vertues, and great excellencies, that thei heale there with greevous and variable diseases." The natives, stated Monardes, called this remarkable tree "Pauame," but "the French menne dooeth call it Sassafras." (The *Oxford English Dictionary* believes *sassafras* to be a Spanish adaptation of a Native American word. It deems Monardes and his French menne unlikely.) Among the greevous and variable diseases reputedly vanquished by the sassafras were headache and toothache, kidney stones, barrenness in women, "griefes" of the stomach, the "poxe," "large importunate fevers," arthritis, and other crippling conditions — sassafras being beneficial, wrote Monardes endearingly, for "them that bee lame and creepelles and them that are not able to go." Monardes also promoted sassafras as a cure for "Quotidian Agewes" — malaria — an error perpetuated for centuries and providing for sassafras the common name Ague Tree.

Of "Sassafras or Ague Tree," wrote John Josselyn in *New-Englands Rarities Discovered*, "the Chips of the Root boyled in Beer is excellent to allay the hot rage of Feavers, being drunk. The leaves of the same Tree are very good made into an Oyntment from bruises and dry Blows. The Bark of the Root we see instead of Cinnamon; and it is sold at the Barbadoes for two shillings a pound. And why may this not be the Bark the Jesuit Powder was made of, that was so Famous not long since in England, for Ague?" There's no good answer to this last query, except perhaps tough luck: the Famous Jesuit Powder was derived from a different tree altogether, the South American *Cinchona*. The cinchona, a native of the Andes, ranged no further north than Costa Rica, and never figured among the rarities of New England. The tree was named for the Countess Cinchon, wife of a seventeenth-century Viceroy of Peru, who brought some of the medicinal bark home with her to Spain, and thus introduced quinine to western Europe.

The less medicinally efficacious sassafras made it to England in the 1580s, under the aegis of Sir Francis Drake. Drake landed in Roanoke, Virginia, in 1586, where he collected a load of discouraged colonists, and heard the story of a group of Roanokers who, lost for weeks in the wilderness, had survived on sassafras soup. Impressed, Drake packed in a load of sassafras, which he described to the recipients back home as a "wondrous roote which kept the starving alive and in fair goode spirit." Sassafras was the first plant product exported from New England, beating out the Pilgrims' prosaic load of white-oak clapboards by some eighteen years. The exporter was Bartholomew Gosnold, who, on board the *Concord*, sailed down the coast of New England in 1602, discovering and naming along the way Cape Cod, Martha's Vineyard, and the Elizabeth Islands. Accompanying him was naturalist John Brereton, who subsequently published "A briefe and true relation of the discourie of the north part of Virginia" in which he waxed enthusiastic over the sassafras, "a tree of high price and great profit." (Brereton set the price of sassafras at three shillings a pound, a bit up from the going rate in Barbadoes.) Gosnold and company persuaded the local Indians to help them "cut and carie" a load of sassafras to their ship, in which they soon returned to England, presumably counting their chickens all the way.

In 1603 a group of Bristol merchants, egged on by historian Richard Hakluyt, financed a sassafras-collecting expedition to Virginia. They dispatched two ships "plentifully victualled for eight monethes, and furnished with slight Merchandizes thought fit to trade with the people of the Country, as Hats of divers Colours, greene, blue, and yellow, apparell of coarse Kersie and Canvasse readie made, Stockings and Shoes, Axes, Hatchets, Hookes, Knives, Sizzers, Hammers, Nailes, Chisels, Fishhookes, Bels, Beades, Bugles, Looking-Glasses, Thimbles, Pinnes, Needles, Thread and such like." The ships landed and loaded up in Connecticut, but made little headway with their "slight Merchandizes" — the local Indians proved unfriendly and had to be driven off by banging on a brass cannon. There is no record that the Bristol merchants persisted in their sassafras venture.

Gosnold, however, did. Still aiming for a fortune in sassafras, he ended up in Jamestown. There, at the height of the sassafras craze, the colonists were eventually saddled with a governmental sassafras mandate: each man was required to produce one hundred pounds of sassafras per year, or pay a penalty of ten pounds of tobacco. Gosnold never had a chance to produce much. He died in 1607 of swamp fever, a disease for which sassafras, ironically, was said to be a sure-fire cure.

Sassafras, at the peak of its career as a wonder drug, was shipped to Europe in quantities rivalling that of tobacco. Sassafras tea was sold on the streets of London and served — with milk and sugar — to the clientele of the urban coffeehouses. In its heyday, sassafras was said to cure scurvy, syphilis, and dropsy. The odor of the wood alone was held to ward off illnesses, evil, and vermin. A ship with a sassafras hull was deemed safe from shipwreck. Cradles, spoons, and Bible boxes were fashioned of sassafras; hen roosts were built of it, in the belief that it repelled chicken lice; bedsteads were built of it, in the belief that it repelled bedbugs. Similarly, in this thoughtful anti-vermin vein, southern plantation owners often directed that their slave cabins be constructed with sassafras floors.

The Pilgrims once evaded disaster by a timely application of sassafras. Edward Winslow, amateur physician, managed to cure the Indian chief Massasoit of some troublesome malady by scraping his tongue with a silver tongue scraper and administering a tincture of sassafras and strawberry leaves. The treatment, miraculously, was successful, and Massasoit, in gratitude, subsequently warned the Plymouth settlers of impending Indian attack.

Sassafras unfortunately never managed to live up to its spectacular medicinal press, and eventually dwindled over years of frustrating trial and error to the level of a spring tonic, drunk for the health and for the thinning of winter-thickened blood. Elizabeth Lawrence in *Gardening for Love* quotes an advertisement from the Georgia *Farmer's Market Bulletin* for "strong red sassafras roots," sold by the quart or half-gallon, diced and ready to make "table-use tea." Sassafras roots come in both white and red, color depending on age, size, and growth rate of the root. Older roots have a narrow layer of white sapwood just beneath the bark and a larger nonfunctional central core, dull orange-red in color, corresponding to the heartwood of the tree trunk. These "red roots" are held to make the best tea, and Euell Gibbons recommended them for sassafras jelly.

The active ingredient in sassafras roots of whatever color is *safrole*, a cyclic chemical (officially, *p-allylmethylenedioxybenzene*) which makes up 70–90 percent of oil of sassafras. It is also found, in lesser amounts, in cocoa, nutmeg, star anise, black pepper, mace, and cinnamon. Safrole, once used routinely to flavor commercial rootbeers, was pulled from the American market in the early 1960s, after experiments showed that both it and its metabolites caused liver tumors in rats and mice. Nowadays Pappy's Sassafras Tea, an evil-looking molasses-colored brew bottled in Columbus, Ohio, is safrole-less. It still makes a tasty, if not blood-thinning, cup of tea.

The sassafras tree is distinctive not only for its appealing scent and flavor, but for its indecisiveness in the matter of leaves. Sassafras leaves come in three different shapes: an unlobed ellipse, four to six inches long; a double-lobed mitten shape, with either a right- or left-handed thumb; and a three-lobed model, with a larger and longer central lobe. This lackadaisical habit inspired the sassafras' original scientific name: *S. varifolium*, or "variably leaved." The leaves are glossy green, with chalk-white undersurfaces, and, in the fall, put on a color show perhaps rivalled only by New England's scarlet maples, turning orange, yellow, salmon-pink, and vermilion. The fruits — botanically drupes, like peaches and plums — ripen on the trees in September, about half an inch long, dark blue on bright red stalks. Birds adore them.

The sassafras is on the short side in the world of trees, only reaching thirty-five feet or so in the northern part of its range. It does better for itself in the sunny South, averaging eighty to ninety feet at maturity, with a trunk up to six feet thick. The champion sassafras tree in this country is located in Owensboro, Kentucky, and is 100 feet tall and 5½ feet in diameter. The wood is soft and weak, but durable — the pioneers used it for fence posts, barrels, and buckets. It is fairly light — thirty-two pounds per cubic foot, dry — and shrinks very little — only about 10 percent — during the drying process, which contributes to its stability. Other uses include small boats and dug-out canoes, window and door sills, interior trim, and an occasional piece of furniture.

A notable non-use is as firewood. It was once thought unlucky to burn sassafras: an old Indian legend held that the tree was sacred to the Great Manitou, who became angry if it were cut and burned. The divine annoyance seems to take the form of violent popping and crackling when the wood is thrown on the fire — "like a package of Chinese firecrackers," writes one experimenter. "The wood itself is of no use in husbandry," wrote Peter Kalm of the American sassafras, "for when it is set on fire it causes a continual crackling and gives no good account of itself." Any wet wood will spark, crackle, and snap when burned: water trapped within the wood cells turns to steam, which eventually builds up enough pressure to cause an explosion. (The same principle applies to popping popcorn.) Some uncooperative woods continue to pop and spark even when dry, usually due to trapped gases generated by heated oils, resins, and pitch. Such pyrotechnic firewoods include birch, eucalyptus, balsam fir, pine, and spruce, as well as the explosive sassafras.

In Cajun country, sassafras leaves are used to make filé powder, a trick picked up from the American Indians. *The Picayune's Creole Cook Book*, originally published in 1901, explains: "'Filé' is a powder manufactured by the remaining tribe of Choctaw Indians in Louisiana, from the young and tender leaves of the sassafras. The Indian squaws gather the leaves and spread them out on a stone mortar to dry. When thoroughly dried, they pound them into a fine powder, pass them through a hair sieve, and then bring the Filé to New Orleans to sell . . . ." Filé powder was used to thicken soups, stews, and gumbos — this last a traditional Creole dish for which *The Picayune* lists ten recipes, variously based on chicken, "The Remains of a Turkey," squirrel, rabbit, okra, crab, oysters, shrimp, veal, and cabbage. *The Picayune* deems gumbos "exquisite and delicious," but master cook James Beard, in his *American Cookery* is tepid: "a history-making item," writes Beard, "but not one to repeat often." The definitive opinion on the debatable sassafras may come from Edward L. Sturtevant's classic *Edible Plants of the World*, first published in 1919. "A peculiar flavor," writes Mr. Sturtevant fastidiously, "much relished by those accustomed to it."

A S H

*W*hen Henry L. Aaron, known to baseball fans as Hank, hit his all-American lifetime record of 755 home runs, he did it with a stick of ash. White ash, to be exact: *Fraxinus americana*, a tree that in the virgin forests of North America lived three hundred years and grew to be 175 feet tall. While the average person, on the upgraded diet of the twentieth century, has been steadily getting bigger, however, the ash tree has been dwindling. According to the National Register of Big Trees, the present champion white ash, located in Palisades, New York, is a piddling ninety-five feet tall, with a trunk girth of twenty-five feet, four inches. The shrinkage of the American ash can be largely blamed on those same baseball bats. White ash, an impressively strong, elastic, and shock-resistant wood, traditionally has been the material of choice for utensils used to whack things with. Hence the popularity of white ash for baseball bats, tennis racket frames, hockey sticks, and polo mallets. In earlier days, ash was the material of choice for spear handles — both Beowulf and King Arthur toted ash spears — and the lances that figured so heavily in tournaments in the sport-minded Age of Chivalry had ash hafts. The American colonists used ash, in a practical vein, for hoe and shovel handles and oars, and, because it is easily bent, in scythes, hayforks, and plows. Its acrobatic bending qualities led to its use in the nineteenth century in the formidably bent bentwood chair.

The versatility of ash wood has certainly led to the depletion of the white ash tree, which is now becoming noticeably scarcer, despite its immense range and persistent growing habits. *F. americana* can be found from Nova Scotia to Florida, and west into Minnesota and Texas. Once cut, it sprouts again from the trunk, and is thus one of the better trees for coppicing. As firewood goes, white ash is fair to middling, delivering 20 million BTU of heat — the equivalent of 204 gallons of No. 2 fuel oil — per cord.

With the increasing scarcity of white ash, ash users have begun to shift their attention to green ash, *F. pennsylvanicum.* Green ash has an even greater range than its white relative, extending from Quebec and Maine to Florida, and then west into Montana and New Mexico. The "green" designation comes from its distinctive bright green shoots. Green ash is a touch heavier than white — forty-four pounds per cubic foot as opposed to forty-one — but is similarly tough, shock-resistant, and elastic. Chances are if you paddle your own canoe these days, you do so with paddles of green ash.

American ashes are a nominally colorful bunch — as well as the white and the green ash, there's the red ash, named for its cinnamon-colored inner bark; the black ash, named for its sooty winter buds; and the blue ash, named for the blue dye the pioneers reportedly managed to extract from its bark. All told, there are some seventy species of ash worldwide, sixteen of which are native to North America. All are members of the Olive family — *Oleaceae* — a clan that also includes the invaluable Mediterranean olive, privet, jasmine, forsythia, and lilac. The ash is the oddball of the olives: while the majority of the family are warmth-loving evergreen trees, the ashes are all deciduous; and, while many of the olives are noted for their prominent sweet-smelling flowers, the average ash flower is nondescript, petal-less, and scentless. Unable to attract anything in the way of pollinators, the understated ash flower for pollination relies on the wind. True to its origins, however, ash wood contains an inflammable oil, chemically similar to olive oil.

The Original Ash, according to Norse legend, was a monster specimen named Yggdrasil, the Tree of the World, whose roots grew down to the depths of the earth and whose branches reached the heavens. Why the ash ranked as World Tree is uncertain. One hypothesis suggests that it was because of the tree's size: among the far northern trees, which tend toward the puny end of the spectrum, the ash stands out as relatively massive. Another attributes it to the ash's strength, which was well respected in Scandinavia. The handles of Viking battleaxes were made from ash. Norse legend further holds that Odin, the one-eyed king of the gods, created the first man from an ash tree, and somewhat uncreatively named him Ask, which meant "ash" in ancient Norwegian. Woman, meanwhile, was created from the less impressive alder, a relative of the birch.

The Vikings were not the only people to claim descent from an ash tree. The Greek poet Hesiod in *Works and Days* describes how Zeus created "the third generation of men" from a collection of ash spears. The men so created reportedly turned out strong, violent, and bloodthirsty, and the ash was subsequently consecrated, by those who admired such traits, to the war god, Ares. The blood-thirstiness of ash-derived persons makes mythological sense: the ash itself had a grim beginning. According to Hesiod, the original ash sprang from the blood of Uranus, the first ruler of the universe, who was simultaneously deposed and castrated with a flint sickle by his youngest son, Cronus. Cronus in turn was less messily ousted by Zeus, who somehow managed to keep all of his own obstreperous sons under his thumb and thus held on to the Olympian throne.

The Algonquian Indians held that humankind began when the Creator shot an arrow into the heart of an ash tree, from which human beings (both male and female) then emerged. On Walpurgis Night, witches were said to nibble the buds of the ash tree as a prelude to their annual supernatural bash; conversely, in the superstitious sixteenth century, ash keys — the crispy single-winged samaras that comprise the ash fruit — were held to ward off witches and serpents. Gilbert White, in *The Natural History of Selbourne*, describes the going eighteenth-century belief in the powers of the ash:

In a farm-yard near the middle of this village stands, at this day, a row of pollard-ashes, which, by the seams and long cicatrices down their sides, manifestly show that, in former times, they have been cleft asunder. These trees, when young and flexible, were severed and held open by wedges, while ruptured children, stripped naked, were pushed through the apertures, under a persuasion that, by such a process, the poor babes would be cured of their infirmity. As soon as the operation was over, the tree, in the suffering part, was plastered with loam and carefully swathed up. If the parts coalesced and soldered together, as usually fell out, where the feat was performed with any adroitness at all, the party was cured; but, where the cleft continued to gape, the operation, it was supposed, would prove ineffectual. . . . We have several persons now living in the village, who, in their childhood, were supposed to be healed by this superstitious ceremony, derived down perhaps from our Saxon ancestors, who practised it before their conversion to Christianity.

While the ash, to the cold modern eye, appears ineffective at the warding off of serpents or the curing of ruptures, its usefulness as the material of staffs and walking sticks goes unchallenged. The staff with which the suspicious Little John bested Robin Hood was almost certainly of ash. The practice of battling with staffs was known as *staving*, a term that survives to the present day. Whenever we speak of staving off disaster, we hark back to the days when the ash staff meant business. "To ash," in past centuries, meant to beat with an ash stick, and, in the same spirit, a diet of "ash beans and long oats" in the nineteenth-century streets of London meant a thrashing.

The most famous of all fighting staffs is perhaps the Irish shillelagh, which, regrettably for purposes of this chapter, was made not of ash, but of oak or blackthorn. The name, according to the *Oxford English Dictionary*, derives from an oak forest — variously called Shelela or Shilleley — in County Wicklow where the best staffs and cudgels once were cut. The shillelagh forest was levelled in the early eighteenth century, along with a large part of all other Irish woodlands. Irish deforestation occurred under the English-imposed Penal Laws following the defeat of the Catholic King James II by his Protestant son-in-law, William of Orange, at the Battle of the Boyne. Under the Penal Laws Irish citizens were forbidden to own or rent land, to participate in government, to pursue a profession or trade, to attend church or school, or to contract legal marriage — and Irish trees, targeted for immediate execution, became the property of the English crown. Much of the Irish aristocracy, faced with this discouraging scenario, fled to France. The felled Irish trees were shipped to England, and those citizens remaining behind were reduced to fueling their fires with peat and cutting their shillelaghs from blackthorn hedges.

The blackthorn, *Prunus spinosa*, is a shrubby native of Europe and western Asia, anywhere from three to twelve feet tall, and heavily branched, which makes it good hedge material. The multiple side branches extending off the main stem form heavy knobs or knots when the blackthorn stick is cut and trimmed, adding considerably to the heft and effectiveness of the finished shillelagh — a weapon referred to by one admirer as "an ancient Hibernian tranquillizer." The fruits of the blackthorn are the size of cherries, blue-black in color and astringent in taste. Called *sloes*, these are used for flavoring in beverages, as in sloe gin fizz, and, in the nineteenth century, were used by unscrupulous purveyors of liquor, who soaked them in brandy and sold the result as "fine old port."

British subalterns, by the late nineteenth century, routinely carried small canes known as ashplants in honor of the tree from which they were cut — though by this stage in British military history, the ashplant was carried primarily for show, and any subaltern worth his salt subdued the natives with sword and firearm. European ashplants were ordinarily cut from the European ash, *F. excelsior*, which is slightly larger than the American ash and is distinguished by its coal-black buds.

While the American or white ash is most valued for solid sticks of wood, the black ash, *F. nigra*, is prized for its ability to split into thin strips, called splints. George Washington, in his surveying notes, referred to this tree as a hoop ash. The early settlers, from its most common use, dubbed it the basket ash. Black ash forms basket splints so readily due to the manner in which its annual increment of new wood is laid down. In ash, the springwood — the paler portion of the tree ring — is notably weak, consisting mostly of large pores sparsely interspersed with wood fiber. Black ash thus tends to split along the line of cleavage formed by this weaker wood, forming thin splints of the darker, tougher summerwood. These splints were used for barrel hoops, woven chair bottoms, and woven mats to be laid over the tops of the rope supports in pre-box-spring beds to keep feather mattresses from poking down through the holes between the crisscrossed ropes. Ash splints were also fashioned into eel traps, fishing creels, animal muzzles — to keep the horses from nibbling the crops while working in the fields — and a mind-boggling diversity of baskets.

Baskets, says one present-day basket-weaver, were "the paper bags of the colonies." Baskets were made for every conceivable purpose. There were egg, apple, cotton, and potato baskets, cheese baskets, sewing baskets, bonnet baskets — used at home for storing clothes and on the road as suitcases — and feather baskets, for the storing of feathers, made with a lid that slid up and down the handles, but didn't come off, so that the efficient housewife could pluck her chicken and stuff the feathers into the basket, all with one hand. Peach baskets were designed with flared sides, which distributed the weight of the soft fruit and kept the peaches at the bottom from squashing. Wool-drying baskets featured open-weave sieve-like bottoms and four to six legs, so that the new wool, hot off the sheep, could be washed, rinsed, and set out to dry all in the same handy container. Cradle baskets lulled many a colonial infant, starting with the arrival of the first cradle on board the *Mayflower*, a woven basket set on a wooden base with wooden rockers. Many of the colonial baskets were based on Indian designs and techniques — the Algonquian Indians of New York, for example, were famed for their ash-splint baskets.

The Indians may also have introduced the settlers to *F. quadrangulata* — the blue ash — a smallish tree that ranges from Ohio to Tennessee, and westward into Oklahoma. The geometric scientific name derives from its square — or four-angled — twigs and young shoots, the colorful common name from the blue dye supposedly obtainable from the inner bark. The sap of the blue ash also turns blue upon exposure to air, and a broken blue ash twig, stirred in a glass of water, will turn the liquid blue. Ash-blue, however, never managed to compete with the much bluer imported indigo, and by the nineteenth century was usually neglected in dye manuals or passed off in offhand one-liners. The wood was used for tool handles.

As well as the genuine white, black, blue, green, and red ashes, North America boasts a number of bogus ashes, most so-called from their ash-like leaves. The leaves of the typical true ash, borne in opposing pairs, are compound. In *F. americana*, for example, each consists of five to nine six-inch-long leaflets. (Odd tree out is the southwestern singleleaf ash, justifiably named *F. anomala*, which routinely produces simple two-inch-long leaves.)

One imitator of the conventional ash is the prickly ash or toothache tree (*Zanthoxylum americanum*), whose foot-long leaves consist of five to eleven smaller leaflets. *Z. americanum* is a hardy member of the Citrus family, found from Quebec to North Dakota, and south into Florida and Oklahoma. It bears lemony-smelling pea-sized red fruits which, held in the mouth, provided an old-fashioned remedy for toothache. The bark, similarly aromatic, also has its medicinal uses. The prickly ash is impregnated with an alkaloid called *xanthoxylin*, which chemical — usually derived from the dried bark — is used to combat such physical and social ailments as diarrhea and flatulence. The prickly ash is also home to a markedly unappealing caterpillar known as the orange dog — which resembles, says Donald Peattie, a bird dropping. The orange dog, disturbed, sticks out a pair of red "horns" — actually glands — and exudes a nasty smell. Perhaps as a reward for going through all this in early life, the orange dog eventually metamorphosizes into the spectacular giant swallowtail butterfly.

Poison sumac (*Rhus vernix*), according to Peattie, is sometimes unfairly referred to as poison ash — though where I come from it has always been uncompromisingly labelled poison sumac, in tones of loathing. Much more likeable is the mountain ash, which is actually a rowan (genus *Sorbus*) and as such a member of the vast Rose family. "The American mountain-ash, *Sorbus americana*," writes Alan Mitchell, "is scarcely more than a shrub and the European species is preferred for planting in parks and gardens." The European mountain ash (*Sorbus aucuparia*) tops off at about sixty feet, more than twice the maximum height of its dwarfish American relative. Both bear ash-like compound leaves up to ten inches long, consisting of eleven to seventeen (American) or thirteen to fifteen (European) leaflets. The European mountain ash traditionally has been touted as a potent anti-witchcraft agent: one touch of a rowan branch, the story goes, and the true witch will be immediately whisked off by the Devil to suffer her just deserts. Crosses made of rowan were prudently tacked up over the doors of houses and barns, and an ancient ballad titled "The Laidley Worm of Spindelston Heughs" describes a ship's mast made of rowan wood, which reputedly protected the vessel from hexes. Given the maximum size of the rowan tree, however, it must have made for a puny mast.

Another legend has it that the mountain ash or rowan was the wood of the True Cross, though this legendary distinction isn't as distinguished as it might be, due to the volume of the competition. Among the trees implicated in the construction of the definitive Cross are, as well as the mountain ash, the cypress, cedar, pine, and holly. Whether or not it was actually present at the crucifixion, the rowan has retained a religious aura. John Evelyn, in his seventeenth-century diary, describes it as "so sacred that there is not a churchyard without one of them planted in it." The churchyard rowan was not simply planted in a spirit of disinterested piety: contemporary belief held that the presence of a rowan tree would keep the dead firmly in their graves until Judgement Day. The mountain ash is thus a sure-fire protection against threats supernatural — and any nervous bump-hearing homeowner who has prowled downstairs at midnight clutching a baseball bat knows *F. americana* to be a comforting handful in the face of threats natural. Given the state of the world, it's not a bad combination.

BASSWOOD

*P*erhaps the most delightful treehouse of all time was that built for the 1960 movie rendition of *The Swiss Family Robinson*, a towering structure of ladders, platforms, and goat pens perched in a giant saman tree on the island of Tobago. The saman, *Samanea saman*, also called the rain tree or the monkeypod, is a member of the Legume family and is reported by *Hortus III* to average eighty feet tall at maturity. The Family Robinson's tree, however — which, incidentally, flourished not on a deserted beachhead, but in a corner of the local cricket grounds — was a monster of its kind, measuring 200 feet high and 250 feet side to side. Such vast canopy spreads make the saman a prime shade tree, a characteristic intimidatingly termed "umbrageous" by horticulturists, from the Latin *umbra*, meaning "shadow." Beneath these shady boughs, the tree also rains of its own accord: the leaves drip moisture on the casual passer-by, shade-sitter, or presumably, hapless treehouse dweller. The source of this rain is thought to be at least in part an arboreal overflow system. One theory holds that the saman sucks up more water through its roots than can be eliminated through transpiration. It therefore drips — rains — to get rid of the excess. Other sources claim that the saman's personal rain results from simple condensation on the under surfaces of the leaves, in the same manner that water droplets form on the outside of a cold glass of lemonade sitting on a hot front porch. In either or both cases, the rain tree seems a dankly uncomfortable choice for a treehouse.

The (dry) treehouse has a long history, dating back to Roman times. The Emperor Caligula, in a rare pleasant moment, had a spectacular dining platform for fourteen erected in the branches of one of his palace trees. Legend has it that he referred to this structure coyly as his "regular nest." During the Middle Ages, treehouses — usually simple arboreal seats or roofed boxes — proliferated to serve as retreats for meditative monks or contemplative commoners, anxious to physically distance themselves from earthbound concerns. The ancient Chinese seem to have pursued their meditations with feet firmly planted on the ground, but the Japanese built upper-air tree walks on stilts, for the use of dedicated leaf-lookers, and the Mogul emperors of India occasionally whiled away the summer days perched on tree platforms known as "garden thrones."

Treehouses of the sixteenth and seventeenth centuries were increasingly elaborate affairs. Often entire green rooms were constructed in the treetops. The roofs and walls were formed by bending and training the upper branches around a floor of planks. Such treehouses were specialties of the Italians. Montaigne admired a palatial example at Pratolino, complete with winding staircase and bannisters; and a description survives of a treehouse in the garden of one of the Medicis, enclosed in the branches of a holm oak. The latter treehouse, however, was somewhat overwhelmed by the other attractions of the garden, which included a field for tilting matches, a fountain topped by a bronze statue of Hercules, and a grotto filled with life-sized stone animals, prominent among them a rhinoceros with a real horn.

The English, not to be outdone by the vulgar Medicis, fashioned their own treehouses. John Parkinson, author of the gardening text *Paradisi in sole* (1629) — the title was a Latin pun on his name, and doubtless sent innumerable seventeenth-century readers into stitches — admired a massive treehouse at Cobham in Kent. The tree, Parkinson wrote, held three immense rooms, one above the other, connected by staircases. Each room was large enough to hold fifty men, and Parkinson, much impressed, described the edifice as "the goodliest spectacle mine eyes ever beheld for one tree to carry." Treehouses in Parkinson's day were routinely referred to as "roosting

places" and were said to have been much favored by the ladies —
a plus for British womanhood, since getting in and out of a tree in
full seventeenth-century female regalia must have challenged even
the most athletic.

Treehouses on this grand scale seem to have been few and far
between on our side of the Atlantic, though one gardening history
describes a notable example from the late eighteenth century. This
treehouse, the property of a Mr. John Ross of Pennsylvania, consisted
of a platform some ten to twelve feet above the ground, capable of
holding twenty people and a table. Food and drink were replenished
from the main house upon demand, when Mr. Ross yanked upon
a cunningly connected bell wire. In this forest bower, Mr. Ross was
wont to serve iced wine on the Fourth of July.

The modern treehouse, an endearing but often rather slipshod
affair, is generally considered the preserve of children, though the
occasional perceptive adult still finds them irresistible. One such still
delights the descendants of Haig Markarian of Tenafly, New Jersey:
a motorized treehouse, operated by foot pedal, which rises in elegant
elevator-like fashion fifty feet into the branches of a backyard oak
tree. In it and its arboreal equivalents scattered across the country,
harassed citizens of the twentieth century meditate, nap, read novels,
avoid mowing the lawn, and generally escape — in the words of one
Elizabethan treehouse aficionado — "the frequent disturbances of
your Family and Acquaintance." It's an entrancing picture.

The best trees for treehouse-building, experts agree, are deciduous — evergreens, which ooze pitch, are too sticky — unencumbered by such inconveniences as telephone or electrical wires,
and not too far from home base. One authority sets a one-mile outer
limit: farther than that and treehouse-building takes on all the
logistical problems of Napoleon's march on Moscow. The ideal
treehouse tree should be at least a foot thick in the trunk and should
feature, in the best of all possible worlds, three or four sturdy
branches eight to ten inches in diameter, extending outward at about
the same level from the ground. Such building sites are found in the
maple, the sycamore, the black oak, the Northern catalpa, the

Southern hackberry, and the white ash. The favored tree in Merrie England, through which the Elizabethan ladies capered in their petticoats and farthingales, was the basswood, better known on the continent as the linden or lime.

The basswoods, lindens, or limes comprise some thirty species of trees of the north temperate regions. Three of these are native to North America, though taxonomic dickering has at times upped the tally to as many as eighteen. Most prominent among them is *Tilia americana* — variously called the basswood, the whitewood, or the American linden — which ranges from New Brunswick to North Dakota, and south to Virginia and Texas. A more southerly version, *T. heterophylla*, the white basswood, is found from West Virginia southward into Florida and Alabama. Both bear largish heart-shaped leaves. Those of the white basswood are, appropriately, white underneath, while those of *T. americana* are green above and below. Young shoots and branches of the American basswood are similarly green, while those of the white basswood tend toward rusty-brown.

The basswoods are beloved for their fragrant yellow flowers, which appear in midsummer, long after most flowering trees have settled down to the serious business of seed-making. The small scented blossoms hang downward in complex little clusters, known to the botanically correct as *cymes*, between ribbony green bracts. "There is only one great summer-flowering tree," writes Helen Van Pelt Wilson of the basswood in *The Fragrant Year*, "but having this we hardly need another." Strictly speaking, *we* don't quite have it: Ms. Wilson stigmatizes the American basswood as "coarse and unrefined" in comparison to the delectable European lindens, which smell variously of honey and grape-flowers, with a touch of mock-orange. To the uncosmopolitan honeybee, however, all are equally enticing. When the linden is in bloom, ambitious hives are said to store up to fifteen pounds of honey in a single day. The popularity of the tree among bees has led to the common nickname "basswood beetree." If you can beat off the bees, the flowers can be gathered, dried, and used to make tea.

The overall attractiveness of the linden tree doubtless contributed to its pleasant place in myth and legend. The Greek dryads — tree spirits — were said to be wedded to linden trees, and in Roman mythology, the linden figures in the tale of Baucis and Philemon, recounted in Ovid's *Metamorphoses*. Baucis and Philemon were the homely heroine and hero in an uplifting fable of rewarded virtue, in which Jupiter and Mercury, bored with high living in Olympus, disguised themselves as poor travellers and wandered through Phrygia seeking food and shelter. The shortsighted Phrygians inhospitably refused them, until the increasingly annoyed gods at last happened upon the humble cottage of Baucis and Philemon. There they were given seats by the fire, offered wine, and fed cabbage soup, hardboiled eggs, and radishes. The gods, who held their grudges, punished most of Phrygia by drowning it and its inhabitants under a great lake. Baucis and Philemon, however, were rewarded for their generous behavior, living out the rest of their long lives in a marble palace with a roof of gold, and finally being transformed together into a pair of trees. Baucis became a linden and Philemon an oak, the two growing out together from one trunk. The linden ever after has been a symbol of conjugal love and fidelity — and, lest we forget, hospitality.

Basswood is a pale creamy wood, resembling poplar, much favored by woodcarvers because of its workability — it is said to "cut like cheese" — and its even grain. In past centuries it was thus the wood of choice for cigar-store Indians and ships' figureheads. Nowadays it is used for broom handles and beehive frames, piano keys and sounding boards, and for the acoustically dead structural portions of guitars. As firewood, basswood leaves a lot to be desired. It generates a mere 11.7 million BTU of heat per cord, less than half the heat output of an equivalent amount of oak or hickory. Lists ranking potential firewoods invariably place basswood at or near rock bottom, along with such other fireplace calamities as balsam fir, hemlock, and poplar.

Basswood bark, however, is notably useful. The thick inner bark is fibrous and, stripped from the tree, can be twisted and woven into cords, ropes, and matting. This practice was common among the northeastern Indian tribes, and was observed by the ever-curious Peter Kalm in his travels through upstate New York in 1749: "The French called the kind of linden which grew abundantly in the woods *bois blanc* (white wood). They had with them bags in which they carried their food, which were made by the natives from the bark of this tree. The Indians take the bark, boil it in lye, and pound it to make it soft. It becomes like coarse hemp." The colonists similarly soaked, softened, and pounded basswood bark strips to make brushes suitable for spreading paint, glue, or pitch.

Michael Weiner in *Earth Medicine, Earth Food* reports that the northeastern Indians used the water in which basswood bark was boiled as a burn remedy. The applied liquid soothed and softened scorched skin, and was effective enough to attract the attention of the American Medical Association, which mentioned it approvingly in a report of 1849. The Romans, less effectively, used an infusion of the bark of the European linden to prevent intoxication, and occasionally wore garlands of linden leaves at parties to offset incipient hangover. Such hopeful recipes for relief from the inevitable morning after have persisted in one form or another to the present day. Hangover cures historical and modern include raw owls' eggs, eel with almonds, ground swallows' beaks and myrrh, broth of boiled cloves, fried canaries, chicken soup, raw tomatoes, chunky peanut butter, and ice cream. Samuel Pepys recovered from his nights of merrymaking with brews of whey, horseradish ale, and turpentine; Lord Byron relied upon sermons and sodawater; modern Mainers recommend rolling naked in the snow. Other sufferers take a more negative view. "There is no cure for the hangover," wrote Robert Benchley tersely, "save death."

WILLOW

he willow, historically, has earned itself a reputation as a miserable and mournful tree. The captive Israelites, according to the Bible, sat down and wept under it by the rivers of Babylon; Desdemona sang sadly about one just before being strangled by Othello; Ophelia, clutching a bouquet of wildflowers, fell in a brook and drowned underneath one. In keeping with such doleful associations, the willow was a popular mid-eighteenth-century gravestone motif, running neck and neck with the winged skull, the urn, the depleted hourglass, and the stone finger pointing heavenward.

Gardeners of the Romantic era favored the willow — or the similarly dejected-looking yew or cypress — for the enhancement of contemplatively mournful moods. In the same manner that dog-owners come to look like their dogs, gardens inevitably reflect the personalities of the attendant gardeners. The Elizabethans, a fun-loving bunch, filled their gardens with picnic tents, peacocks, archery butts, and bowling greens. William III, an incorrigible war-monger, planted a topiary fortress called Troy Town, with green battlements of clipped yews and variegated hollies; Louis XIV, that most pompous and pretentious of monarchs, presided grandly over the vast and immaculately formal acres of Versailles. The eighteenth-century Romantics, who liked life at the emotional edge, preferred the dramatically sinister. The ideal Romantic garden was a "landscape picture" of mood-evoking structures — resident Romantics wandered among broken columns, Greek temples, rusted water-wheels, grottoes (with imitation stalactites), cascades, wildernesses, and blasted heaths. The hallmark of the Romantic garden was the ancient ruin, and those lucky homeowners who actually possessed one designed entire estates around such crumbling windfalls. For the ruinless majority, professional ruin-builders moved in to fill the gap — presumably adhering to the dictates of Thomas Whateley, who, in his *Observations on Modern Gardening* (1770), laid down the aesthetic guidelines for the construction of effective ruins. Clients most commonly demanded Gothic churches; similarly popular were Stonehenges, made from plastered timbers. One German Romantic, in an excess of enthusiasm, added a derelict wing to his mansion. Over all, to ensure the proper atmosphere of gloom, one horticulturist urged the central installation of an iron forge, going full blast and belching out "a black cloud of smoak."

Suitable plants for such outdoor stage productions were a problem. Mood was all: the great garden of Stourhead in Wiltshire, an acknowledged Romantic masterpiece, is said by some to have been much damaged by extensive twentieth-century plantings of cheerful orange rhododendrons. Trees, in the Romantic mode, had to be gnarled, bent, and withered — or possibly stone dead, which melancholy state, wrote landscape gardener William Kent, lent "a greater air of truth to the scene." Some living specimens were acceptably tragic. Various dark-hued conifers were favored, and the garden of poet Alexander Pope was praised for its double avenues of cypresses, terminating mournfully at Pope's mother's tomb. Willows, drooping dismally by a lake, were also romantically suitable, and beneath them meandered many a prospective poet, tragically brooding.

In the Victorian language of flowers, the willow represented forsaken love, and those nineteenth-century unfortunates who "wore the willow" moped after an unfaithful suitor. The willow also represented mournfulness in general. "Beware that your Northern laurels do not change to Southern willows," wrote Charles Lee dampingly to a buoyant General Horatio Gates after the surrender of Burgoyne at the Battle of Saratoga — surely among the most grudging congratulations on record.

Saddest of all the willow trees is, inevitably, the weeping willow. This drooping form, which so inspired the Romantics to melancholy, is not restricted to the weeping willow, but appears in many of other species as well, among them the weeping beech, weeping spruce, weeping Japanese cherry, weeping mulberry, weeping holly, weeping juniper, weeping ash, weeping birch, weeping cedar, and even weeping giant sequoia. Horticulturists, who tend to be coldly unemotional in their assessment of trees, refer to this form as *mounding.* As such, it is one of the six standard shapes assumed by the fully leafed-out tree — the other five being the oval, the pyramidal, the columnar, the round, and the irregular.

Most deciduous shade trees tend toward the oval, a shape that has been perceptively compared to an egg perched on a golf tee. White and red oaks, buckeyes, walnuts, hickories, most maples, beeches, and basswoods are, in silhouette, oval. Most conifers are pyramidal, a shape that obsesses many of us each December in the seasonal search for the perfect Christmas tree. Columnar trees feature a svelte silhouette nearly as narrow at the bottom as at the top; these essentially hipless trees are termed *fastigate* by horticulturists. A common example is the Lombardy poplar. Round trees, other than in topiary gardens, are relatively rare, though some sugar maples and elms are natural spheres. Irregular trees, each possessing what Roger Yepsen tactfully terms "a certain picturesque unbalanced quality," are determined eccentrics. Yepsen cites old Scotch pines, dogwoods, and true cedars as classic examples of arboreal irregularity. It's often the line of the lone irregular tree that gives Japanese prints their peculiar beauty.

The weeping (or mounding) willow is believed to have originated in China, where, since ancient times, it has appeared in literature and legend, pottery, painting, and silk embroidery. The willow motif has also been co-opted by western artists desiring to appear Chinese. Among these was a potter's apprentice named Thomas Minton, who, in 1780, conceived the willow-pattern design for china. This design, reputedly inspired by an old Chinese legend, depicts in shades of blue the garden of a mandarin, through which a pair of lovers are nervously eloping over an arching bridge, beneath the branches of a weeping willow tree. Minton's pseudo-Chinese tableware leapt to popularity with the craze for all things Oriental that swept Europe in the nineteenth century. Enthusiasts wallpapered their parlors with Chinese prints, draped their daughters in Chinese silk embroideries, and erected pagodas in their gardens. Minton's willowware, much in demand, was rapidly copied by the major European pottery factories, and eventually — in a curious circle of imitation — began to be produced and exported by the Chinese themselves.

The weeping willow was similarly exported. It travelled at first along overland trade routes to the Middle East, where it was apparently established in time for the homesick Israelites to hang their harps on it, as recorded in the 137th Psalm: "By the rivers of Babylon, there we sat down, yea, we wept, when we remembered Zion. We hanged our harps upon the willows in the midst thereof." Some skeptics, who view biblical botany with a suspicious eye, hold that these were not willows at all, but poplars. Linnaeus, however, accepted the psalmist at face value, and thus classified the weeping willow as *Salix babylonica*, which name it still bears today.

If not by the rivers of Babylon, willows indisputably grew in the gardens of the ancient Persians, along with tulips, hyacinths, saffron crocuses, and the famous Persian roses. The roses, legend has it, sprang up from the sweat of Mohammed. One early caliph, by name El-Mutavekkel, was so taken with them that in rose season he wore only rose-colored clothing and had all the royal carpets sprinkled with rosewater. Persian roses reportedly reached Europe through Spain, via the eighth-century Moorish conquest. The willow seems to have arrived somewhat later. It reached England in the late 1500s, reportedly in the hands of an English merchant named Thomas Vernon, who had spotted a specimen of the tree in Aleppo, growing on the banks of the Euphrates River. Mr. Vernon took a cutting from the tree and brought it home, where he planted it on his estate at Twickenham on the Thames River. The willow flourished. A cutting from this tree, the story goes, was given to Alexander

Pope, who planted it in his famous garden. There it became such a drawing card for tourists and garden gapers that, in 1801, a later owner of the garden had the tree cut down, to ensure himself a little peace and privacy.

Before its demise, however, at least a portion of Pope's weeping willow made the transatlantic crossing to North America. According to William Cullen Bryant, the introduction of the willow was effected by one Samuel Johnson, an Anglican clergyman, philosopher, and author, and first president of New York's King's College. (King's College, hastily renamed in the days of the Revolutionary War, is now known as Columbia University.) Johnson, while travelling in England, visited Pope's garden, where he was so taken with the legendary weeping willow that he acquired cuttings to take home. He planted them in his own garden in Stratford, Connecticut, on the Housatonic River, where they flourished and multiplied.

George Washington was an early admirer of the weeping willow. In the days when he was first establishing the Mount Vernon plantings, he directed his plantation manager — Lund Washington, his cousin — to obtain for the southern grove "all the clever kinds of trees (especially flowering ones) that can be got such as crabapple, Poplar, Dogwood, Sassafras, Laurel, Willow (especially Yellow and Weeping Willow, twigs of which may be got from Philadelphia)." His diary entry for March 13, 1786, mentions more willows: "The ground being in order for it, I set the people to forming the mounds of Earth by the gate in order to set weep willows thereon." Despite the doleful impact of the trees on most viewers, Washington seems to have regarded his willows quite cheerfully: the mounds bearing the latest Mount Vernon trees were positioned flanking the Bowling Green. Thomas Jefferson put in twenty-four hundred weeping willow cuttings at Monticello in March of 1794; and James and Dolly Madison grew a few on their Virginia estate, Montpelier, a fact that Dolly recorded with pride in her memoirs.

The importation and establishment of the weeping willow on the American continent, though an admirable botanical accomplishment, was in cold truth a case of carrying coals to Newcastle. The willows are the largest group of trees native to North America, consisting of some sixty-five to one hundred true species and fifty or so hybrids. The Indian tribes had exploited their regional willows for centuries. The Plains Indians built sweat baths of willow poles draped with buffalo skins, framed their war shields with bent willow branches, and smoked in their ritual pipes a mixture called *kinni-kinnick,* made from shaved willow bark and buffalo fat. Farther north, the Ojibwas cured moosehide for their moccasins over a willow fire and, in meteorological emergencies, fashioned willow snowshoes. The Paiutes wove exquisite water jugs from fine willow twigs, an art somewhat perverted in the nineteenth century, when native American weavers began to model their creations on U.S. Army canteens.

Worldwide the total number of willow species is estimated at between three and four hundred, with a vast distribution ranging from Chile to the Arctic Circle and from Spain to Japan. The precise number of extant species remains questionable due to the willow's irresponsible predilection for interbreeding, which carefree prom-iscuity has produced a botanical *gemisch* referred to by willow students as "a field naturalist's nightmare." All, whether of pure or mixed ancestry, are members of the family *Saliceae. Saliceae* is commonly known as the Willow family, though to be fair, the family name is shared by two other genera, including some thirty to forty comparatively puritanical species of poplars.

For dendrologists, willow-counting is sometimes complicated by difficulties in determining precisely what is and what is not a tree. Of the North American willows, over half are less than tree-sized, ranging from large upright shrubs or borderline trees, down to four-inch prostrate mats. The latter, occasionally cited as the world's smallest tree, is *Salix arctica,* the arctic willow, whose tiny low-lying habit allows it to survive in its inclement far-northern environment. Both botanists and linguists, however, balk at designating as "tree" a plant that habitually crawls across the tundra, barely raising its head over four inches skyward. On the other hand, opinions vary as to what does constitute a tree. A tree, states *Hortus III,* somewhat cagily, is "a woody plant that produces one main trunk and a more or less distinct and elevated crown." A tree, states the *Oxford English Dictionary*, also gracefully skirting the issue, is "a perennial plant having a self-supporting woody main stem or trunk . . . and growing to a considerable height and size." One man's considerable, however, is another man's puny, which leaves us with a no-man's-land occupied by large shrubs and/or small trees, over which botanists bicker in the same way philosophers haggle over those half-full (half-empty?) glasses of water. Some tree writers simply grab the bull by the horns. Alan Mitchell, in *The Trees of North America*, decrees that a mature willow, to qualify as a tree, must be over thirty feet tall on a single stem. Thus eliminated from tree status are over half of the American willow species, including the familiar pussywillow, *Salix discolor*, whose furry gray catkins are regarded as a harbinger of spring throughout the Northeast. *S. discolor*, deemed by *Hortus III* a "large shrub or small tree," never makes it much taller than twenty feet.

Pussywillow catkins are indisputably all-male, which means that those of us who were raised on the old nursery riddle

> *I know a little pussy*
> *Her coat is silver gray*
> *She lives down in the meadow*
> *Not very far away*

have been misled by poetic pronouns. Left to themselves, in their preferred swamps and marshes, the furry catkins will blossom, revealing bright-gold stamens laden with pollen. Ernest Thompson Seton, incidentally, claims that the common name "pussy" willow comes not from the pussycat-like fur of the catkins, but from the French *pousse*, which means "budded." Nearly all willows — except for a few odd hybrids of *S. babylonica* — are, like the pussywillow, dioecious, and all are insect-pollinated. To attract potential pollinators, each miniscule willow floret comes equipped with a gland at the base, which secretes honeysuckle-scented nectar, irresistible to honeybees. Often pussywillows provide prowling bees with their first honey of the new year. After pollination by such grateful bees, seeds develop, to be released at maturity in white clouds of silky down. They are dispersed — effortfully — by wind, being a bit on the heavy side for air transport, and more easily by water, which is why so many young willows spring up along stream and river banks.

The bright and early spring growth of willows led children, in bygone days, to the making of willow whistles — a tuneful spring tradition that seems to have gone the way of marbles, May baskets, and hoop-rolling in the park. Willow whistles were made by slipping the new green bark off the young willow twig — a feat which can be performed only in early spring; older and more settled bark loses its slipability. Removal of the outer bark reveals new, immaculately white wood beneath; it's this young willow wood that we refer to when we use the phrase "clean as a whistle."

WILLOW WHISTLE

In early spring, cut a length of green willow twig about as thick as your thumb and approximately six inches long. About two inches from one end, cut a ring through the bark; about two inches from the other, cut a deep notch. Tap the green bark until it loosens and can be pulled off as an intact cylinder. Whittle down the bare wood at the notched end to form an air passage. Replace the bark cylinder. Blow.

Barely making tree status is the slightly larger osier or basket willow (*S. viminalis*), a European native imported in colonial days and now naturalized throughout the Northeast. One story holds that the osier was introduced to this country by Ben Franklin, who noticed some willow baskets — sprouting — on a wharf in Philadelphia, and urged that such an indefatigable plant be grown for American use. *Hortus III* considers the osier a "shrub or small tree" — but in the same breath states that it reaches thirty feet at maturity, which renders it, by Mitchell standards, a definite tree. Harvested by basketmakers, the osier seldom manages to reach full height. In European villages, osiers are grown and managed like a coppice, cut annually for a crop of whippy six-foot wands. Such a harvesting practice, properly pursued, can continue almost indefinitely — even, wrote seventeenth-century gardener John Evelyn, until "World's End." Chances are that it was twigs of osier upon which, as late as 1826, the English Exchequer recorded payment of taxes. A twig was notched to indicate the amount of tax paid, then split lengthwise. The taxpayer kept half, as a receipt; the tax collector kept the other. When English tax records were converted to paper, the enormous and obsolete files of willow twigs were taken out and burned. The fire ran amok and burned down the Houses of Parliament.

While the osier is the tree of choice for the basket professional, almost any willow will yield slender wands suitable for weaving. Collectively known as withy, such pliable branches were used by colonial coopers as hoops, to bind the staves of barrels, buckets, tubs, and churns.

Largest of the native American willows — and by anyone's standards a tree — is the black willow, *S. nigra*. Mature black willows occasionally manage to reach 140 feet in height, with trunks four feet in diameter. Found throughout the eastern and central United States, and west as far as Texas and Mexico, *S. nigra* is most likely the tree Jacques Cartier's eye fell upon when he wrote of a "pleasant countrey full of all sorts of goodly trees, Ceders, Firres, Ashes, Boxe and Willowes." The "black" designation derives from the color of the bark: deep brown to black in mature trees, with a tendency to peel off the trunk in strips. *S. nigra* is one of the few willows with any claim to usefulness as a timber tree: it holds nails well, resists splitting, and is durable in water, which traits were valued by the makers of waterwheels and certain types of boat keels. In general, however, willow is a soft, light, and wimpishly weak wood. As firewood, it's no great shakes, averaging 13.2 million BTU per cord, which puts it well down the list of woodpile candidates, along with red pine and hemlock. The colonists scorned it.

The black willow, like so many of its willow relatives, is a waterlover, thriving along the edges of streams and rivers, where its waterborne seeds tend to plant it. The scientific name for the willow genus — *Salix* — is held by some to derive from the Celtic *sal* (near) and *lis* (water), in honor of this propensity. The mighty Mississippi, along which the young Sam Clemens cautiously maneuvered his riverboat, has been called a river of willows. Along its edges grow black willows, peachleaf willows (*S. amygdaloides*), and sandbar willows (*S. interior*). Sandbar willows are non-trees by the Mitchell ruling, generally reaching no more than fifteen feet, but they compensate for their lack of inches by sheer reproductive enthusiasm. These large shrubs or small trees spread, like strawberries, by means of underground stems — *stolons* — and eventually spring up in such numbers that they form dense thickets. The thickets are colloquially known as willow bats or willow slaps, which is what the springy branches do to unfortunates blundering through them. The American Indians put these willow thickets to good use: Prince Maximilian von Wied Neuweid, sightseeing along the Missouri in 1833, noted nervously in his diary that the local Indians habitually lay in ambush among the river willows. Modern hunters favor them for duckblinds.

A major advantage of riverside willows is their effectiveness as erosion-controllers. Willows, large and small, all form wide-spreading root systems, which function to hold unstable riverbanks in place and thus keep obstreperous rivers within bounds. This same invasive root system makes the willow the bane of city water commissioners: the willow has been known to strangle water pipes and wreak havoc upon septic systems. On the riverbank, however, such underground grabbing is appreciated. Among the first to exploit the willow for erosion control was the army: Captain Oswald Ernst of the Army Corps of Engineers, stationed in St. Louis on the banks of the overflowing Mississippi in 1878, initiated an intensive willow-planting program to combat flooding. He was aided in this task by the growth properties of the willow, which takes root easily from cuttings casually stuck into the ground. Once established, the willow grows by leaps and bounds, some species reaching eighty feet in as little as fifteen years. Noting this, medieval historian Dorothy Hartley suggests that the early Christian missionaries carried willow staffs, since so many of them dramatically took root and sprouted when thrust into the ground.

Slightly smaller than the impressive black willow are the white willow (*S. alba*) and the crack willow (*S. fragilis*), both colonial-era imports from Europe. The crack willow was established — ironically — under the auspices of the British government for the making of charcoal, which in turn was used in the manufacture of gunpowder. Both the common name "crack" and the scientific *fragilis* derive from the brittleness of the tree's branches, easily snapped by storms.

The white willow was originally propagated for more peaceful purposes. Since the time of the ancient Greeks, it had been known that infusions of white willow bark could dull pain. Medical practitioners, both amateur and professional, thus used teas of willow to treat toothache, earache, headache, gout, and rheumatism. Powdered willow bark was applied to the navels of newborn babies; mashed poultices of leaves and bark were plastered over wounds to staunch bleeding; boiled leaves and twigs were mixed with wine and used as a dandruff shampoo. Willow sap was promoted as an eyewash in the treatment of cataracts; bark decoctions were touted as a cure for venereal disease.

The white willow's medical reputation stemmed from a chemical named *salicin*, first isolated from willow bark by French chemist Henri Leroux in 1827. Salicin itself was medicinally unusable, since it could not be taken internally without dire side effects. Its discovery did, however, point researchers in the right direction. Related compounds were subsequently isolated from other plant sources: methyl salicylate from birch oil; salicylic acid from meadowsweet, a white-petalled wildflower then scientifically known as *Spiraea ulmaria*. (It is now, in living testimony to the inconstancy of scientific truth, known as *Filipendula ulmaria*.) The problem of finding a pain-killer that could be swallowed without ill effect was not solved until 1899, when a filial German named Felix Hoffman began seeking a cure for his father's arthritis. He came up with the soon-to-be-famous acetylsalicylic acid. The new drug was first mass-produced by the pharmaceutical firm of Friederich Bayer & Co., who dubbed their product "aspirin" — *a* for acetyl, *spirin* for *Spirea* — which, though catchy, is unfair, since *Salix alba* was there first.

192

Today aspirin is the world's most frequently taken medicine. Americans consume some thirty-five tons of it daily. About 65 percent of aspirin-poppers take it to alleviate headaches, though half of all aspirin sold is purchased by arthritis sufferers. Prescribed for everything from influenza to premenstrual tension, aspirin has enjoyed a further upsurge in popularity with recent evidence that a tablet a day may keep heart attacks away. An aspirin held tightly between the knees was recommended in pre-sexual-freedom days as an effective form of birth control; and my husband's grandma (who had six children) recommended an aspirin in each Mason jar to keep dill pickles crisp. Neither of these exemplary uses was foreseen by Felix Hoffman.

POPLAR

he poplars — all thirty to forty species of them — are members of the aforementioned Willow family. The genus name *Populus* is said to derive from the Roman use of the trees as the sites of public meetings — hence *arbor populi*, or "people's tree." Others claim that the name comes from the Latin *papelin*, meaning "to babble," in honor of the incessant rustling of the poplar's restless leaves. Along these lines, the regrettably sexist Greeks had a saying that a woman's tongue is like poplar leaves (i.e., never still) — though if the surviving literature is anything to go by, male Greeks seem to have held their own in conversation.

Botanical convention today assigns the world's poplars to four major groups: the white poplars, which include both white and gray poplars and the enchanting quaking aspen; the black poplars, which include the soldierly Lombardy poplar and the Eastern, Plains, and Fremont cottonwoods; the balsam poplars, which include the group namesake balsam poplar, the black cottonwood, and the Balm-of-Gilead; and a fourth assemblage known primly as *Leucoides* ("white-poplar-like"), represented in America by only a single native species, the swamp (or river) cottonwood of the Southeast. The swamp cottonwood (*Populus heterophylla*) holds the dubious distinction of being the best saw timber of all the poplars. Over 50 percent of all the excelsior used in the United States, states Donald Culross Peattie, is shredded from the downed bodies of swamp cottonwoods. *P. heterophylla* also furnishes wood for crates.

Perhaps the most exquisite of the native poplars is the less useful *P. tremuloides*, commonly known as the quaking, trembling, or golden aspen, or occasionally, the quiverleaf. The quaking aspen boasts the widest range of any North American tree, and is found from Newfoundland south through Delaware, and west in a broad swathe to the Alaskan coast. Aspen thickets are found throughout the Rocky Mountains, where, each fall, the ever-active leaves turn a bright butter-gold. Aspens in the West, impartial observers say, put on a better display than aspens in the East. This may be due, suggests Donald Peattie, to the sunlight, which in the unpolluted West shines through the leaves "like a clear, sustained blast on angelic trumpets." Cynical easterners attribute it to the lack of competition in the conifer-heavy Rockies.

A distinguishing feature of *P. tremuloides* is the unceasing shiver of its "silver dollar" leaves, which nervous habit led the Onondaga Indians to dub the tree *Nut-Hi-e*, or "noisy leaf." The noisy rustling was given sinister interpretations by some early observers. In Christian legend, the aspen was the tree upon which Judas Iscariot hanged himself, and the leaves, two thousand years later, suppos-edly still tremble in vicarious shame. Another story holds that, in the flight from the infant-slaughtering Herod, the Holy Family passed through a dense forest. All the trees pulled back to let them through except the thoughtless aspen — which was given such a baleful look by the Baby Jesus that the leaves have trembled ever after in humiliation. According to Father Pierre-Jean de Smet, nineteenth-century missionary to the Indian tribes of the Northwest, the French *coureurs du bois*, or trappers, claimed that the aspen leaves' shamed trembling commemorated the tree's use for the wood of the Cross. In the Victorian language of flowers, the unfortunate aspen — per-haps for all of the above reasons — symbolized scandal, lamenta-tion, and fear. In cold fact, the quivering of aspen leaves predates the construction of the Cross and the demise of the dishonorable Judas by some seventy million years. The quivering is due to the structure of the aspen leaf-stalk, which is both long — markedly longer than the leaf blade — and flattened contrary to the plane of the blade, such that the stalk acts as a pivot in the wind.

The aspen is a white poplar, classed by botanists with the Old World white poplar (*P. alba*). The trees are characterized by a coating of white fur on new shoots and leaves. The bark is also distinctively pale. As the trees reach maturity — no great age for aspens, which are mature at twenty-five, old at fifty, and doddering at one hundred — the bark bleaches to a chalky white. The white bark is reminiscent of the equally chalky paper birch, but unlike birch, aspen bark — "smooth as flesh," writes Donald Peattie — does not peel. Aspen bark, chewed or brewed in tea, is nastily bitter, which perhaps contributed to its early reputation as a medicinal. The Indians used it to treat coughs; the colonists prescribed it for fever. The effectiveness of these concoctions was due to the presence of salicin in aspen bark, which, once choked down by the sufferer, probably exerted an aspirin-like effect. Bark of the related white poplar, also impregnated with salicin, was listed by the *U.S. Pharmacopoeia* as late as 1936 as a specific for fever and menstrual cramps.

A large number of animals, unencumbered by the picky taste buds of the human being, rely on the aspen as a source of food. Moose, porcupines, snowshoe hares, and cottontail rabbits nibble buds and branches; grosbeaks and purple finches eat the buds. White-tailed deer browse on it: in some areas, aspen twigs constitute a quarter of the deers' diet. Sapsuckers, woodpeckers, and chickadees nest in hollows in aspen trunks; bears use aspens as scratching posts.The most enthusiastic user of the aspen, however, is the beaver. Beavers, like other aspen-eaters, consume leaves, buds, and twigs, but their main staple — the real basic of beaver food — is the inner bark, particularly the juicier, tastier bark of the young limbs at the top of the tree. Since the beaver, possessed of a decidedly low center of gravity, does not climb, often the only way to get at this superior bark is to gnaw down the entire tree. While the busy beaver thus wreaks havoc in the pond-side aspen grove, beavers do — to their credit — utilize their downed trees as thoroughly as the Plains Indians utilized the buffalo. Edible portions are eaten; strong sticks go to build dams and lodges; and no beaver worth his salt would face winter without a good supply of aspen sticks thriftily buried in the mud for cold-weather mealtimes. The aspen-beaver relationship is so well established that beaver-seeking fur trappers — back in the days of the beaver-hat craze — zeroed in on aspen thickets as telltale signs of beaver domiciles.

Aspen wood is less appealing to humans than to animals — though structurally strong enough for the average beaver lodge, aspen is too light and weak for more ambitious construction. Out west, it was used for mine props and corral fences, and occasionally — since it weathered kicking, gnawing, and other equine misbehaviors without splintering — for horse stalls. The non-splintering feature has led to the modern use of aspen in toys, tongue depressors, and popsicle sticks. Though it doesn't splinter, it shreds well, which means that running it through an excelsior machine (U.S. Patent No. 75728) turns it into that shredded-wheat-like packing material used for the cushioning of such delicate edibles as watermelons, avocados, and cantaloupes; and for stuffing in the upholstery of furniture and coffins. Aspen is also used in high-quality paper pulp, the sort that eventually appears in glossy magazines advertising aspen-surrounded Rocky Mountain getaways.

As firewood, aspen is relatively worthless, though the fur traders reportedly burned it through the long cold winters at Hudson's Bay Company trading posts. Aspen puts out a mere 12.5 million BTU per cord. An anonymous early poet stigmatizes it and its kin in the cutting verse: "Poplar gives a bitter smoke / Fills your eyes and makes you choke." It also burns rapidly. One modern user refers to it resignedly as "gopher wood" — because you continually have to go for more. Fast burn and bitter smoke aside, an advantage of aspen firewood is its availability. Aspen and related poplars are excellent wood for coppicing; they reproduce enthusiastically by suckering and grow rapidly — so explosively, in fact, that potential poplar planters are warned against setting them too close to walkways, roads, or buildings. You can't actually *see* them grow, like some farmers claim for their telescoping cornstalks, but close. Morton Fry of Ephrata, Pennsylvania, a professional poplar grower, calculates that his hybrid poplars — offspring of the Eastern cotton-wood (*P. deltoides*) and the Lombardy poplar (*P. nigra*) — pack on an impressive 59.8 million BTU per acre per year. Such magic-beanstalk-like growth by far outstrips the plodding maple (an annual 47 million BTU per acre) and hickory (32.3 million BTU per acre), and illustrates the competitive advantage of sheer quantity.

Such reproductive verve suggested a use for poplar on another fuel front. During the ominous days of the 1974 Arab oil embargo, poplars were proposed as a possible fossil fuel substitute. Rapidly growing poplars, it was suggested, could supply immense quantities of wood chips, either for conversion to alcohol — and eventually gasohol — or for reduction in wood gasifiers to combustible gases (hydrogen and carbon monoxide), which would in turn fuel steam boilers or generators. With the — at least temporary — abatement of the oil crunch, however, many alternative energy proposals were put on the national back burner. Not so on the Fry poplar plantation: using wood gasifiers, the Frys use their poplar chips to heat and power the family greenhouses — and to fuel one of the family pickup trucks. "This truck runs on wood only," proclaims a sign on the poplar-powered vehicle's side. Its owners claim twenty miles to the two-by-four.

The Eastern cottonwood (*P. deltoides*) is a black poplar, dis-tinguished from its white relatives by the green undersides to its leaves, and a generally larger size. Variously and confusingly known as the big cottonwood, the yellow cottonwood, the whitewood, the necklace poplar, the Carolina poplar, and the Southern cottonwood, it is scattered across the eastern United States from Vermont to Michigan, and south into Texas. The common name *cottonwood* derives from the impressively vast quantities of tiny cotton-embed-ded seeds ("objectionable," says *Hortus III*) released from enclosing pods by female trees in early summer. The Eastern cottonwood exists in a number of geographical forms, among them, recent evidence suggests, the midwestern Plains cottonwood. Though the Plains cottonwood has enjoyed its own species name — *P. sargentii* — for many years, the going belief these days is that *P. sargentii* is simply a western form of the Eastern cottonwood. Luckily for those states claiming the cottonwood as state tree, all have maintained a cautiously political vagueness as to species: both Kansas ("To The Stars Through Difficulties") and Nebraska ("Equality Before the Law") claim an unadorned cottonwood, as does Wyoming ("Equal Rights"). The Wyoming cottonwood, however, is generally assumed to be the balsam poplar, of which more later.

The Plains or Western cottonwood ranges from Alberta east to the Dakotas, and south through Texas and New Mexico — overlapping with the Eastern cottonwood in the crucial territory of Kansas and Nebraska, which may explain the taxonomic caginess of the State Tree legislators. The Plains cottonwood is generally a smaller tree than its eastern alter ego — averaging fifty to seventy-five feet, as opposed to the Eastern cottonwood's ninety, with trunks four to six feet thick. It flourishes across the Great Plains wherever low moist ground can be found, springing up along streams and creeks, around waterholes and old buffalo wallows. Pioneers camped beneath cottonwood trees along the Santa Fe and Oregon trails. Trappers along the Missouri River cut them for *pirogues*, the vast dugout canoes that, lashed together two by two, were capable of carrying fifteen tons of mountain men and beaver pelts. Cottonwood bark served as winter forage for livestock: the Plains Indians fed their horses on it. So, according to his diary, did George Armstrong Custer, during the winter campaign of 1868–69, when the flamboyant general was engaged in driving the Arkansas Indian tribes out of their winter encampments.

Unsurprisingly, in a region notably scarce in trees, many Western cottonwoods sprang to prominence as trail markers and gathering sites. Among the most famous was the late Lone Sentinel cottonwood of Kansas, located at the crossing of the Arkansas River where Dodge City, stalking ground of Wyatt Earp, sprang up in the early nineteenth century. At the arrival of the first pioneers the tree was reportedly one of only three that existed between Dodge City and Pueblo, Colorado. As such, it was revered by the local Indians and became a landmark for western travellers. In 1920, the Dodge

City Business and Professional Women's Club acknowledged their ancestors' debt to the Tree by attaching to it a bronze tablet bearing the doleful lines:

> *A lonely sentinel of the Kansas Plains,*
> *Which marked the ford for wagon trains,*
> *A campsite on a weary ride,*
> *A bit of shade for those who died.*

The tree itself died in 1934.

Of more limited fame, but similarly cherished, was the Cattle Trail Cottonwood, located on the banks of Stinking Water Creek within spitting distance of the Old Texas Cattle Trail. The Trail was in heavy use during the period 1875–1884, by Texas ranch hands driving their stock north to the railroad loading pens. At some point during this active decade, an entrepreneurial settler erected a small building under the cottonwood tree, stocked it (solely) with whiskey, and went into business. Business — offering the last liquid refreshment until the end of the line — flourished, and the sheltering cottonwood became fondly known among the trailriders as the Saloon Tree. Today, tastefully renamed the Cattle Trail Cottonwood, the tree stands on land owned by the Maddux Cattle Company, in Chase County, Nebraska.

The far western version of the Eastern and Plains cottonwood is called the Fremont cottonwood (*P. Fremontii*) in honor of John Charles Frémont, its formal discoverer. The Fremont cottonwood ranges from California to Nevada, and south into Arizona and New Mexico. Within this range, it is a common inhabitant. The Mohave Indian women made skirts of the fibrous inner bark — somewhat like the Hawaiian grass skirt, twisted strips hanging from a waistband. The early Spanish settlers frequently remarked upon the tree and dubbed it *alamo*. Thus the old Spanish mission in which Davy Crockett and his compatriots came to such a bloody end in the winter of 1836 was named for its peaceful grove of cottonwood trees.

John C. Frémont was born in Savannah, Georgia — native

territory of the aforementioned swamp cottonwoods — in 1813. He began his career as a mathematician, surveyor, and sometime map-maker in the employ of the federal government. It seems to have been his map-making expeditions — mostly in the region of the upper Mississippi and Missouri rivers — that left him with a thirst for wilderness adventure. In 1841, he married Jessie Benton, daughter of Senator Thomas Hart Benton of Missouri — and in 1842, under the auspices of his influential father-in-law, his travels in the West began. As an explorer, modern sources agree, Frémont was highly overrated. He displayed a distressing predilection for disastrous mid-winter mountain crossings; and, though romantically nicknamed "the Pathfinder," historians argue that all Frémont-found paths had been perfectly well known for decades by trappers, traders, and Indians. His military career was similarly overblown: his involvement in the liberation of California and the establishment of the Bear Flag Republic led to a court-martial under President Polk (for mutiny, disobedience, and conduct prejudicial to military discipline); his part in the Civil War ended when he was relieved of his command by Abraham Lincoln. He made a fortune in gold during the California Gold Rush days, but lost it all in unwise investments. However, despite the ups and downs of his hectic career, Frémont was — when he had time — a competent and conscientious naturalist.

His first record of the tree that came to bear his name was made near Pyramid Lake, Nevada, on the night of January 6, 1844. In company with the now-legendary Kit Carson, Frémont came upon a spring, bordered by "some trees of the sweet cottonwood, which, after a long interval of absence, we saw again with pleasure, regard-ing them as harbingers of better company." He noted the trees again in April, in California's San Joaquin Valley, and somewhat later in "beautiful green" profusion along the Mohave River. The Fremont cottonwood, like its eastern relatives, favors river and stream banks, and waterholes. It reaches heights of ninety to one hundred feet at maturity, and bears glossy, vaguely triangular, toothed leaves. It has a tendency to fork at the base into several equal trunks, a charac-teristic referred to by botanists as *multi-boled*, and by lumbermen, who view their trees in board feet, as undesirable. The wood of Frémont's cottonwood is, in several respects, undesirable: like that of other *Populus* species, it is soft, weak, brittle, and generally lacking in staying power.

One of Frémont's cottonwoods bears the distinction of being an authenticated hanging tree. Though many trees of the mid- and far west saw mayhem during the hot-tempered settlement years, few entered the twentieth century with the historical details of the dreadful deeds intact. One such is the Hanging Cottonwood of Genoa, Nevada — one of the first settlements in the Utah Territory, established by Mormons in 1849. In Genoa, on November 25, 1897, Adam Uber — generally characterized as a drifter and ne'er-do-well — shot and killed Hans Anderson, a popular and respected home-town boy, in an ill-considered argument over twenty-five cents. Uber was promptly arrested, but before justice could take its course, a mob of nameless vigilantes broke into the jail, removed Uber, and hanged him from a handy cottonwood tree. Though the members of the freelance hanging committee were never apprehended, some of the local citizenry eventually regretted their rash action and had the hanging limb cut from the cottonwood, to ensure that the tree would never again be used for such a purpose. So far, it hasn't.

The yellow poplar — as opposed to the legitimate white and black — is not a poplar at all, but a member of the Magnolia family. Donald Peattie, in fact, refers to it as "King of the Magnolias," and even *Hortus III*, a volume not given to superlatives, terms it "one of the noblest of American trees." It is the tallest hardwood tree in North America, reaching heights of up to two hundred feet in its favored stomping grounds in the southern Appalachians. Diameters reach eight to ten feet. John Lawson reported an awe-inspiring specimen in North Carolina, "wherein a lusty Man had his Bed and Household Furniture, and lived in it till his Labour got him a more fashionable Mansion." The yellow poplar is the state tree of ("Commerce & Agriculture") Tennessee.

Scientifically the yellow poplar is known as *Liriodendron tulipifera*; colloquially, it is called the tuliptree. Both names pay tribute to the tree's exquisite, two-inch-long tulip-shaped flowers, the petals colored a pale greenish yellow banded at the base in orange. Once fertilized, by ecstatic bees, the flowers give way to narrow little conelike fruits borne erect on the branches. These remain in place through the winter, long after the release of the ripe winged seeds, and look, on the winter-barren trees, like misshapen candelabra.

The yellow poplar is also sometimes called the canoewood: the Indians — and later the settlers — hollowed the tall straight trunks to make canoes. Daniel Boone and family, all packed in a sixty-foot tuliptree canoe, sailed down the Ohio River in 1799 to start a new life in Spanish Missouri. Today canoewood is used less romantically to make crates, boxes, and plywood, and it is pulped to make high-grade book paper.

The balsam poplar (*P. balsamifera*), unlike the bogus yellow, is a genuine poplar. It is a tree — often the only tree — of the arctic prairies, found in a chilly northern sweep from Labrador to Alaska, with forays into northern New England, the Dakotas, and the mountains of Idaho, Wyoming, and Colorado. The word *balsam*, like *balm*, is said to derive from the ancient Hebrew *bot smin*, meaning "the chief of oils" — which refers, in *P. balsamifera*, to the stickily fragrant resin secreted by the large leaf buds in winter and early spring.

Scented resins have been valued by many cultures since antiquity. Perhaps the most famous, historically, are frankincense and myrrh — those mysterious offerings toted to Bethlehem on camelback by the biblical Three Kings, Gaspar, Melchior, and Balthazar. Frankincense, traditionally burned as an incense, is secreted in canals beneath the bark of *Boswellia carteri*, a bizarre Middle Eastern tree resembling, according to one authority, a "decomposing animal." The tree features stiff, low branches, small curling leaves, and an intimidatingly thick bark which the local Bedouins fashion into buckets. Myrrh — used in embalming — is produced by *Commiphora myrrha*, a scraggy thorn tree and one of the less prepossessing relatives of the cedar. Both trees are restricted

203

in range to the southern tip of the Arabian peninsula, in the area of modern Somalia, Yemen, and Oman. There, in the centuries before Christ, Arab merchants monopolized the profitable incense trade in the same manner that their descendants now exploit their vast deposits of oil. The harvested resins were shipped overland by heavily guarded caravan, and were eventually sold at Mediterranean trade centers for an estimated modern equivalent of $500 per pound (frankincense) and $4,000 per pound (myrrh) — either way a 500 percent profit for the Arab distributors.

Both frankincense and myrrh, strictly speaking, are gum resins, mixtures of resin and gum. Resins, chemically, are composed of polymerized terpenes and volatile oils — stubbornly insoluble in water, which is why casual dabblers in resins tend to stay sticky indefinitely. Resins are actively synthesized and secreted by plants, presumably as deterrents to hungry insects and other potential plant-eaters. They have also been shown to exhibit some antibacterial activity, which may be why the ancients optimistically prescribed them for infections and fevers, vomiting, dysentery, tremors, ulcers, carbuncles, gonorrhea, leprosy, and hemlock poisoning. Gums, on the other hand, are not actively synthesized by plant cells, but are produced only in cases of emergency, in response to external injury. Following, for example, a slash in the bark, the traumatized tree will exude gum — formed from the breakdown of compounds in the damaged cells — as a wound sealant. Chemically, gums are sugar-based — polysaccharides of acid salts of sugars — and as such are water-soluble. They wash off.

The resin of the balsam poplar — though less romantic (and less expensive) than frankincense and myrrh — also has a history of medicinal use. The Ojibwas prepared a salve of the resinous buds mixed with bear fat, which was used as a Vicks-Vaporub-like nasal decongestant; the colonists used the buds in cough syrups. Balsam poplar buds — which smell, and reportedly taste, of turpentine — were also recommended as a cure for scurvy. Alternative, and presumably more palatable, antiscorbutics included wild garlic, persimmon leaves, mountain ash berries, cranberries, pine needle tea, and

— doubtless the most popular of the lot — spruce beer.

The tree from which this curative resin comes is commonly known as the tacamahac — from the Spanish *tacamahaca*, which in turn came from the Aztec name for a resin-producing, but totally unrelated, Mexican tree. It reaches, under ideal circumstances, heights of eighty to ninety feet, and bears broadly oval leaves in two shades of green — dark above, pastel below. The balsam poplar boasts a number of similarly sticky relatives, disjointedly divided between North America and northeast Asia. On the American side, its most prominent relation is the black or Western cottonwood, *P. trichocarpa*, noted for its size. *P. trichocarpa*, which has been known to reach heights of two hundred feet, is the largest poplar in North America — possibly the largest poplar in the world — and the largest broad-leaved tree in the West. It flourishes in the far west, from Alaska south to Baja California. While *P. trichocarpa* is a common tree of the western wilds, its smaller relative, the Balm-of-Gilead, is unknown outside the boundaries of civilization. The Balm-of-Gilead, *P. candicans*, is now believed to be a hybrid or selection of the balsam poplar. It is thought to have been planted and propagated by the early settlers, who made medicinal ointment from the resinous buds. To get this resin, they competed with the local honeybees: bees gather the sticky resin of the balsam poplars and use it to seal cracks and crevices in their hives. From this busy practice comes the common name for balsamic resin: bee glue. The trees today are often found planted near apiaries.

The Balm-of-Gilead, as befits its romantic name, holds a romantic place in tree history. Perhaps the saddest of its stories is that of the Scythe Tree of Seneca County, New York, near the town of Waterloo. This tree, in the sunny autumn of 1861, grew in the yard of the Johnson farm; the scythe belonged to young James Johnson, who suddenly, in the midst of mowing the family hayfield, decided to join the Union Army. Before he marched away with the rest of the 85th New York volunteers, he hung his scythe in the crotch of the farmyard tree with the injunction that it be left there until he returned home. James never did return home. He served with the army until April 1864, when he was wounded in battle at Plymouth, North Carolina. He was taken to the Confederate hospital at Raleigh, where, one month later, he died. The elder Johnsons, grieving, left the scythe in the tree. Eventually the wooden handle fell off, and the tree over the past century has gradually swallowed most of the iron blade. Only a few inches of James Johnson's scythe protrude from the now-massive poplar tree, where, over a hundred years ago, an optimistic young man left it to go with Mr. Lincoln's army.

Equally gallant — and a happier memorial — are the Balm-of-Gilead trees of Vicksburg, Colorado. Vicksburg, in the early 1890s, was a mining town of some 150 people, located in the mountains of western Colorado. The miners had high hopes of their tiny town, and at some point during this booming decade, four Vicksburg citizens made the long trip over the mountains to bring in fifty Balm-of-Gilead saplings, on the backs of burros. The saplings were planted in rows down what passed for Vicksburg's main street. Vicksburg never lived up to the hopes of its early citizens; it is now one of Colorado's many ghost towns. The mines are deserted. The Balm-of-Gilead trees, however, are still green and growing — a fitting memorial for Sam McGowan, James Ross, Jim Metcalf, and Alfred Bedore, who laid down their pick-axes long enough to plant trees.

PINE

The first European to comment on the vast pine forests of early North America was Christopher Columbus, who wrote poetically in his diary of "trees stretching to the stars with leaves never shed." The first European to bring a pine tree home with him, however — Columbus having settled conservatively for parrots and Indians — was Captain George Weymouth of the British Royal Navy. Captain Weymouth's souvenir was an Eastern white pine — *Pinus strobus* — cut in 1605 in country that would eventually become the state of Maine. Back in England, Captain Weymouth's pine caused a small sensation. It was declared a national treasure by the naval board, which had been racking its collective brains for some decades over the disastrous national deficit in mast trees. By the early 1600s, England was fitting her ships with masts of Scotch pine (*P. sylvestris*), most of which was imported from Russia, Sweden, and the Baltic countries. Such masts were generally unsatisfactory — the smallish Scotch pines had to be pieced together to make a mast massive enough for a state-of-the-art British battleship — and their availability depended on a series of touchy political relationships with foreign monarchies. The new North American pine, known gratefully in England as the Weymouth pine, was the answer to a naval power's prayer.

Modern estimates calculate that the virgin white pine forests of the eastern United States once held some 750 billion board feet of timber. A pioneer saying boasted that a squirrel could travel through those forests for a squirrel's lifetime (nine to twelve years, in the case of the eastern gray) without once setting paw on the ground — and the trees through which the squirrels cavorted were awesome specimens. Early settlers routinely reported pines upward of 150 feet — and occasionally over 200 feet — in height. The trees, cut, were sent to the shipyards of England by specially designed transport ships, vast vessels capable of carrying twenty to forty white pine trunks in their holds. Diarist Samuel Sewall — whose seventeenth-century journals abound with accounts of failed courtships and favorite dinners — recorded the loading of a massive mast tree: "'Twas a very notable sight," wrote Sewall, adding with awed precision that the tree required "36 yoke of oxen" to haul it harborward.

Such trees, at least by unauthorized colonials, were to be admired, but not touched. The Royal Navy understandably took a dim view of potential mast material being cut down willy-nilly in the clearing of New England farmland, and under William III the first laws were passed reserving the prime pines of New Hampshire and Maine for the crown. By 1761, it was decreed that a clause be appended to all future land grants "to reserve all white or other Sort of Pine Trees fit for Masts, of the growth of 24 Inches Diameter and upwards at 12 inches from the Earth, to Us, our Heirs & Successors, for the Masting of Our Royal Navy, and that no such Trees shall be cut — without our License — on Penalty of the Forfeiture of such Grant, & of the Land so granted reverting to the Crown; & all other Pains and Penalties as are or shall be enjoined or inflicted by any Act or Acts of Parliament passed in the Kingdom of Great Britain." To make sure that no mistake be made over precisely which trees were meant, crown-appointed surveyors marked those designated for the navy with a triangular blaze known as the "king's broad arrow."

Unfortunately, the resident colonists proved strenuously unco-operative in the provisioning of His Majesty's battleships. American lumbermen cut as many broad-arrow-marked trees as possible, often deceitfully duplicating the king's blaze on neighboring trees of inferior size and straightness. Ornery farmers and frontiersmen cut, sawed — and sometimes burned — the king's pines. In areas where British law enforcement was vigilant, these dastardly acts were often performed at night, the perpetrators artfully disguised as Indians. The annoyed Crown then decreed that anyone wearing a disguise while cutting trees should be flogged. Annoyed colonists retaliated by attacking the royal surveyors. (At least one was thrown off a twenty-foot ledge and only survived because he landed in mud.) Disloyal British agents, tempted by the financial rewards of the lumber industry, invested in American sawmills; loyal British agents smashed saws with crowbars and set American sawmills on fire.

The escalating pine tree controversy was settled — or rather, superseded by — the Revolutionary War. In 1774, the brand-new American Congress officially halted all exports, including pine masts, to Britain. All masts cut subsequently went to outfit America's own fledgling fleet, including John Paul Jones' *Ranger*, which sailed on November 1, 1777, under "three of the tallest white pine masts that ever went to sea." In it, Jones racked up a spectacular record in naval victories before his transfer to the *Bon Homme Richard* — from which, in 1779, he bellowed, "I have not yet begun to fight!" at the stunned captain of the British *Serapis*.

By 1777, John Paul Jones sailed under the Stars and Stripes, but the first flag of the Revolutionary forces — flown at the Battle of Bunker Hill — was that adopted by the state of Massachusetts, bearing a single white pine tree and the motto "An Appeal to Heaven." The pine tree motif was the same as that on the first American-made coin, the silver pine-tree shilling, made in Boston for a thirty-year period from 1652 to 1682. Every one of these shillings was imprinted with the original date of issue — 1652 — in an attempt to deceive the British authorities, whose established policy was to keep their colonial citizenry chronically short of cold cash.

Such official symbols were appropriate: the Eastern white pine was the wood synonymous with colonial America. It was used to construct the earliest pioneer cabins and for much of what antique dealers nowadays refer to as "primitive" furniture: seventeenth-century settles, chests, bedsteads, and cupboards. "Tables," states one source, "were made 2½ feet wide from a single board, without knot or blemish" — which impressive slabs of wood, a quick calculation shows, most certainly measured 24 Inches in Diameter 12 inches from the Earth, and as such had no business appearing in anything other than a royal mast. The church pews upon which the Puritans sat for at least four chilly hours every Sunday were also made of pine.

Ships' figureheads were carved of "pumpkin pine" — an ancient smooth-grained form of white pine that reminded its users of slices of ripe pumpkin. Coffins and covered bridges, boardwalks and bobsleds, were made of pine, and by 1805, according to that peripatetic botanist François Michaux, the United States boasted half a million white pine houses. Pine shingles were produced in amounts that Donald Peattie states are "beyond calculation" — in a mere one-quarter of the last century, the combined states of Michigan, Wisconsin, and Minnesota turned out 85,000,000,000. In the pre-Industrial Age, such shingles were made by hand, using a knife-like wedge called a frow or froe — or, by the English, a fromard or rending-ax. The frow was whacked with a frow-club — a bowling-pin-shaped wooden mallet — thus neatly shaving a block of white pine into shingles, a process formally known as "riving." An expert shingle-shaver, equipped with frow and frow-club, could turn out five hundred shingles a day. All this — including , in 1912, some seventy-two million board-feet-worth of matchsticks — was made from the wood of *Pinus strobus*, one of thirty-six native North American pine trees.

The pines are conifers, cone-bearing evergreen trees, and members of the family *Pinaceae*, which comprises some 110 species worldwide. The conifers first appeared on earth 225 million years ago, neck and neck with the first unprepossessing ratlike little mammals. Both eventually flourished, the conifers more rapidly than the mammals, who, in the early days of the Jurassic period, were severely outclassed by the dinosaurs. The high card held by the conifers in the evolutionary game was the seed. The seed contains a miniature preformed embryo plant, primed to sprout, plus a stock of food, which gives seed-producers a reproductive edge over the older and simpler spore-bearing plants. Conifers and their like are *gymnosperms*, from the Greek meaning "naked seed" — thereby sharing linguistic roots with *gymnasium*, where athletes once trained naked, and *gymnosophist*, an adherent of a mystical Hindu sect which abjured clothing. The seeds of gymnosperms, such as the conifers, the cycads, and the bizarre gingko, lack an outer case or protective covering — hence "naked" — and are usually (but not always) borne in cones. In the white pine, a typical gymnosperm, male and female flowers (cones) develop on the same tree, females at the tree top and males at the bottom. Since all conifers rely on the unreliable wind for pollination, the reproductive strategy of the male cones is that of overkill: vast quantities of pollen are produced. Each male pine cone annually releases an estimated one to two million pollen grains — and the immense coniferous forests of Sweden have been calculated to spew out seventy-five thousand tons of pollen every spring.

Some fraction of these bright yellow grains are blown successfully to the female cones, all geometrically clever constructs designed to function like wind turbans, channelling the pollen toward the ovules. Each female cone consists of a series of scales, arranged around a central axis like the treads of a spiral staircase. The spiral in question is what mathematicians call a logarithmic spiral; similar symmetrical coils appear in the sunflower and the chambered nautilus. Within the cone, each scale bears a pair of ovules on its upper surface, each of which exudes a sticky pollen-trapping fluid. Pollen grains, thrown by the wind into the female cone's funhouse-like spiral channels, are caught and held in this attractive glue. Once pollinated, the cone closes up tightly and remains so for two years until the seeds mature. Such unopened cones were viewed by the Romans as symbols of virginity: virgins, or those who wished to appear as such, wore garlands of closed evergreen cones at ceremonies.

At maturity, the cones become dry, the scales hard and woody, and open to release the winged seeds. The cones of some species have lost the ability to open gracefully of their own accord. Cones of the Rocky Mountain white bark pine (*P. albicaulis*), the jack pine (*P. banksiana*), and the knobcone pine (*P. attennata*) remain tightly sealed for years, often only opening — "exploding like popcorn," writes Rutherford Platt — when subjected to the blazing heat of forest fire. Such monumentally closed cones gave some cause for concern — the French-Canadian lumberjacks believed that any woman who passed near a jack pine, with its load of stubbornly inaccessible seeds, would become permanently sterile.

The cones of the historically contended *P. strobus* measure four to six inches long, which is middling for a pine tree. The largest pine cones are produced appropriately enough by the largest of pine trees: the sugar pine (*P. lambertiana*) of Oregon and California, which John Muir deemed the "largest, noblest, and most beautiful of all the pine trees in the world." The tree reaches heights upwards of two hundred feet and bears Brobdingnagian cones some fifteen to twenty-four inches long. The "sugar" moniker derives from its sweet-flavored resin, which, when the tree is wounded, coalesces into candylike crystals with a taste reminiscent of maple sugar. Unfortunately, this sweet treat has a discouraging side effect: sugar pine resin acts as a purgative on the unwary consumer. The Indians, said John Muir, ate it in "only small quantities," and bears, despite their notorious sweet teeth, avoid it. Some — perhaps those once burned — refer to sugar pine resin spitefully as "false manna."

Other big-cone pines include the Coulter pine (*P. coulteri*), which produces the heaviest cones of any American pine, each weighing between five and eight pounds green. Coulter cones measure ten to twenty inches long and look like great medieval weapons, each scale tipped with a 1½-inch-long curved claw. Smaller, but still sizeable, are the cones of the digger pine (*P. sabiniana*), which average six to seven inches in length and weigh about a pound dry; and the cones of the Jeffrey pine (*P. jeffreyi*), six to twelve inches long, prickly, and shaped, says Donald Peattie, "like an old-fashioned beehive." The digger pine grows solely in California, where its common name commemorates an old racial slur against the local Indian tribes — all of whom were contemptuously referred to by the encroaching pioneers as "diggers," from their habit of digging roots for food. (In the same nasty spirit, the Adirondack Mountains perpetuate an old insult: *adirondack* is an Indian word meaning "bark-eater," a taunting term for members of defeated tribes who fled to the mountains and survived by eating the inner bark of the pine trees.) The Jeffrey pine, a more imposing tree than the maligned digger, ranges from southern Oregon to Baja California, and is distinguished by its resinous odor. Interpretations of the Jeffrey's scent appear to vary with the olfactory make-up of the smeller. It has been likened to oranges, tangerine rinds, violets, pine-apples, mellow apples, and vanilla extract.

When the botanically precise Marquis de Chastellux toured New England in 1780, he noted in his journal his annoyance at the ignorant American natives, who referred to all conifers indiscriminately as "pine trees." Such scientifically fuzzy thinking was emulated by taxonomists, who originally lumped all conifers into one massive Pine family. Conifer classification today has become more varied and complex, but the Pine family is still massive: it includes nine genera and about 210 species of trees, including the pines, the firs, the spruces, the hemlocks, and the larches. The larches, black sheep among the pines, are deciduous. Non-pine conifers are mainly distributed among three other families: *Taxodiaceae*, which includes the arthritic-looking bald cypress and the awesome sequoias; *Cupressaceae*, the Cypress family, which includes the cypress, the cedar, the arborvitae, and the juniper; and *Taxaceae*, the Yew family, which includes both yews and torreyas.

The pines are distinguished among conifers by the packaging of their needles, which are grouped in bundles (called *fascicles*) of two, three, or five, bound together at the base by a sheath, and attached to short shoots. The needles of two-needle pines tend to be thick and stiff, and are semicircular in cross-section; three-needle pines produce thinner, triangular needles; and the foliage of five-needle pines is the thinnest of all, pliable, and drooping.

"The options for a leaf," writes Roger Swain, "are the same as for Greek heroes — a short and glorious life, or a long and tranquil one." Conifer needles have opted for the latter: they are thus excluded from the spectacular technicolor display of the deciduous October, but are exempted from falling off the tree and dying at the end of the season. The advantage of the tranquil needle over the glorious broad-bladed leaf is several-fold. The needle is generally resistant to temperature extremes and to breakage, impervious to insects, and conservative of moisture. The camel-like pine, for example, loses only one-tenth as much water through transpiration as does a comparably sized broadleaf tree. Deciduous leaves are quick and cheap to produce and, once developed, are rapid photosynthesizers — which is why they can be insouciantly jettisoned each autumn. In contrast, the production of the physically and chemically well-equipped needle is metabolically effortful and expensive — and, once the needle is complete, it's a slow photosynthesizer. Deciduous leaves photosynthesize up to four times faster than needles. The needles, therefore, have to stick around a while for the parent tree to get its money's worth. Human beings make similar keep-or-discard decisions: you may buy a new bathing suit every summer, but you like to get a few years' wear out of your down parka.

Nonetheless, evergreen does not mean green forever — even the heavily fortified needle eventually wears out, turns brown, and bites the dust. Survival time varies from conifer to conifer. Needles of the white pine last two years, hemlock three, and Sitka spruce nine to eleven. The aged bristlecone pine (*P. aristata*) hangs onto its needles for fifteen years or more, but the longest-lived needles appear to belong to a stubborn relative of the bristlecone, *P. longaeva*, a denizen of the mountains of California, Utah, and Nevada. These last an average of twenty-five to thirty years, which gives them a lifespan about the same as that of the horse.

The age of the average pine needle is barely a patch on the age of the tree— which, in the Pine family, can be impressively Methuselan. In fact, more so: while Methuselah, the biblical patriarch, survived only a paltry 969 years, the bristlecone pine, oldest living thing on earth, lives over 4,000. The bristlecone, like the sugar and white, is a five-needle pine, but an ugly one — Rutherford Platt damns this most ancient of trees as a "gaunt runt." It grows primarily at cold and wind-battered elevations, eight thousand feet or more up in the mountains of Colorado, Arizona, New Mexico, and Nevada. The most notable bristlecone groves, however, are found on twenty-seven thousand government-restricted acres in central California's White Mountains. Here, in the Inyo National Forest's Schulman Grove — named for Dr. Edmund Schulman of the Tree Ring Laboratory at the University of Arizona, who discovered the great age of the bristlecones in 1957 — lives the oldest of the old, a tree known as Methuselah. This Methuselah is believed to be 4,715 years old, which means that its first sprouts were poking out of the stony soil when the Egyptians were building the Great Sphinx at Gizeh. It is one thousand years older than Stonehenge, two thousand years older than the Acropolis, thirty-seven hundred years older than Westminster Abbey. Such age is almost beyond human comprehension, and is somewhat disappointing to discover in such gnarled, twisted, and dwarfish specimens as the oldest bristlecones.

Early naturalists had high hopes for more distinguished-looking trees. Alexander von Humboldt, impressed by the monstrously barrel-like African baobab, deemed it "the oldest organic monument of our planet"; John Muir claimed oldest status for his giant sequoias, on one stump of which — in 1880 — he recorded counting a full four thousand rings. The stump could never be relocated, so Muir's estimate was never confirmed. Biggest, however, proved not to be oldest. The most elderly of giant sequoias are a mere thirty-two hundred to thirty-five hundred years, over a thousand years younger than the oldest bristlecones. Lesser pines are more ephemeral. Most live two hundred to three hundred years, though the massive sugar and ponderosa pines survive an average 450 years.

Though mere adolescents as the bristlecones measure time, the majority of pines have more than adequate lifespans to develop into timber trees. Conifers, en masse, yield 75 percent of the world's timber and practically all of the pulp for its paper — of which

Americans use 187,000 tons daily, enough to cover 1,350 square miles, or an area the size of Long Island. Conifers are generally referred to as "softwoods," a term that refers not to the softness of the wood per se but to the internal structure of the tree. The xylem — water-conducting tubules — of softwoods is composed primarily of *tracheids*, long tubular soda-straw-like cells that conduct water only through openings in their sides. The xylem of hardwoods, in contrast, consists of vessels — shorter, plumper cells that conduct water straightforwardly through openings at either end — plus tracheids and assorted other cells. Softwood is thus a less complex and more uniform wood than hardwood, and is therefore more easily workable. Pines — softwoods all — are further subdivided into "soft pines" and "hard pines," again depending on the uniformity and workability of the wood. The Eastern white pine — probably the most important timber tree in nineteenth-century America — is a soft pine, as are the sugar pine, the bristlecone pine, and the peculiar resinless whitebark pine.

The two- and three-needle pines are generally deemed hard pines. Of these, among the most valued commercially are the four major trees of the southern piney woods: the longleaf (*P. palustris*), shortleaf (*P. echinata*), slash (*P. elliottii*), and loblolly (*P. taeda*) pines. All are referred to indiscriminately as southern yellow pine by the insensitive lumber industry. The longleaf and shortleaf pines are named for the distinctive lengths of their needles: respectively, up to sixteen inches (long) and down to two (short). "Loblolly" is a bit more of a puzzle. According to the dictionary, a loblolly is either (1) a lout or clownish fellow, or (2) a thick gruel or mudpuddle, neither of which quite fills the bill for a respectable one-hundred-foot-tall, five-foot-diameter tree. Donald Culross Peattie explains that in North Carolina a "loblolly" is a natural pocket or depression in the landscape, in which grows, aptly enough, the tree we know as the loblolly pine. For those dissatisfied with "loblolly," *P. taeda* possesses a vast number of alternative common names, perhaps a record of a sort among pine trees. It is variously known, depending who and where you are, as the bastard, black foxtail, black slash, bull, cornstalk, frankincense, Indian, longshucks, longstraw, meadow, old field, rosemary, swamp, torch, North Carolina, Virginia, and yellow pines — which, what with "loblolly" and the lumberman's "southern yellow," adds up to a grand total of twenty aliases.

Largest of the hard pines is the ponderosa or Western yellow pine (*P. ponderosa*) — also, to be fair, occasionally referred to as the bull, blackjack, Western red, big, heavy, Sierra brownbark, Western longleaf, or ponderosa white. The ponderosa pine was first formally described and named by the indomitable Scottish naturalist David Douglas, whose strenuous collecting trips to North America — he called them "healthful perambulations" — took place between 1823 and 1834 under the aegis of the Royal Horticultural Society of London. Douglas' botanizing excursions in the largely unexplored territories of the American West were fraught with disaster. He was attacked by Indians, grizzlies, and red ants; braved rapids, thunderstorms, blizzards, and avalanches; suffered from cold, fever, loss of eyesight, and hunger. Several times he was driven by starvation to eat his painstakingly collected berries, seeds, and dried animal skins; twice he was forced to eat his horse. He was shipwrecked at least once, and once he was swept out to sea in a hurricane, where he and his companions managed to keep afloat for two days by continuously bailing with their hats. Douglas took it all in stride, entering only the most understated of Scottish complaints in his journal: " . . . travelled thirty-three miles, drenched and bleached with rain and sleet, chilled with a piercing north wind; and then to finish the day experienced the cooling, comfortless consolation of lying down wet without supper or fire. On such occasions I am very liable to become fretful." Douglas was killed in Hawaii in 1834, as spectacularly as he lived: while travelling across the mountains toward the village of Hilo, he fell into a pit dug as a cattle trap, and was gored to death by a wild bull. He was thirty-five years old.

In the course of his journeys, Douglas collected and catalogued a truly phenomenal number of plant species — over eight hundred in California alone, many previously unknown. Among them were the Monterey pine; the Sitka spruce; the digger pine (its scientific name, *P. sabiniana,* honors Joseph Sabine, director of the Royal Horticultural Society and Douglas' patron); the massive sugar pine (Douglas was in the act of shooting down a few specimen cones with his shotgun when he was accosted by a party of hostile Indians in full warpaint); and the ponderosa pine, so named by Douglas for its impressive size. The ponderosa — second in height only to the sugar pine — averages heights of 80 to 150 feet, with diameters of up to eight feet. Prospective fathers among the Zuni Indians ate ponderosa pine shoots if they wanted their wives to bear sons.

Both sugar and ponderosa pines, however, are dwarfed by the tree best associated with Douglas — the towering Douglas fir. Douglas himself, when he first came upon these coniferous behemoths in 1825, thought the new tree was a pine, and tentatively referred to his find in letters home as *Pinus taxifolia.* The tree's original discoverer —botanist Archibald Menzies of the 1792 Vancouver expedition — similarly plumped for pine, and throughout the nineteenth century, the Douglas fir answered to the name of Oregon pine. Common parlance then waffled between Douglas fir and Douglas spruce, while botanists — caught between colloquialisms — protested that neither was scientifically accurate. The Douglas fir refused to fit comfortably into any existing biological niche. It bears drooping, rather than erect, cones, which distinguishes it from the true firs (*Abies*). The spruces (*Picea*) also bear drooping cones — a hopefully harmonious sign — but, unlike any known spruce cone, the cones of the Douglas fir bear protruding three-pronged bracts between their scales, which gives them a distinctive shaggy and unkempt appearance. The wood of the Douglas fir is resinous, which differentiates it from the true hemlocks (*Tsuga*), and its needle-like leaves are flat with a prominent mid-rib, borne singly on short stalks — which differentiates it from the true pines (*Pinus*). The taxonomists eventually settled matters to their own satisfaction by assigning the problematical pine to a new genus, dubbing it *Pseudotsuga Menzies.* The common name, however — despite the diplomatically proposed "Douglastree" — stubbornly remained Douglas fir.

David Douglas' fir is the third (or fourth) tallest tree in the world, averaging 250 feet in height, with champion specimens over 300. The Douglas fir is to the twentieth century what the Eastern white pine was to the seventeenth and eighteenth: the dominant timber tree. Today a quarter of all the timber cut in the United States is Douglas fir. Fittingly, in 1925, when the great white pine masts on Old Ironsides were deemed beyond repair, the only appropriate available replacements were three massive trunks of Douglas fir.

The pines — like the aforementioned balsam poplar — are producers of resins, water-insoluble terpene polymers from which people since historical times have obtained pitch, turpentine, and rosin. Such sticky compounds have traditionally been termed "naval stores," since the navy, in presynthetic days, was resin's largest consumer. The navy used its pine-derived pitches and tars for caulking and for waterproofing wood, rope, and canvas — which is why sailors, since the 1600s, have been referred to as "tars." The practice of sealing one's ship with pitch dates at least to biblical times. Among the instructions that God gave Noah for the construction of the Ark was the somewhat redundant directive to "pitch it within and without with pitch." Pine pitch was used by the seafarers of ancient Egypt, Greece, and Rome; the Egyptians sealed their mummy wrappings with pine pitch; and the Greeks smeared pine pitch on the inside of their clay wine vessels to prevent leakage. The pitch coating gave a resinous flavor to the wine, which the Greeks came to enjoy; pine flavoring is still added to Greek wines, giving retsina its distinctive taste. The unappreciative liken it to turpentine.

Pitch became increasingly necessary in the sixteenth and seventeenth centuries as Europe — bent on profitable colonization — sent more and more ships into tropical waters. There, their wooden hulls fell victim to *teredo navalis*, a tiny marine mollusc whose propensity for boring into ship bottoms spelled naval disaster. The only effective defense against these indefatigable creatures was to coat the hull with an impenetrable layer of pine pitch. Pitch, in this period, was obtained by slowly cooking great chunks of resinous pine wood in a pit, then collecting the exuded tarry substance, distilling it, and packing the molasses-like product in barrels. Chronically wood-short England, which had begun to look to its American colonies for mast trees, similarly depended on them for supplies of pitch and tar. In 1705, Parliament passed the Bounty Act, which offered the cash-hungry colonists a five- to ten-shilling bonus on every barrel of pitch they shipped back home, and Queen Anne, in an appeal to their better natures, sent out a team of public-relations officers "to convince the inhabitants how necessary it is to assist the views of the Mother Country." By 1725, the convinced Americans were supplying four-fifths of England's pitch and tar. This happy situation ended abruptly with the advent of the Revolution, during which the rebelling colonists applied some of their plentiful pine resins to loyal Englishmen in an uncomfortable process known as "tar and feathering." This painful and sticky punishment was not an American innovation. Back in 1189, Richard I (the Lion-hearted) decreed it by royal ordinance an appropriate penalty for theft in the navy; and in 1623, the outraged Bishop of Halverstade is said to have used it on "a party of incontinent friars and nuns." The American colonists applied it liberally to a large number of persons of unpopular political views, and threatened the Royal Governor of Massachusetts, Thomas Hutchinson, with it in 1774. Hutchinson managed to exit the country untarred.

Probably the first of the American pines to be exploited for its resin was the pitch pine (*P. rigida*), found from Maine south through the mountains of Georgia. This is the predominant pine of Cape Cod and of the famous pine barrens of New Jersey, where the Mafia used to bury the remains of their opposition. This early pitch pine was called "candlewood" by the pioneers: bundles of resinous splinters or knots were attached to hickory withes and lit for outdoor torches. In the 1600s, the town criers carried flaming pine knots in an iron cage suspended from a pole — a contraption referred to by Eric Sloane as "the first streetlight." The wood of the pitch pine, due to its abundance of resin, makes a risky firewood — it sparks excessively and coats chimneys with a tough and dangerously inflammable soot. For construction purposes it is similarly less than ideal.

The wood holds nails and bolts so poorly, states Donald Peattie, that ships built of it have been known to abruptly come apart at sea.

The principal sources of pitch these days are two of the lumber industry's "southern yellow" pines, the longleaf and the loblolly. Much of the usable resin is derived from stumps left standing after the trees have been cut for lumber. Rosin — which precipitates from crude resin — is brittle when dry, sticky when heated. Baseball players rub their hands with it to improve their grip on the bat; ballerinas dip their toe shoes in it to improve their grip on the stage; violinists drag their bows across blocks of it to enhance friction with the strings. Turpentine is distilled from liquid left over after the removal of rosin, and is known today primarily as a solvent and cleaning agent for oil-based paints. Chemically, however, turpentine serves as a jumping-off point for the synthesis of an impressive number of useful substances, among them deodorants, shaving lotions, medicines, and limonene, the lemon flavoring found in lemonade, lemon pudding, and lemon meringue pie.

Among the most popular of resin products is linoleum, the slick, easily scrubbable floor covering that our delighted great-grandmothers laid down by the acre over their hardwood floors. Linoleum was invented in 1860 by English chemist Frederick Walton, who discovered that a mixture of linseed oil, resin, and cork particles rolled onto fabric yielded a superb kitchen floor. The resin initially preferred for linoleum-making was not pine, but dauri resin, derived from *Agathis australis*, a New Zealand gymnosperm. Today linoleum resins are wholly synthetic.

Among the most expensive of resin products is amber, which bears the distinction of being the only jewel of plant origin. Variously opaque to transparent, and colored golden-yellow to dark brown, amber consists of fossilized terpenoid resins, largely from long extinct pines. In ancient times, it was believed to shield the wearer from asthma, rheumatism, and witchcraft. The best of it comes from Russia. Other than amber, perhaps the most unusual of resin products is the nest of the *Dianthidium* bee, which builds its nest of pebbles and pine pitch.

In the Southwest, the Navajos boiled pitch from the piñon pine with sheep and goat hooves to make glue, which they then used to cement turquoise into silver settings, thus producing — among other works of art — their heavily elaborate squash-blossom necklaces. The Hopi mixed it with sumac leaves and yellow clay to yield an inky-black dye for wool, and smeared it over their woven baskets to make waterproof jugs. Cooks among the Pueblo and Navajo Indians coated stone griddles with piñon pitch to create a non-stick surface — a sort of primitive Teflon, writes Ronald Lanner in his treatise on the piñon pines — essential in the baking of blue cornmeal wafer bread. Various tribes used the resin medicinally. It was applied externally to open wounds, burned and the resulting fumes inhaled for head colds, and — in the late 1800s — drunk in tea by the Zunis, in a brave attempt to cure syphilis. The Hopis believed that a dollop of piñon pitch on the forehead would protect those venturing outdoors in December from sorcerers.

The prize feature of the piñon pines, however, is not their resin, but their deliciously edible seeds — a snack known inaccurately to modern eaters as pine nuts. The first Europeans to lay eyes on the piñon pine were probably Alvar Núñez Cabeza de Vaca and company, who, shipwrecked in the Gulf of Mexico in 1528, marched determinedly across Texas, New Mexico, and Arizona, to California, where they were finally rescued eight years later. En route, they were introduced to the pine nut by local Indian tribes, and received it with gratitude: "The nuts," wrote Cabeza de Vaca later, "are better than those of Castile."

Botanists distinguish between four and eleven species of piñon pines, with a collective range extending from the Great Basin of Nevada and western Utah south to Mexico. The two most prominent are the Colorado piñon, *P. edulis* — the tree that sustained Cabeza de Vaca — and the singleleaf piñon, *P. monophylla,* a botanical anomaly that bears its needles in singletons rather than convivial bundles, and thus is unique among pine trees. The first of these to be presented to science was the singleleaf piñon, whose cones were collected by John C. Frémont in 1844. Frémont promptly shipped the cones off to botanist John Torrey, with a patronizing cover letter explaining that the seeds of such trees were located between the scales of the cones. Torrey took this in stride and set about — slowly — naming the new find. He was toying with the idea of *Pinus pignon*, when Frémont, beside himself with impatience, suddenly named the tree himself: *Pinus monophyllus*, to be commonly known as the nut pine. The species name was later modified by Latin-conscious taxonomists to *monophylla*.

It has been suggested that Frémont's frenzy to get his tree into the official literature stemmed from the guilty knowledge that the "nut pine" was not his tree at all. The singleleaf piñon had actually been discovered some eleven years previously by a party of trappers under Captain Joseph Walker. Starting from Bear Lake, Utah, in 1833, Walker and company made the second successful overland trip to California. (The first was in 1826, led by mountain man Jedediah Smith.) The record-keeper of the Walker expedition was an obser-vant Pennsylvanian named Zenas Leonard, who noted — in Septem-ber 1833 — "the pinone tree, bearing a kind of must [mast], which the natives are very fond of, and which they collect for winter pro-visions." Leonard published, but — luckily for Frémont — without noticeable public impact. Frémont got credit for the tree.

The piñon pines, collectively, fed the southwest Indian tribes for at least six thousand years, and the local wildlife — to include squirrels, chipmunks, wood rats, black bears, desert bighorns, porcupines, wild turkeys, and the irrepressible bright blue piñon jay — for even longer. "Just as life on the plains was fitted to the habits of the buffalo," writes Lanner, "life in the Great Basin was fitted to the homely, thin-shelled nut of the singleleaf piñon." The Indians ate the piñons raw, or roasted — which makes them taste, claims Donald Peattie, like a mixture of pine, popcorn, and peanuts — ground them into flour, mashed them into nut butter, or mixed them with cornmeal and sunflower seeds. The nuts are notably nutritious, containing up to 15 percent protein; the Colorado piñon consists of a further 62–71 percent fat and 18 percent carbohydrate; the singleleaf piñon 39 percent fat and 54 percent carbohydrate. One pound of Colorado pine nuts is good for 2,880 calories, which is about the energy equivalent of a pound of butter.

As such, these healthful tidbits were — at least, indirectly — responsible for the survival of the notorious Donner Party, which was stranded, starving, in the Sierra Nevadas in the winter of 1846. Winter began with five feet of snow in October, and by December a desperate group of fifteen — styling themselves the "Forlorn Hope" — set out on homemade snowshoes in a last-ditch attempt to get help from the settlements of California. Nine died along the way, and the surviving six made it as far as an Indian village, where the generous-spirited inhabitants took them in and revived them on acorn bread and pine nuts. With that under their belts, and the help of an Indian guide, "Forlorn Hope" finally reached an enclave of settlers' cabins. The Donner Party was rescued in January.

Piñons are smallish nuts, about a quarter of an inch long, white, and shaped like grains of puffed rice. Also edible are the more substantial seeds of the digger pine (28 percent protein, 51 percent fat), which are about the size of lima beans, and the seeds of limber and whitebark pines. In Europe, the edible seeds of the Italian stone pine (*P. pinea*) are marketed as *pignolias* or *pinocchios* — as in the long-nosed puppet who after so many misadventures managed to turn into a real boy. In Russia, the nuts of the Siberian stone pine (*P. sibirica*) are processed commercially to yield a cooking oil.

"What the apple is among fruits, what the oak is among broad-leaved trees of the temperate zone," wrote horticulturist Liberty Hyde Bailey, "the pines represent among conifers . . . " — which may be why ten states have chosen the pine as their emblematic Tree. Arkansas ("The People Rule"), Minnesota ("The North Star"), and North Carolina ("To Be Rather Than to Seem") all boast a nonspecific interdenominational pine. Nevada ("All for Our Country") and New Mexico ("It Grows As It Goes") are both represented by piñon pines; and Montana, which has the nation's only non-English state motto ("Oro y Plata"), by the ponderosa pine. The state tree of Alabama ("We Dare Defend Our Rights") is the resinous longleaf pine; Idaho ("Let It Be Perpetual") lays claim to the Western white, and Michigan

("If You Seek a Pleasant Peninsula, Look About You") the Eastern white pine. The state tree of Maine, the Pine Tree State — whose motto is the unpleasantly bossy "I Direct or I Lead" — is also the Eastern white pine, but Down Easterners have taken pine devotion one step further. Their state flower is the pine cone.

SPRUCE

$\mathcal{T}$he spruces comprise some forty-five species of northerly trees, seven of which are native to North America. All are characterized by a scaly bark, dangling cones, and nasty sharp needles, borne singly on the twigs in spiral ranks such that they bristle out in all directions like an aggressive bottlebrush. Many spruces bear needles evilly tipped with spines: hence the Asiatic dragon (*Picea asperata*) and tigertail (*P. polita*) spruces, so named for the painful effect of grabbing them.

Prickliest of the American spruces is the Sitka spruce, *P. sitchensis*, state tree of Alaska ("North to the Future"). Alaska's tree also bears the distinction of being the biggest and fastest-growing spruce in the world. Under favorable circumstances, along Washington's Pacific coast, Sitka spruce specimens have been found over three hundred feet in height and fifty feet or more around the base. Smaller, but similarly spiky is the blue spruce (*P. pungens*), state tree of both Colorado ("Nothing Without Providence") and Utah ("Industry"). Its one-inch blue(ish) needles are stout, stiff, and hostilely pointed. The species name — *pungens* — comes from the Latin for "sharp," as in puncture wound.

These militarily erect needles, plus the punctiliously conical form of the trees overall, probably inspired early observers to bestow the common name "spruce" — which term, since the sixteenth century, has meant smart, dapper, or fashionably put together. "Spruce" in this sense came into vogue in England during the reign of Henry VIII, when fashion-conscious courtiers adopted the flashy dress of Prussian noblemen: broad-brimmed plumed hats, satin cloaks, red velvet doublets, silver and jeweled neck chains. Anything from Prussia had been for some centuries referred to as "pruce"; with an *s* added, in the mysterious manner of evolving language, these well-tricked-out clotheshorses were said to be in "spruce fashion." Spruce, by the nineteenth century, had expanded to "spruce up," meaning to tidy, neaten, and generally whip into shape, as in "go spruce up for supper." Spruce trees — naturally tidy, neat, and shapely — are unmistakably spruce, which makes this explanation of their common name appealing. A less romantic source suggests that the trees were so named because they originated in Prussia.

The spruces are aromatically, as well as physically, sharp, due to their complex content of volatile oils. A key identifying feature of the various spruces is the odor of their crushed needles. Just what these distinctive odors resemble is, unfortunately, a matter of debate. For example, the white spruce (*P. glauca*) is uncharitably nicknamed the skunk spruce for what has traditionally been described as the skunk-like smell of its crushed needles. Alan Mitchell, however, thinks that *P. glauca* smells of mouse, and a few kind-hearted souls compare its effluvia to black currant or grapefruit. The Engelmann spruce (*P. engelmannii*) and the black spruce (*P. mariana*) smell — to everybody — medicinally of menthol, but the red spruce (*P. rubens*) is more controversial: the scent of its needles is variously likened to ripe apples or candlewax. Donald Peattie says it smells like orange rind.

The odoriferous spruce needles have a long tradition of medicinal efficacy. Decoctions of the bark and needles were known to the Indians as a scurvy preventive, and it is believed — but not proven — that black spruce saved the lives of Jacques Cartier and his companions, marooned, vitaminless, in Canada in the winter of 1535. Cartier, ice-bound in the St. Lawrence River near the future site of Montreal, had already lost twenty-five of his company to scurvy when he finally turned to the local Indians for advice and assistance. Their proffered remedy was nothing short of miraculous: "It wrought so wel," wrote Cartier in his diary, "that if all the phisicians of

Mountpelier and Lovaine had been there with all the drugs of Alexandria, they would not have done so much in one yere, as that tree did in six days . . . ." Frustratingly for posterity, the identity of the wonder-working tree is left in doubt. "The tree is in their language called Aneda or Hanneda," wrote Cartier. "This is thought to be the Sassafras tree." Some skeptical historians believe the "Sassafras tree" phrase to be an officious aside inserted in the original text by an early translator. A more probable scurvy cure, modern sources agree, was a tea of pine, hemlock, or — most likely — black spruce.

Spruce beer — a beverage that dates back to early sixteenth-century England — was antiscorbutic, with the additional advantage of being alcoholic. The beer was fermented from the young shoots of the black or red spruce, and was often straightfacedly touted as a wholesome tonic. Henry David Thoreau describes drinking it in *The Maine Woods*: "a lumberer's drink, which would acclimate and naturalize a man at once, — which would make him see green, and, if he slept, dream that he heard the wind sough among the pines." It is difficult to reconcile such a magical image with the no-nonsense recipes of the times. The *American Economical Housekeeper* (1850), for example, provides the following instructions for the brewing of spruce beer: "Take three gallons of water, lukewarm, three half-pints of molasses, a tablespoonful of essence of spruce, and the same quantity of sugar; mix all together, and add a gill of yeast; let it stand overnight and bottle it in the morning." "It will be ready for use," the *Housekeeper* concludes ominously, "in twenty-four hours."

"Essence of spruce" was a concentrated spruce extract, made by boiling green shoots until the water became pungent and red-brown, then straining off the liquid and re-boiling until the solution was reduced to half its original volume. The "essence" was then bottled for year-round use — one of the most frequent of which was as a substitute for hops as a preservative in colonial beer.

The red spruce ranges from Nova Scotia to Ontario and south through the Adirondacks to Pennsylvania, New Jersey, Virginia, and Tennessee. Throughout its range, the red spruce is found cheek by jowl with the balsam fir, and in the southern mountains this inseparable twosome goes by the common names he-balsam and she-balsam. The fir is the she-balsam, on the principle that the resin-filled blisters under its bark are comparable to breasts filled with milk; the flat-chested red spruce is the he-balsam.

Despite this milkless reputation, the spruces, like the firs, are resinous trees, enough so that the genus name for spruce — *Picea* — comes from the Latin for "pitch." The most famous exudation of the spruce trees is spruce gum, a conglomeration of linked carbo-hydrate molecules released from the walls of certain plant cells upon injury. The gum flows in to seal the wound, hardening to a trans-parent amber-colored mass upon contact with the air. These tangily chewable chunks have a long history as a human snack. Rural Europeans have been masticating spruce gum for centuries, and in early Sweden, where the gum was scraped off the local *Picea abies* (unfairly known as the Norway spruce), spruce gum was considered a prime present for a potential sweetheart — the Scandinavian equivalent of the latter-day box of chocolates. The American colo-nists probably acquired their spruce-gum-chewing habit from the Indians, who in turn — suggests Robert Hendrickson, author of *The Great American Chewing Gum Book* — may have picked it up from the bears, who have been observed, prehibernation, to gulp down hunks of spruce gum that were as big as a man's fist. The Indians reportedly chewed to quench thirst; the pioneers, suggests one source, chewed to relieve the nervous strain of anticipated attack by the Indians.

The colonial chew is not altogether to the sugar-conditioned modern taste — Hendrickson compares it to "sinking your teeth into frozen gasoline" — and it turns hard and crumbly when stuck to the bedpost overnight. Francis Parkman, in 1842, wrote in his journal of an attempt to mend a leaking canoe with chewed spruce gum: the next day the gum disintegrated, "water spouted in like a stream from a pump," and the hapless canoe "burst all to pieces." For purely recreational purposes, however, spruce gum did just fine.

The first person to exploit the gum commercially was an ex-sailor from Maine named John Curtis. Curtis, with his son — a second

John — whipped up the first saleable batch of spruce gum in 1848, on the Franklin stove in the family kitchen in Bangor. The result was peddled profitably with horse and wagon throughout New England as "State of Maine Pure Spruce Gum." Purity was debatable. The initial Curtis gum recipe was relatively rough and ready: gobs of raw gum, fresh off the tree, were boiled in a kettle until they reached the consistency of molasses. Floating bark and any other noticeable non-gum substances were then skimmed off the top, and the liquid gum poured out to cool. When partially cool, but still malleable, the gum was rolled out into quarter-inch-thick sheets and sliced into pieces. Eventually the individual pieces were dipped in cornstarch, wrapped in twists of tissue paper, and sold — either in packets of twenty in wooden boxes, or by the piece, at two chunks for a penny.

The spruce gum business was so successful that in 1850 the Curtises relocated to Portland — where, two years later, they built the Curtis Chewing Gum Factory, three stories high and the first chewing-gum factory in the world. At the height of their popularity, the Curtises employed two hundred workers and turned out eighteen hundred boxes of gum each day. By the last quarter of the nineteenth century, so many Americans were hooked on spruce gum that the Maine Forest Service estimated the state's annual gum harvest at 150 tons (some $300,000 worth of gum). Other sources put the annual total as high as fifteen hundred tons. Among the devoted chewers was Mark Twain's Tom Sawyer, who, in the throes of young love, shared a wad of spruce gum with Becky Thatcher one afternoon after school.

Most of this chewable gum was (and is) collected from the black or the red spruce — and usually in the early spring, when the gum is less sticky than in the heat of summer. (The traditional stickiness of summertime gum has given us such foreboding phrases as "gum up the works," which is what happened to things in the days before SNAFUs.) A good gum-gatherer — on snowshoes, armed with a long pole ending in a chisel — could bring in sixty pounds of gum a day. Robert Frost immortalized this bizarre profession in his poem "The Gum-Gatherer":

. . . We know who when they come to town
Bring berries under the wagon seat,
Or a basket of eggs between their feet;
What this man brought in a cotton sack
Was gum, the gum of the mountain spruce.

He showed me lumps of the scented stuff
Like uncut jewels, dull and rough.
It comes to market golden brown;
But turns to pink between the teeth.

I told him this is a pleasant life
To set your breast to the bark of trees
That all your days are dim beneath,
And reaching up with a little knife,
To loose the resin and take it down
And bring it to market when you please.

There is only one company left in America that makes spruce gum, the Kennebec Spruce Gum Company in Maine. You can buy their product — 24 hours a day, 365 days a year — from L.L. Bean. Most of the raw gum nowadays is shipped south from Nova Scotia, where the pleasant life of a gum-gatherer will earn you a fat $1,000 per year.

The death of the spruce gum industry was brought about in part by the increasing public demand for newspapers, which led to massive reductions in the size of the spruce forests, and hence in the availability of raw gum. The gum factories thus turned to alternative chewables. They first attempted to use paraffin, an offshoot of the fractional distillation of petroleum. Paraffin never made a particularly good gum, despite the fact that it was the first to come in a fancy wrapper with enclosed "picture cards." It survives today in more-or-less edible novelties, such as wax mustaches, wax buck teeth, wax fangs, and wax false tongues. A more successful substitute was chicle, a chewable latex secreted by the Mexican sapodilla tree. Chicle was wildly successful (except for a brief period in the 1920s, when spoilsports blamed it for the post-World War I influenza epidemic). By the 1930s, the United States was importing fifteen million pounds of chicle each year, enough to make 5,750,000,000 sticks of gum.

Any number of enterprising businessmen made their fortunes off chicle-based chewing gum, but the first to make it to multimillionairedom was William J. White, a brash ex-popcorn salesman from Cleveland, Ohio. William White — who, at the apex of his career, thrust a pack of gum upon King Edward VII — developed the first effective process for flavoring chicle and founded the vast American Chicle Company (manufacturer of Chiclets) in 1899. He was also elected mayor of Cleveland, served for a term in Congress, and made and lost three fortunes before he died, broke, of a fall on the Cleveland ice in 1923. The Curtis Chewing Gum Company, in the meantime, outlived both Johns and was purchased in the early 1900s by the Sen-Sen Chiclet Company, which in turn merged with William White's American Chicle. The Gemini V astronauts took American Chicle gum along with them into space, which, in the historical view, seems a long journey for the stuff started in 1848 on John Curtis' kitchen stove.

Chewing gum today is composed mostly of synthetic plastics, among them such mouth-boggling compounds as butadiene-styrene rubber, polyethylene, and polyvinyl acetate. Newspapers, however, are still made of spruce, turned out in this country at the rate of 62.5 million issues daily, printed on some twenty-three thousand tons of newsprint. One bumper issue of the *New York Times* consumes an estimated 988 acres of softwood forest.

Wood pulp was first used for the manufacture of newspaper in the late 1860s and 70s; the first all-wood *New York Times* came out on August 23, 1873. Prior to that, American news was printed primarily on paper made of linen or cotton rags. As the demand for paper increased in the eighteenth century, however, papermakers rapidly ran short of rags. By the time of the Revolutionary War, a national rag-collecting campaign had been initiated, comparable in scope to our modern can- and bottle-recycling programs. To implement this, the Massachusetts General Court in 1776 appointed official rag-receivers for each population center, to oversee the collection of rags and speed them on their way to the paper mills. Nervous newspapers urged every family to maintain a rag-bag, and begged that children be taught their "rag lesson"— namely the importance of saving every cotton or linen scrap. Some advertisers, knowing the ways of their fellow men, stooped to bribery: "4 pounds of rags will buy a pair of handsome buckles," wrote the *Cheshire Advertiser* of New Hampshire in 1793, "or the famous 'History of Robinson Crusoe,' who lived 28 years on an uninhabited island . . . ." Despite such appealing ploys, rags in sufficient quantities for the insatiable papermills were simply not there. Scientists and inventors worldwide therefore plunged into a concerted search for alternative fibers for papermaking.

One of the earliest proposals — made in 1684 by Englishman Edward Lloyd — outlined a plan for making paper out of asbestos, a process which — luckily for our ancestors — proved impractical. Later, less lethal, suggestions covered a vast range of fibrous materials, among them potatoes, pine cones, cattails, cabbage stalks, corn husks, caterpillar cocoons, seaweed, straw, thistles, poplar and willow bark, walnut leaves, and dandelion roots. Perhaps the most bizarre solution to the paper problem was that of Dr. Isaiah Deck of New York, who in 1840 came up with a heretofore unexploited source of rags. Egyptian mummies, wrote Dr. Deck, contain up to thirty pounds of linen wrapping per mummy, at which rate a mere 13,500,000 mummies per year should be able to supply the total rag requirements of all eight hundred American papermills.

In the 1860s, at least one American papermaker put this proposal into practice: I. Augustus Stanwood of Gardiner, Maine — a gentleman whose name is doubtless a hissing and a byword to this day among archaeologists — imported shiploads of mummies to be converted into brown wrapping paper. This wrapping paper was purchased largely by grocers and butchers: thus in the days of the Civil War, Maine housewives carried home their Sunday lambchops wrapped in the funerary raiment of ancient Egyptians. Apparently

Mr. Stanwood's only competition for mummy wrappings during this period was the Egyptian railroad, which, in its salad days, used mummies (whole) as its sole source of fuel. Mummy wrappings, in the long term, were unable to solve the paper industry's fiber problem. The mummy supply, contrary to popular belief, was limited; and at least once Stanwood's ancient rags were blamed for an epidemic of cholera among Maine mill workers.

A more viable substance for paper-making was wood pulp, a fibrous mash that became readily available with the invention of a wood-grinding machine, patented in 1840 by a German weaver named Friedrich Keller. The first wood-grinder to be installed in the United States was put in place by one Albrecht Pagenstecher, owner of a mill near Stockbridge, Massachusetts. (Pagenstecher got the idea, he said, from his cousin Alberto, who in turn got it from a casual remark of Theodore Steinway, of piano fame.) Pagenstecher's paper was initially shunned by the newspapers, who considered it shoddy stuff, generally unfit as a carrier for America's news. Its cheapness and printability, however, were irresistible, and eventually the wood-based paper carried the day. It succeeded so well, in fact, that subsequent decades — by grace of wood pulp — are sometimes referred to by historians as the Paper Era. Inspired paper manufacturers produced not only wood-pulp-based newsprint, but paper shirtfronts, cuffs, and collars — one Boston manufacturer boasted an annual paper collar output of seventy-five million — bonnets, aprons, hats, boxes, buckets, curtains, carpets, and cuspidors. One enterprising soul — in 1869 — turned out paper coffins. Roofing and building papers were introduced for the construction trade — first used extensively in this country after Mrs. O'Leary's cow carelessly set off the Chicago Fire of 1871. The new paper was used for lining some ten thousand new houses, rapidly put up for those dispossessed by the blaze. Rensselaer Polytechnic Institute put a paper dome on their campus observatory; the crew teams of Harvard, Yale, and Columbia sped to victory (or defeat) in paper racing shells. Bell Telephone insulated its telephone cables with paper; Chicago blacksmiths introduced paper horseshoes — said to be more comfortable for the horses than old-fashioned iron. One section of a Washington, D.C., street was experimentally paved with blocks of paper. Here, however, the paper industry over-reached itself; paper pavement was a failure. Paper milk bottles came in in 1906; by 1915 California was drying its famous raisins on paper trays. During World War II, naval experts estimated that sixteen tons of blueprint paper were required to build a battleship.

Paper consumption these days, according to one source, totals 640 pounds per person per year — of which, according to another, we collectively throw away 150,000 tons daily, in the form of boxes, bags, and miscellaneous wrappers. These figures, multiplied out, don't quite mesh, but the message remains the same: Americans use a lot of paper. That paper comes in many different incarnations, from tissue paper to posterboard to corrugated cardboard — and a good deal of it lately comes in the form of fluff, packaged in disposable diapers. The lion's share of wood pulp in this country is made from softwoods — mostly white spruce, along with fir and hemlock.

Unpulped spruce yields a creamy-white, lightweight, even-grained wood — World War I fighter planes, including Sir Thomas Sopwith's "Camel," were built of it; it is still used for gliders, sailplanes, and racing sculls. Also largely spruce was Howard Hughes' aptly named "Spruce Goose" — the massive wooden flying boat with the largest wingspan in the world (319 feet, 11 inches). Hughes, who spent $40 million on the Goose, flew it himself on its initial run in 1947. It travelled a thousand feet, landed in the harbor at Long Beach, California, and never got off the ground again.

In the nineteenth century, less excitingly, spruce was used for bandboxes, pantry boxes, and — in limited quantities — for spruce gum boxes, the eminently collectible paperback-book-sized boxes carved by northern lumbermen for storing their sticky spruce chewing gum. The most famous use of spruce wood, however, is due to its resonant qualities — for which reason the musically vibrating spruce is used in the manufacture of guitars, mandolins, organ pipes, piano sounding boards, and the top plates — or bellies — of violins. Foremost among violins are the acoustically exquisite three-hundred-year-old instruments of Antonio Stradivari of Cremona, Italy — each topped with wood of the Norway spruce (*Picea abies*) and backed with maple. The secret of the Stradivarius violin has eluded musicians, craftsmen, and scientists for centuries. Until recently, most agreed that the source of the incomparable Stradivarius sound lay in the — unfortunately irreproducible — seventeenth-century varnish. Modern violinists were thus forced either to resign themselves to inferior instruments or to shell out the one million (or so) dollars, which is the current asking price for a Stradivarius original.

The latest research, however, indicates that such problems may be things of the past. At Texas A&M University, Dr. Joseph Nagyvary, a nucleic-acid chemist, has analyzed wood samples from the violins of Stradivari and his fellow craftsmen using electron microscopy. Results showed that the wood was full of distinctive open holes, the result of microbial degradation. The Cremona violin-makers, Nagyvary explains, used wood that had come — as green logs — from the Alps, floated south by river into Italy. In the warm Italian river water, the logs were invaded by bacteria and fungi, all producing batteries of cell-wall-dissolving enzymes. Internal destruction by these hungry microorganisms increases wood's permeability as much as fifty-fold, without altering its strength. Once dried, the fungus-chewed wood is lighter and more porous than that of normally seasoned commercial wood — and the tone it creates is richer and warmer.

The havoc wreaked by the fungi and bacteria also allows a deeper penetration of the finishing coats of varnish, which, Nagyvary contends, also contribute to the Stradivarius sound. Nagyvary — who reads Latin — accordingly travelled to Italy, where he translated volumes of ancient varnish recipes. The varnishes were based primarily on plant resins — notably the dark-red resin known as "dragon's blood," obtained from a palm-like tree of the Canary Islands — bizarrely supplemented with powdered glass, amber, and rubies, crab eyes, egg shells, white vitriol, and porcelain. Nagyvary then analyzed samples of old violin varnishes by X-ray spectroscopy and now, data in hand, is well on the way to reproducing the Stradivarius sound deep in the heart of Texas.

For future owners of such musical prizes, both science and art recommend regular practice. The wood cells of the violin body become more elastic with constant vibration, but stiffen arthritically if neglected—for which reason the instruments in museum collections are routinely picked up and played. If left long enough, even the greatest of violins can die. Paganini's spruce-bellied violin — played once again after spending fifty sacrosanct years in a museum in Genoa — was found, tragically, to be a music-less shell.

CHRISTMAS TREE

"*My* complaint," writes Eleanor Perényi, in her enchanting book of essays, *Green Thoughts*, "is against our national preference for [evergreens] that look like Christmas trees. This conical image endlessly imprinted upon the retina makes me sigh for an oak . . . ." This Scroogelike sentiment precedes a pitch for the planting of more innovative evergreens in American gardens — or, at least, for the planting of fewer of the old coniferous standbys, shaped so tidily like isosceles triangles.

The first settlers of New England were similarly anti-Christmas tree, though for religious, rather than aesthetic, reasons. The Puritans considered it sinful to subscribe to any practice not specifically mentioned in the Bible, and the Pilgrims, conscientious readers of the Good Book, spent their first Christmas in the New World dourly splitting logs. As increasing numbers of incipient merry-makers infiltrated early Massachusetts, however, it became necessary — in 1659— for the faithful to level fines against anyone caught celebrating Christmas. Some determined celebrants went ahead anyway and damned the consequences. Samuel Sewall of Salem, on Christmas Day in 1705, groused about the noisy exuberance of carousing Anglicans. In general, however, Puritan vigilance paid off. New England remained essentially Christmas-less well into the nineteenth century.

Elsewhere the Christmas season customarily carried more comfort and joy, its early proponents indulging themselves in fireworks, parades, brass band music, and big dinners. Occasionally —

but not often — the festivities included a Christmas tree. The origin of the modern Christmas tree tradition is uncertain. Some claim the tree idea can be traced to the ancient Druids, who yearly decked their sacred oak trees with candles and gilded apples in celebration of the Winter Solstice; others attribute it to Martin Luther, who, one sixteenth-century Christmas Eve, saw fir trees outlined against a background of stars. Impressed by their beauty, he cut a small tree, brought it home, and placed lighted candles in its branches in memory of the fabled Star of Bethlehem. The first known record of a Christmas tree is indeed German — which seems to support the Luther theory — but dates to 1604, fifty-eight years after Luther's death. Perhaps the idea was slow to catch on.

From Germany, the Christmas tree spread throughout northern Europe and across the Atlantic to America. The first Christmas tree in England was erected by Prince Albert of (German) Saxe-Coburg-Gotha, husband of Queen Victoria, in celebration not only of Christmas, but of the arrival of their first son, Albert Edward, born in November 1841. The Christmas tree is said to have been introduced to America by homesick Hessian (German) mercenaries during the Revolutionary War; however, the oldest mention of an American holiday tree dates to 1747, indicating that the custom was established well before the arrival of George III's hired strongmen. The tree of 1747 was erected in the (German) Moravian community of Bethlehem, Pennsylvania, and — like many of the earliest Christmas "trees" — consisted of a wooden pyramid covered with cut evergreen boughs, decorated with candles and apples. Such Christmas trees were rare at first, largely confined to the immigrant communities of Pennsylvania through the early nineteenth century. In the 1830s, the Christmas tree was still such a novelty that a Philadelphia ladies' bazaar was able to exhibit a decorated sample for an admissions charge of 6¼ cents per ticket. The Christmas tree was not admitted to the White House until 1856, when the first one was decorated by the family of President Franklin Pierce — a politician otherwise noted for putting stickum on the backs of postage stamps.

Most of these early Christmas trees were tiny, either center-piece-like wooden pyramids like that of Bethlehem's Moravians, or table-top-sized trees trimmed — in Pennsylvania Dutch country — with gingerbread, pretzels, gilded nuts, strings of raisins, and marzipan. From the predominance of edibles, these evergreens were sometimes called "sugartrees." As the Christmas tree became more popular, however, it also became increasingly bigger, until the towering floor-to-ceiling evergreen was a seasonal fixture. The addition of such sizeable trees to the Christmas repertoire had its attendant problems. The taller the tree, for example, the harder it was to keep it upright. Prior to the 1870s, this was accomplished somewhat tipsily, by nailing the tree to a cross of wooden boards, or by planting it in a large tub filled with rocks and earth. In 1876, the first Christmas tree stand came along, patented by a pair of festive Pennsylvanians, Hermann Albrecht and Abram Mott of Philadelphia. It consisted of a three-legged iron holder which could double as a flagstand on the Fourth of July.

Once stabilized, such large trees also called for numerous decorations, which, in the first half of the nineteenth century, were necessarily almost entirely handmade. The first commercial ornaments — glass icicles and balls — arrived from Germany in the 1860s. Over the next decade, the Christmas bauble business skyrocketed. Soon trees were hung with molded wax cherubs on ribbons, cornucopias, trumpets, and drums of colored isinglass, tiny satin pillows embroidered with uplifting mottoes, colored paper flowers, and silver- or gold-embossed cardboard cutouts of birds, animals, circus horses carrying dancing girls dressed in real silk tutus, and steamboats with silver portholes, their smokestacks puffing cotton smoke. Fake icicles came along in 1878, made of silver tinsel using a French process developed centuries earlier for putting glitter on military uniforms. By the 1920s they were made of lead foil, which hung straighter, still glittered, and cost less. Lead icicles were banned in the 1960s by the federal government, fearful that America's children might eat them and contract seasonal lead poisoning. Fake icicles nowadays are made of plastic.

In some circles, the annual tree became an exercise in individuality. An account of 1897 describes a tree trimmed by a gleeful Klondike miner with $70,000 worth of gold nuggets; in rural Pennsylvania, in 1898, an enthusiastic group of budding taxidermists decked their tree with stuffed squirrels and chipmunks. In 1900, spirited students in the University of Pennsylvania's Department of Biology trimmed their tree with strings of vertebrae, beetles, crabs, stuffed snakes, birds' nests filled with eggs, and a couple of stuffed monkeys.

The trees were originally — and often disastrously — lit with wax candles; nineteenth-century newspapers are peppered with tragic accounts of catastrophic Christmas conflagrations. By the end of the century, however, the first electric Christmas tree appeared, strung with hand-blown bulbs and wired up in Menlo Park by Thomas Edison's laboratory assistants in 1882. It was also about this time that the first artificial Christmas trees were introduced, for the heavily urbanized. They were available by mail order from Sears, Roebuck, and Company: thirty-three limbs for fifty cents, fifty-five limbs for a dollar.

These days Christmas trees — real or artificial — are invariably evergreen, but nineteenth-century holiday-makers were less selective. Often "winter-barren" — deciduous — trees were cut, brought indoors, and their bare branches wrapped in cotton quilt batting to simulate snow. A favorite deciduous tree for such purposes was the sassafras, a species which — except among medicinal tea fanciers — was considered expendable. In the 1860s, the favored Christmas evergreen was the cedar — a fragrant tree which fell from grace because it lost its needles too rapidly in the warm, dry indoors. The cedar was briefly replaced by the hemlock, whose branches proved too flimsy and flexible to support much in the way of ornament. Pines and spruces then ruled the Christmas roost until the 1890s, when they were ousted by the balsam fir. The first shipment of these arrived in Boston's Faneuil Hall marketplace from Maine in 1892.

The balsam fir (*Abies balsamea*) ranges from Labrador to the Yukon, and in the United States south through New England into West Virginia. Within this range, the tree grows to seventy-five feet in height and bears the flat, blunt-tipped needles — dark green above, silvery below — that are used to stuff the spicily scented balsam pillows said to prevent headaches and bad dreams. Balsam resin, which collects in blisters on the bark — hence the common name "blister pine" — is much favored by biologists, being the source of Canada balsam, a fixative used for mounting specimens on glass slides for the microscope. The resin, which simultaneously holds the cover slip to the microscope slide and protects the enclosed specimen from drying or decay, has the same refractive index as glass; the Canada balsam-and-glass sandwich thus functions as a single optical system. Less scientifically, the resin was recommended by Indians and settlers as a palliative for sore nipples. The balsam fir today remains the favorite Christmas tree of Maine, New Hampshire, and Vermont — though on the modern Christmas tree lot, the trees are considerably pricier than in the Boston markets of 1892, where you could buy a ten-footer for fifteen cents.

The balsam fir retained its lead in the Christmas tree race until the Depression of the 1930s. Then — under the auspices of an enterprising ex-Chrysler salesman, Fred Musser of Indiana, Pennsylvania — it was overtaken by the Scotch pine. The Scotch pine (*Pinus sylvestris*) is native not only to Scotland, but to a wide swathe of wintery territory across northern Europe. Nowadays it's the tree most frequently cultivated on American Christmas tree plantations, despite the drawback of its longish (to three inches) needles, which makes it difficult to trim. Mr. Musser's telling selling point was that the needles, though long, stayed on the tree much longer than those of the balsam fir or spruce. The Scotch pine is also fast-growing: a mere eight years to a six-foot tree, suitable for the holiday trade.

The Scotch pine was briefly eclipsed in the 1960s by the Douglas fir — a thick, soft, and trimmably short-needled tree — but promptly recouped its losses in the 70s and 80s. Today, according to the National Christmas Tree Association, it is the most popular Christmas tree in the north central United States, and in the outlying states of Pennsylvania, Kentucky, and Colorado. The far west — with the exception of California — continues to favor the Douglas fir; 69

percent of Californians usher in the Christmas season with a floppy Monterey pine. The South leans heavily toward the white pine, while New England celebrates largely with balsam fir or white spruce.

The public — as anyone can tell by listening to the altercations at a cut-your-own Christmas tree farm — holds strong opinions on the size and shape of their seasonal evergreens. Consumer studies show that most purchasers prefer a tree between 5½ and 7 feet tall, with a 66⅔ percent taper — which means a tree two-thirds as wide at the base as it is tall. A six-foot tree, for example, would thus measure a perfectly proportioned four feet across the bottom branches. Such a taper suits the small-bottomed spruces and firs, but the pines — generally broader at the base — often look better with a wider taper. A six-foot pine, for example, may measure — still attractively — close to 5½ feet at the base. The ideal pine thus takes up more of the living room than the ideal balsam fir.

The precisely pyramidal shape of the Christmas conifer is due not only to judicious pruning on the part of the tree farmer, but to the natural growth pattern of the tree itself. Though nearly all infant trees begin life with a Christmas-tree-like shape, new branches extending from a single central stem, only the conifers — and a few non-conformist deciduous trees like the pin oak — persist in this pattern into adulthood. The ideal Christmas tree results largely from a phenomenon known to botanists as *apical dominance*, in which the growth zone at the very tip of the main stem — the apex — acts as king-pin, hormonally controlling and restricting the outgrowth of secondary branches beneath it. If the apical bud is nipped off, such controls and restrictions are lifted; and second-string lateral buds promptly develop and take over the dominant role. Such apical nipping and lateral liberation are the basis of pruning — which, done properly, results in a flourish of lush secondary branching.

Secondary branches bud off from the main trunk in a regularly mathematical pattern, either in matched pairs on either side of the parent stem, or in precisely positioned spirals or whorls around it. The exceedingly symmetrical conifers subscribe to the latter pattern: each year a new round of lateral buds sprouts into a new whorl of secondary branches. The pattern is so predictable that the age of the tree can often be estimated by a count of whorls (or whorl scars). The tree grows not only upward, but outward, adding each year, along with its new whorl of branches at the top, new whorls of lateral branches to the side. Branching sideways is similarly subject to apical dominance. In some cases — Christmas trees, for example — the dominating presence is indeed the apical bud; in others, the terminal bud unselfishly aborts itself each year, turning its duties over to the next in line, the uppermost lateral bud. Such a pattern is typical of birches, chestnuts, sycamores, and basswoods — all of which, in consequence, tend to have zigzag twigs.

New lateral buds are inset at an angle on the parent branch, the precise degree of which is again under Big-Brother-like apical control. Usually the buds are set such that the side shoots emerge at a slant of forty to sixty degrees. In some trees, such as the docile spruce, the lateral branches simply grow out serenely at the original insertion angle. In deciduous trees, the lateral branches have a stubborn tendency to bend themselves upright and stay that way, which is why most hardwoods eventually develop rounded crowns. Pines play it both ways: The new lateral shoots rebelliously bend themselves upright, and these pale green perpendiculars, startling obvious against the darker, older foliage, are known as "candles" from their resemblance to the lights on old-fashioned Christmas trees. After this brief period of adolescent struggle, however, the candles bow to the dictates of the terminal bud and return, older and wiser, to the original insertion angle.

In conifers, the horizontally extended side branches — with increasing age and weight — eventually begin to sag. To compensate for this, the tree develops a specialized form of wood, referred to as *reaction wood*— essentially an extra-muscular slab of stiff tissue strong enough to haul the drooping limb back into position. In sagging softwoods, reaction wood, known as *compression wood*, forms on the underside of the overweighted limb. Its composite wood cells, featuring abnormally thick walls and unusually high concentrations of lignin, act collectively to shove the wayward branch back up into place. Hardwoods generally approach the droop problem from the other end. Sagging oak and maple limbs form *tension wood*, layered above, rather than below, the trouble spot, and the collective stresses exerted *pull*— rather than push — the defective branch back into line. Such cleverly corrective surgery allows the middle-aged hardwood to lift its leafy arms to pray, and keeps the branches of the middle-aged softwood from collapsing downward like a closed umbrella. In the latter case, the internal efforts are not wholly effective, however, since mature conifers still show a clear progression of branch angles, from the perkily slanted youngsters at the top to the elderly compression-wood-supported horizontals at the bottom. The aging evergreen branch, like the aging human being, fights a continuous battle with gravity. Which is why, when all is said and done, the bottom branches of Christmas trees are parallel to the floor.

The National Christmas Tree Association estimates an annual harvest these days of about forty million trees — essentially all axed from tree plantations, where evergreens are raised for the express purpose of ornamenting America's living rooms on December 25th. Christmas trees of the last century, in contrast, were simply cut from the closest forest. The first American Christmas tree business, accordingly, was based in the tree-laden Catskill Mountains of New York, founded in 1851 by Mark Carr — who, in that year, was cozily described by the *New York Times* as "a jolly woodsman." By the 1880s, the depredations of the jolly Mr. Carr and his like were a source of concern to naturalists and conservationists, and dedicated friends of the forests were vociferously promoting the tree-less Christmas. The *Ladies' Home Journal* urged its readers to substitute for the holiday tree a "Jacob's ladder," made from a cheesecloth-covered stepladder festively trimmed with greens, candles, and gifts. In 1904, President Theodore Roosevelt set an example for the nation, announcing that his family would forgo the traditional Christmas tree, and urging other environmentally aware citizens to do the same. Such high ideals were too much for the Roosevelt children, and one particularly disappointed son — Archie — smuggled a Christmas

245

tree into the White House and concealed it in his bedroom closet. The illicit tree soon came to the attention of the President, who sent his obstreperous offspring to see Gifford Pinchot, head of the newly organized National Forest Service. Pinchot, to the boys' glee, came down on the side of Christmas, explaining that the worst threats to the national forests were posed by fires, not the cutting of Christmas trees. The proper cutting of Christmas trees, stated Pinchot, accompanied by planned reforestation, was in fact beneficial to timberlands. TR gave in.

Today the National Christmas Tree Association estimates that 80 percent of the nation's Christmas tree acreage is in plantations, 20 percent in "natural stands" — with plantations on the rise. Christmas tree growers in the 1980s have been planting roughly eighty million trees each year, with numbers steadily increasing. This indicates that Christmas-minded Americans can — with clear consciences — indulge in their annual Scotch, Virginia, or Monterey pine, white spruce, or Douglas or balsam fir. Christmas might still be Christmas without any presents, but the season would be emptier by far without its eternally green tree.

REDWOOD

*P*eople, since first putting their noses out of the cave, have been obsessed with measuring large objects. Witness the popularity of the *Guinness Book of World Records*, which lists — among other record-making spectaculars — the world's longest alphabet (Cambodian), tallest totem pole, largest okra stalk, most expensive stuffed bird ($23,000 for a Great Auk), and highest extinct volcano. Human beings apparently feel passionately about such things: the *Guinness Book*, originally published in 1956 under the auspices of Benjamin Guinness, Earl of Iveagh, was ostensibly brought out to provide "a peaceful means for the settlement of arguments." Even Alexander the Great — perhaps with future arguments in mind — is said to have paused in the course of conquering the world to measure an awe-inspiring Indian banyan tree. Early correspondence from the American colonies is peppered with impressive accounts and measurements of giant trees, usually massive pines, oaks, chestnuts, beeches, and elms. As big trees go, however, the East Coast pioneers hadn't seen anything yet. Three thousand miles across the continent, and still essentially untouched by human hands, were growing both the world's tallest and the most massive trees — respectively, the coast redwoods (*Sequoia sempervirens*) and the giant sequoias (*Sequoiadendron giganteum*).

The first foreign view of the towering coast redwoods took place, according to legend, in 218 B.C., when a Chinese mariner named Hee-Li inadvertently arrived in California in his trading junk. The junk, some four months previously, had been blown off course by a storm; then a cockroach wedged beneath the ship's compass had forced the directional needle out of kilter, seducing the ship's captain into sailing due east instead of west. The captain, despite such daily cues as sunrise (in the east) and sunset (in the west), persisted in his cockroach-directed error, to the extent of having one hapless crew member — who protested that they were going the wrong way — thrown overboard. Eventually they fetched up on a strange coast, populated by enormous red trees. Once on land again, someone discovered the fatal cockroach, convinced the captain — tactfully — of his error, and Hee-Li turned his junk around and returned home. He subsequently wrote an account of his bizarre journey and filed it in the archives of the city of Si-Ngan-Foo in the province of Shen-si — where, in 1890, an American missionary named Shaw unearthed it, translated it, and sent an excited account of it back home to the American newspapers. The original account, unfortunately, was then lost, and modern historians tend to view Hee-Li's problematical voyage with skepticism.

Impeccably documented, in contrast, is the first redwood sighting by the Portola expedition — the first formal Spanish land exploration of the California coast, under the leadership of Gaspar de Portola, which resulted in the discovery of San Francisco Bay. On October 10, 1769, Fray Juan Crespi, chronicler of the expedition, wrote in his journal that the party had reached "plains and low hills, well forested with very high trees of a red color, not known to us. They have a very different leaf from cedars, and although the wood resembles cedar somewhat in color, it is very different and has not the same odor; moreover the wood of the trees that we have found is very brittle. In this region there is a great abundance of these trees and because none of the expedition recognizes them they are named redwood from their color." Later observers waxed more enthusiastic than the firmly factual Fray Crespi. David Douglas raptly described the coast redwoods as "awful," as in engendering awe; and German architect Eric Mendelsohn referred to them as "God's own flagpoles."

Actually, there remains some question as to whether God's own flagpole is the world's tallest tree. At maturity, the coast redwood reaches heights of up to 370 feet, with the tallest known living specimen — simply named the Tall Tree — measuring 367.8 feet, which makes it a good hundred feet taller than the Statue of Liberty. According to Edwin Menninger, however, even taller trees once grew along a tributary of the Limpopo River — the "great, grey-green, greasy Limpopo" of Kipling's *Just-So Stories* — in northwest Transvaal, Africa. These trees, commonly known as monkey-thorns (*Acacia galphii*), were estimated in 1907 to have heights of up to four hundred feet, the measurements including those parts of the trunks buried in the silt and sand of the riverbank. Unfortunately such record-breaking heights can no longer be confirmed — "These old trees have all been destroyed by fire and storm and have completely disappeared," writes Menninger — which thus effectively eliminates the mysterious monkey-thorn from the tall-tree competition.

Still solidly in the running, however, is an Australian eucalypt commonly known as the peppermint gum, giant string bark, or Australian oak. Turn-of-the-century champion-seekers routinely reported sightings of four-hundred- to five-hundred-foot-tall trees. Such measurements seem to have been overly optimistic, perhaps because, suggests one cynical source, the Australian government offered monetary rewards for tall-tree discoveries. The tallest known peppermint gum today measures 347 feet, which leaves it, at least for the present, in second place. In third place towers the Douglas fir, the grand champion of which measures 330 feet.

Trees appear to have an absolute maximum height, somewhere around four hundred feet — with the limiting factor in continued upward growth being availability of water. Richard Ketchum compares the tree to a kerosene lamp, its internal transport tubules acting as the wick, embedded in a pool of liquid beneath the ground, sucking water up toward the leaves. In the coast redwood, this process entails no mean suck: from the tips of the roots, extending outward as much as one hundred feet underground, to the leaves, over three hundred feet in the air, ground water travels over four hundred feet, much of it straight up. The guiding force behind this spectacular pumping feat is water tension. Water molecules, positively charged at one end and negatively charged at the other, are electrically sticky; within the tree's xylem tubules, they form a long continuously linked strand from roots to leaf tips. At the leaf surface, this strand breaks as water is lost from the leaves, either in the process of photosynthesis or in transpiration, the tree equivalent of sweat. This abrupt shortage of water at the top creates a powerful pull toward the bottom. The result is a steady stream of water, sucked up the tree's conducting tubules like cider through a straw, and then — for the most part — expelled through the leaves into the atmosphere. One study estimates that a tree uses only 1 percent of the water that passes up its trunk. The rest continues skyward, eventually to be redistributed to us as rain. The average adult redwood absorbs and then releases through transpiration some five hundred gallons of water daily — which explains why the thirsty *Sequoia sempervirens* thrives in California's central fog belt, under a soggy hundred inches of rainfall per year. Deprived of water, the redwoods wilt and die from the top down, producing what are colloquially known as "spike-tops" — trees with lushly green underpinnings, but withered brown peaks.

The great majority of (markedly shorter) North American trees grow in drier climates (twenty to forty annual inches of rainfall), with heights generally decreasing as the environment becomes increasingly arid. Once the rainfall level drops below twenty inches per year — the "disaster line," according to dendrologists — there tend to be no trees at all. Such is the situation in much of the western half of the United States, which lies downwind of the rain-trapping Cascade and Sierra Nevada mountain ranges; the resultant vast treeless stretch was known to the appalled pioneers as the "Great American Desert."

Given enough water, the process by which a tree grows upward — in the case of the coast redwood, over three hundred feet upward — is more complex than meets the eye. One explanation was conceived by the German writer Johann Wolfgang von Goethe — author of *Faust* — who devoted some years of his long career to science. Goethe's scientific endeavors never came to much — he spent five years attempting to prove light indivisible, in the teeth of the evidence from Isaac Newton's prism — and he published, in 1790, a work titled *Metamorphose der Pflanzen* (The Metamorphosis of Plants), characterized by fuzzy logic and exquisite botanical drawings. In it, he postulated a force opposing Newton's downward-pulling gravity, to be known as "levity." Levity, hypothesized Goethe, was responsible for all upward movement, to encompass such phenomena as the skyward growth of plants, the fountaining of geysers, the eruption of volcanoes — and, presumably, the popping of champagne corks and the gushing of oil wells. Serious scientific circles today discount Goethe's levity as an active force, and have provided explanations of their own for movements up.

Trees exhibit an instinctive response to the force of gravity — a phenomenon known as *geotropism* — which directs the infant plant to send shoots up and roots down. Scientists believe that plants respond to gravity by a mechanism somewhat similar to the equilibrium-maintaining device that operates in the human inner ear. Within each side of our heads, the up-down sensing organ consists of a pair of ovoid lumps or sacs, called the *utricle* and the *saccule*, and a tiny trio of contorted semicircular canals. All are located just downstream of the eardrum and its accompanying hammer, anvil, and stirrup — which, as any Trivial Pursuit player can tell you, are the body's smallest bones. The inner surfaces of the utricle and saccule are coated with sensory cells, which in turn are covered with a gooey gelatin-like layer containing numerous dense little particles called *statoliths*. The statoliths are composed of calcium carbonate — the same substance that makes up stalactites, stalagmites, the white cliffs of Dover, and the pyramids of Egypt. When you tip your head, the simultaneously tipped statoliths exert greater or lesser pressures on the underlying sensory cells, which in turn relay positional messages to the brain. It's these statoliths, therefore, that are largely responsible for *mal-de-mer*, car sickness, and the wonky feeling suffered by roller coaster riders.

While plants are generally excluded from the positional excitements available to human beings, they do similarly use statoliths to determine which way is up. In the plant world, statoliths appear to be heavy granules of starch rather than calcium carbonate crystals. These are found in specialized cells of the root and shoot tips, where, under the influence of gravity, they sink through the cell sap to settle at the downward end of the cell. When the sunken statoliths fetch up against the cell membrane, the contact apparently effects the distribution of growth hormones and/or growth inhibitors, such that the developing shoot or root grows properly up or down.

While *Sequoia sempervirens* grows impressively upward, its closest relative — now scientifically known as *Sequoiadendron giganteum* — grows impressively outward. These trees are the most massive on earth, both in circumference and volume. Largest of the large is the General Sherman Tree — named for its discoverer's wartime commanding officer — which measures 272.4 feet in height and 101.6 feet in circumference at the base. The tree weighs an estimated twelve million pounds, including 750,000 pounds of roots and 14,000 pounds of bark — and the timber industry calculates regretfully that General Sherman, felled, would yield up 600,120 board feet of lumber. Such behemoths are commonly known as giant sequoias, Sierra redwoods, or — capitalized — Big Trees. "A tree which is 300 feet high, which is 10 feet in diameter, and which weighs 2,000 tons," wrote Walter Fry, one-time commissioner of Sequoia National Park, "is more than a big tree. It is a Big Tree."

The spectacular Big Trees are restricted to a 260-mile-long-by-15-mile-wide strip of California, on the western slope of the Sierra Nevada mountains at elevations of forty-five hundred to seventy-five hundred feet. In contrast, the coast redwood — which, despite its designation as California ("I Have Found It") state tree, lops over into Oregon — extends from southwest Oregon south 450 miles to the Santa Lucia Mountains south of Carmel (home of Pebble Beach). The Big Trees are limited to some seventy-five groves, totalling 35,607 acres. This scarcity probably explains why the Trees were so late in coming to public notice. The first recorded instance of human contact with the Big Trees occurred in 1833, when they were observed by Zenas Leonard, the note-taking member of Joseph Walker's expedition across the Nevada desert and Sierra mountains.

Leonard described the Trees as "incredibly large," and included them, with estimated measurements, in the account of his journey published in 1839. Despite his dramatic disclosures, the book — and Trees — went mostly unnoticed, "probably," writes a modern redwood chronicler, "because the small book was published in Pennsylvania."

The definitive discovery of the Big Trees, most accounts agree, occurred in 1852, when a hunter named A. T. Dowd — employed by the Union Water Company of Murphy's Camp to supply its workers with fresh meat — encountered and chased a grizzly bear. Man and bear ended up in what is now known as the Calaveras Grove, surrounded by truly awesome specimens of *Sequoiadendron giganteum*. Dowd abandoned his bear, and hightailed it back to camp with the news of his find; and from there the word spread. Within a month of Dowd's announcement, an eager collector arrived at the grove and acquired specimens of leaves, branches, and cones. These were sent off with a flourish to Dr. Albert Kellogg, founder of the San Francisco Academy of Sciences and California's premier botanist. Dr. Kellogg, being a man of "leisurely habits," had not yet passed judgement on the specimens or visited the immense trees when — two years later — he shared his information about Dowd's find with British plant collector William Lobb. Lobb — the Hare to Kellogg's Tortoise — promptly streaked off to the Calaveras Grove, where he amassed a specimen collection of his own; then, with barely a pause for breath, he boarded the first boat to England, where he presented his arboreal loot to British botanist John Lindley. Lindley, who seems to have had a keen sense of academic competition, published a paper on the new trees with almost indecent haste, bestowing upon Dowd's find the name *Wellingtonia gigantea*, in honor of Arthur Wellesley, Duke of Wellington, hero of Waterloo. In doing so, he escalated what had been a mild scientific controversy to a political shouting match.

The formal botanical naming of the redwoods began in 1828, when British botanist A. B. Lambert correctly assigned the coast redwood to the family *Taxodiaceae* (sometimes called the deciduous Cypress family), and incorrectly lumped it into the genus *Taxodium*, along with the bald cypress. He proposed the species name *sempervirens* ("ever-living") both in honor of the evergreen foliage and of the redwood's ability — unusual among conifers — to regenerate by sending up sprouts from lateral roots. Shortly thereafter Austrian botanist Stephen Endlicher entered the fray, pointing out a number of telling differences between the bald cypress and the coast redwood, and proposing in consequence that the redwood be given a separate generic name. He proposed *Sequoia*, to commemorate the eighteenth-century Cherokee leader Sequoyah, famed for devising an eighty-three-letter alphabet for the Cherokee language. (Which, incidentally, puts it eleven letters up on the Cambodian, with seventy-two letters.)

The entry of the Big Tree upon the scene inspired a new flurry of scientific naming, beginning with the aforementioned *Wellingtonia*. Dr. Kellogg, still lethargically ensconced in San Francisco, fell in with the bald cypress camp, opting for *Taxodium giganteum*. Other American scientists were made of sterner or touchier stuff: upon learning of Lindley's Wellingtonian nomenclature ("Loud was the patriotic anguish of the American botanists," wrote Donald Culross Peattie), they countered with *Washingtonia californica* and *Taxodium washingtonianum*. An objective — French — botanist, Joseph Descaine, then argued that the closely related coast and Sierra redwoods belonged in the same genus, for which he found Endlicher's designation *Sequoia* more appropriate than any "nationalistic epithet." *Sequoia* the redwoods stayed until 1938, when detailed embryological studies separated them again. Today, political figures forgotten, the coast redwood remains *Sequoia sempervirens* and the Big Tree is known as *Sequoiadendron giganteum*. Both are members of the family *Taxodiaceae*, which includes at least ten genera and fifteen species worldwide, among them the bald cypress, the Chinese fir, the Tasmanian cedar, the Japanese cedar, and the Japanese umbrella pine.

Redwoods and their relatives have been around for some 125 million years. The first evidence for their existence — fossilized cones — dates to the Upper Jurassic period, the heyday of the dinosaurs. In these carefree early years, they flourished across the northern hemisphere; sixty million years ago redwoods grew in what is now Yellowstone Park. Redwood fossils have been found in Texas and Pennsylvania, in Greenland and Alaska, in France and Japan. Climatic changes gradually narrowed this great range, wiping out the majority of the original redwood species, until only three were left. The third extant redwood species is the dawn redwood — *Metasequoia glyptostroboides* — whose real-life story is no stranger than the popular Hollywood fantasies about explorers stumbling upon baby brontosaurs in the depths of the rain forest.

Up until 1944, the dawn redwood was believed extinct; no sign of it had been seen for about twenty million years. Then, in the final year of World War II, a Chinese forester named Wang stumbled upon a living specimen in the wilderness of the Szechuan province in central China. Wang reported his find to the Chinese botanical authorities, who excitedly published, and word of the unprecedented discovery trickled through tree circles, eventually reaching the United States. In 1948, paleontologist Ralph Chaney and Milton Silverman, science editor of the *San Francisco Chronicle*, set off to China to view the miraculous trees *in situ*. They reached their goal after a harrowing journey by boat down the Yang-tze River and on foot over the mountains, escorted by armed soldiers for fear of bandits — which turned out to be no mean precaution: the soldiers killed one bandit and scared off two. Upon their arrival, Chaney and Silverman were rewarded by the sight of entire valleys of dawn redwoods. The trees are considerably smaller than their American cousins, reaching maximum heights of about 140 feet with slender six-foot diameters, and their branchlets are arranged in opposite pairs, rather than in the ascending spirals characteristic of the California trees. And, unlike their evergreen relatives, the dawn redwoods are deciduous. Dr. Chaney, entranced, brought home four dawn redwood seedlings and planted them on the campus at the University of California at Berkeley — thus bringing back a tree that had been absent from American soil since the days of the dinosaurs.

The excitement accompanying the discovery of the dawn redwoods — though intense in rarified botanical circles — barely held a candle to the furor raised over the fabulous Big Tree. Prior to 1850, the chief admirer of the Big Tree was the chickaree, or Douglas squirrel, a clever-pawed little conifer-dweller who favors the fleshy green scales of sequoia cones. The squirrels hold the small cones in their front paws and peel the flesh off the scales with their teeth, somewhat as human beings set about eating an artichoke. The peeling releases and scatters the tiny seeds — ninety-one thousand to the pound — wedged beneath the scales, which thus benefits the redwood tree. The relationship of people to Big Tree, regrettably, has been less mutually beneficial. By the late 1850s, parks, gardens, and arboretums worldwide were clamoring for specimens of *S. giganteum.* This need was initially, if inadvertently, filled by G. H. Woodruff of New York, a disappointed gold-digger. Woodruff, the story goes, was mooning dismally about a Big Tree grove, brooding upon his failures, when he happened — in the aimless way of dismal mooners — to collect a handful of Big Tree cones. He shook the seeds into his empty snuffbox and sent them east, prepaid, by Pony Express to the Rochester, New York, nursery of Ellwanger and Barry. Ellwanger and Barry, who knew a good thing when they saw it, planted Woodruff's seeds and managed to raise four thousand tiny Big Trees. They sold these, profitably, mostly to customers in England, who persisted stubbornly in referring to their new acquisitions as *Wellingtonia.* Woodruff was paid a share of the profits, which came to $1,036.60.

Other exploitations of the redwood groves were less benign than those of the nurserymen. The showmen made minor, but dramatic, inroads. In 1854, a slick businessman named George Trask arrived in the Calaveras Grove, and zeroed in on a monstrous tree known for centuries to the local Indians as "Mother of the Forest." "Mother," at the time of Trask's attack, stood 321 feet tall — the tallest known *S. giganteum* today measures 310 feet — and was over sixty feet in circumference six feet up the trunk. Trask had originally planned to cut the tree and transport it east, lock, stock, and barrel, where it would be displayed in all its outsized glory. One look at the tree was enough to disabuse him of that notion — and perhaps he also heard stories of the felling of the first Big Tree, a Bunyanesque task that took twenty-five men two weeks of work, and even then was finally finished off by the wind. The stump of that tree — A. T. Dowd's first giant sequoia, nicknamed the Discovery Tree — was used for a Fourth-of-July cotillion in 1854, and found large enough to accommodate thirty-two waltzers, half of them in hoop skirts, plus musicians. Such overwhelming immensity intimidated even the most determined tree-chopper, so Trask decided to take a simpler approach. Instead of crassly cutting, Trask decided to strip the bark from his chosen tree, to a height of 116 feet. The bark pieces could then be shipped to New York and London, and there reassembled for the edification and amusement of the urban populace. This was, in fact, done; and the bark ended up in the Crystal Palace in London, where it was admired by, among others, Prince Albert and Queen Victoria. It burned, along with the rest of the Palace, in 1866. "Mother," in the meantime, survived in a crippled state until 1908, when it too succumbed to fire.

William Waldorf Astor — for a bet — had a dinner table made from a cross-sectional slice of redwood tree capable of seating forty dinner guests with full place settings of crystal and silver. The Columbian Exposition of 1893, in Chicago, featured "the biggest plank ever sawed" — of coast redwood, sixteen feet, five inches wide. Such demonstrations merely reflected the prevailing attitude toward trees. Madison Grant, president of the New York Zoological Society and one of the founders — in 1918 — of the Save-the-Redwoods League, wrote, "It is scarcely necessary to dwell on the crime involved in the destruction of the oldest trees on earth. The cutting of a sequoia for grape stakes or railroad ties is like breaking up one's grandfather's clock for kindling to save the trouble of splitting logs at the woodpile, or lighting one's pipe with a Greek manuscript to save the trouble of reaching for the matches."

Nonetheless, the lumbermen came. The California town of Eureka, founded in 1850, boasted a population of three thousand people and nine working sawmills by 1853. By 1860, there were an estimated three hundred sawmills in operation along the northern California coast. The Big Trees, for all their spectacular size, proved less than ideal as timber. The mammoth trees tended to shatter when felled, which led — at the height of the late nineteenth-century logging activity — to the waste of at least half of every tree downed. Once downed, each multi-million-pound corpse had to be transported to the coastal sawmills — a task that sometimes involved blasting the trunks into manageable segments with dynamite. The logs were then dragged out of the woods by ox teams, along a skid row of logs laid crosswise to prevent the heavy cargo from sinking irretrievably into the earth — the same technique used by the Egyptians in hauling the huge stones of the Pyramids across the sandy desert.

All in all, the lumber industry found the coast redwood more suitable to their purposes, being tougher, skinnier, and handier to sawmills and harbors. An acre of redwood yields about 100,000 board feet of lumber — with estimates ranging as high as 500,000 — which product, selling for $15 per thousand feet, grossed the mill a neat $1,350 for each $1.25 invested, a profitable prospect irresistible to timber barons. Driven by such fine financial visions, eager woodsmen obliterated over one-third of California's original two million acres of redwood forest between 1850 and 1925.

Prior to the introduction of nineteenth-century commercial logging, the redwoods had remained virtually unmolested by humankind. The local Indians — "amazingly," writes one author — managed to do some redwood logging, using elkhorn wedges and scrapers, and adzes made of mussel shells. The painfully acquired planks were used to build houses. Fallen redwoods were hollowed to make dugout canoes, and several tribes used redwood bark as a building material. The early Spanish generally shunned redwood in favor of adobe, but roving Russians — out after sea otter — built an all-redwood colony in 1812 at Fort Ross, just south of modern Sonoma. They sold it in 1841 to Captain John Sutter, who, eight years later, discovered gold — thus quadrupling the population of California and monumentally increasing the wood demand.

Redwood wood, writes Donald Peattie, is "inferior to practically every timber in all ways except one": it lasts nearly forever. Fray Junipero Serra, the indomitable Franciscan friar who masterminded the building of the California missions, died in 1784 and was buried in a redwood coffin under the floor of the Mission San Carlos Borromeo in Carmel. The adobe mission eventually crumbled to dust, but the coffin was unearthed ninety-eight years later, still intact. Today redwood is favored for such weather-worried items as stadium bleachers, shingles, picnic tables, fences, and backyard decks. Milwaukee brewers and California vintners prepare their wares in redwood vats; redwood is used for water tanks, water pipes, and septic tanks, and is occasionally sold abroad for railroad ties. The trains of Peru run on redwood.

The legendary longevity of the redwood is due to its militarily astute multiple lines of defense. Redwood bark owes its rich cinnamon color to a high content of tannins, astringent chemicals off-putting to tree-eating pests. Coast redwoods have also been shown to produce a pair of more specific anti-insect and anti-fungal compounds, named — for their manufacturers — sequirin A and B.

The very thickness of the bark is in itself a defense. One to two feet thick in mature trees, the bark renders the redwood essentially fire-resistant. One fallen tree, meticulously examined in 1934 by Emanuel Fritz of the University of California, was found in its 1,204-year life to have survived nine fires — including a major scorcher in 1820, which killed 40 percent of its circumference — and seven floods. It was the fire of 1820 that eventually did the tree in, destroying enough of the root system that the tree developed a lean — which lean, some 114 years later, tipped the tree over on its side. Redwood bark has been used as insulation for electric water heaters, fur storage vaults, and iceboxes. Some of the virtues of the whole tree are believed to persist in the sawn planks: redwood siding in houses is reportedly fire-resistant due to its lack of (flammable) resins. The once largely redwood city of San Francisco is said to have had no severe fires until the fatal fifty-second earthquake of 1906.

The name most often associated with California's redwoods is that of John Muir, the Scottish-born naturalist and conservationist, and the founder — in 1892 — of the Sierra Club. Muir is generally credited with ensuring federal protection for the Grand Canyon, the Petrified Forest of Arizona, Yosemite, and Sequoia National Park, this last formally set aside in 1890. Much of the groundwork for protection of sequoias and coast redwoods was reportedly laid on a camping trip taken by Muir and president Teddy Roosevelt in May of 1903 — during which the president slept on a makeshift bed of army blankets and it snowed. The president emerged from Muir's woods an impassioned defender of redwood trees: "I feel most emphatically," wrote TR, "that we should not turn into shingles a tree which was old when the first Egyptian conqueror penetrated to the valley of the Euphrates . . . ." John Muir was crisper and more to the point. "Any fool can destroy trees," wrote Muir — in whose honor, in 1907, the 503-acre Muir Woods National Monument was established in Marin County, just north of San Francisco.

Poet Gerard Manley Hopkins — who was thinking of other trees — may have said it the best of all:

> *What would the world be, once bereft*
> *Of wet and wildness? Let them be left,*
> *O let them be left, wildness and wet;*
> *Long live the weeds and wildness yet.*

BIBLIOGRAPHY

Abbey, Edward. "The Crooked Wood," *Audubon,* November 1975, pp. 24-27.

Adkins, Jan. *The Wood Book,* Little, Brown and Company, Boston, 1980.

Adrosko, Rita J. *Natural Dyes and Home Dyeing,* Dover Publications, Inc., New York, 1971.

Austwick, Peter, and Robin Mattocks. "Naturally occurring carcinogens in food," *Chemistry and Industry 3:* 76-83, 1979.

Auvergne, Caroline. "The American Black Walnut," *Early American Life,* October 1986, pp. 59-61.

Bainbridge, David. "The Grain That Grows on Trees," *Mother Earth News,* September/October 1984, pp. 80-84.

Bainbridge, David A. "The Use of Acorns for Food in California: Past, Present, and Future," presented at the Symposium on Multiple-use Management of California's Hardwoods, San Luis Obispo, California, November 12-14, 1986.

Bellamy, David. *Bellamy's New World: A Botanical History of America,* British Broadcasting Corporation, London, 1983.

Bennett, Jennifer. "Tough Nuts," *Harrowsmith,* March/April 1987, pp. 89-93, 125-130.

Block, L. S. "A New Battle for Perfect Apples," *Yankee,* April 1982, pp. 86-93.

Bodanis, David. *The Secret House,* Simon & Schuster, Inc., New York, 1986.

Borland, Hal. *A Countryman's Woods,* Alfred A. Knopf, New York, 1983.

Brock, William E. "Bozeman Chain Saw Massacre," *Discover,* November 1987, pp. 79-85.

Brown, John Hull. *Early American Beverages,* Bonanza Books, New York, 1966.

Brown, Robert C., ed., *The Garden and Farm Books of Thomas Jefferson,* Fulcrum, Inc., Golden, Colorado, 1987.

Brown, Sanborn C. *Wines and Beers of Old New England,* The University Press of New England, Hanover, New Hampshire, 1978.

Buchanan, Rita. *A Weaver's Garden,* Interweave Press, Loveland, Colorado, 1987.

Canby, Peter. "A Ringing in the Maples," *Audubon,* March 1978, pp. 89-91.

Casson, Lionel. "Mystery Behind the Magi's Gift," *San Francisco Chronicle,* December 20, 1987.

Chasan, Daniel Jack. "Twilight of the Great Cedars," *Audubon,* November 1977, pp. 50-55.

Chasan, Daniel Jack. "Varieties come and go, but apples remain a staple," *Smithsonian,* September 1986, pp. 123-132.

Christopher, Thomas. "Willows Worth Whistling At," *Horticulture,* November 1988, pp. 43-47.

Ciesla, Bill. "The Digger: California's Oddball Pine," *American Forests,* January/February 1987, pp. 22-25.

Clary, Mike. "Lightning! Spectacular and Deadly," *Weatherwise,* June 1985, pp. 128-135.

Clepper, Henry, and Arthur B. Meyer. *The World of the Forest,* D.C. Heath and Company, Boston, 1965.

Clouston, Brian, and Kathy Stansfield, eds. *After the Elm,* Heinemann, London, 1979.

Collingwood, G. H., and Warren D. Brush. *Knowing Your Trees,* The American Forestry Association, Washington, D.C., 1974.

Cook, Jack. "Your Back-yard Fruit and Nut Orchard," *Country Journal,* May 1984, pp. 30-39.

Cook, Jack. "A Crop for Christmas Yet to Come," *Country Journal,* December 1986, pp. 36-41.

Cook, Jack. "Elm Street Revisited," *Country Journal,* October 1987, pp. 52-56.

Cronin, William. *Changes in the Land: Indians, Colonists, and the Ecology of New England,* Hill and Wang, New York, 1983.

Cure, Karen. *An Old-Fashioned Christmas,* Harry N. Abrams, Inc., New York, 1984.

Cutwright, Paul Russell. *Lewis and Clark: Pioneering Naturalists,* University of Nebraska Press, Lincoln, Nebraska, 1989.

Dathe, Michael. "Sassafras in Spite of Itself," *Horticulture,* September 1984, pp. 19-24.

De Forest, Elizabeth Kellam. *The Gardens and Grounds at Mount Vernon,* The Mount Vernon Ladies' Association of the Union, Mount Vernon, Virginia, 1982.

Dent, Alan. *World of Shakespeare: Plants,* Taplinger Publishing Company, New York, 1971.

Diamond, Nancy K., Richard B. Standiford, Peter C. Passof, and John LeBlanc. "Oak trees have varied effect on land values," *California Agriculture,* September/October 1987, pp. 4-6.

Dodge, Bertha S. *Tales of Vermont Ways and People,* Stackpole Books, Harrisburg, Pennsylvania, 1977.

Dow, George Francis. *Every Day Life in the Massachusetts Bay Colony,* Dover Publications, Inc., New York, 1988.

Dowden, Anne Ophelia. *The Blossom on the Bough,* Thomas Y. Crowell Company, New York, 1975.

Duchin, Dian. "Test-Tube Titans," *Garden,* March/April 1987, pp. 20-22.

Dudley, Ruth H. *Favorite Trees of Desert, Mountain, and Plain,* Funk and Wagnalls Company, New York, 1963.

Earle, Alice Morse. *Customs and Fashions in Old New England,* Charles E. Tuttle, Inc., Rutland, Vermont, 1973.

Earle, Olive L. *State Trees,* William Morrow and Company, New York, 1960.

Earle, Olive L. *Nuts,* William Morrow and Company, New York, 1975.

Emsley, John. "Plant a tree for chemistry," *New Scientist,* October 8, 1987, pp. 39-42.

Evans, George Ewart. *Ask the Fellows Who Cut the Hay,* Faber and Faber Limited, London, 1956.

Fergus, Charles. "Wild Nuts: A Gatherer's Compendium," *Country Journal,* October 1985, pp. 23-32.

Fergus, Charles. "Hunting for Giants," *Country Journal,* January 1989, pp. 57-61.

Flexner, Stuart Berg. *I Hear America Talking,* Simon & Schuster, Inc., New York, 1976.

Flexner, Stuart Berg. *Listening to America,* Simon & Schuster, Inc., New York, 1982.

Flint, Harrison L. "Elms of Yesterday and Today," *Horticulture,* July 1986, pp. 50-57.

Fulbright, Dennis W. "Spread of a hypovirulent strain of *Endothia parasitica* in an American chestnut stand," 78th Annual Report of the Northern Nut Growers Association, July 1987, pp. 193-194.

Furnas, J. C. *The Americans: A Social History of the United States 1587-1914,* G.P. Putnam's Sons, New York, 1969.

Gadowski, Michael P. "Aspens," *The Conservationist,* January/February 1987, pp. 24-26.

Galston, Arthur W. *Green Wisdom,* Basic Books, Inc., New York, 1981.

Garelik, Glenn. "Different Strokes," *Discover,* October 1984, pp. 60-66.

Gibbons, Euell. *Stalking the Wild Asparagus,* David McKay Company, Inc., New York, 1962.

Gibson, Mark E. "Mistletoe as Malady," *Garden,* November/December 1986, pp. 24-27.

Goldsworthy, Andrew. "Why trees are green," *New Scientist,* December 10, 1987, pp. 48-52.

Greason, Michael C. "The White Pine in New York," *The Conservationist,* January/February 1986, p. 17.

Greenoak, Francesca. *Forgotten Fruit: The English Orchard and Fruit Garden,* Andre Deutsch Limited, London, 1983.

Grotz, George. *The Furniture Doctor,* Doubleday and Company, Inc., Garden City, New York, 1962.

Gusewelle, C. W. "The Truffle Hunters," *Country Journal,* February 1986, pp. 37-40.

Halfman, Elizabeth S. *Maypoles and Wood Demons: The Meaning of Trees,* The Seabury Press, New York, 1972.

Hall, F. Keith. "Wood Pulp," *Scientific American 230:* 52-62, 1974.

Hamilton, Edith. *Mythology,* Little, Brown and Company, Boston, 1942.

Hartley, Dorothy. *Lost Country Life,* Pantheon Books, New York, 1979.

Hawke, David Freeman. *Everyday Life in Early America,* Harper and Row, Publishers, New York, 1988.

Hendrickson, Robert. *The Great American Chewing Gum Book,* Chilton Book Company, Radnor, Pennsylvania, 1976.

Hendry, George. "Where does all the green go?," *New Scientist,* November 5, 1988, pp. 38-42.

Hess, Karen. *Martha Washington's Booke of Cookery,* Columbia University Press, New York, 1981.

Hewes, Jeremy Joan. *Redwoods: The World's Largest Trees,* Gallery Books, New York, 1984.

Hirono, Iwao. "Natural carcinogenic products of plant origin," *CRC Critical Reviews in Toxicology 8:* 235-277, 1981.

Hoagland, Edward. "Johnny Appleseed" in *A Sense of History,* American Heritage, New York, 1985.

Hofferber, Michael. "The Duchess of Oldenburg and Other Edible Antiques," *Country Journal,* October 1987, pp. 68-71.

Holan, Frank. "Sugaring Made Simple," *Country Journal,* March 1986, pp. 38-45.

The Hortus III: A Concise Dictionary of Plants Cultivated in the United States and Canada, Macmillan Publishing Co., New York, 1976.

Hunter, Dard. *Papermaking,* Dover Publications, Inc., New York, 1978.

Hunter, Neil. "Molecules of the green machine," *New Scientist,* April 28, 1988, pp. 60-63.

Huxley, Anthony. *Plant and Planet,* Viking Press, New York, 1974.

Huxley, Anthony. *Green Inheritance,* Doubleday, Garden City, New York, 1985.

Isherwood, Justin. "The King's Broad Arrow Tree," *The Conservationist,* January/February 1986, pp. 13-15.

James, Anne Scott, and Osbert Lancaster. *The Pleasure Garden,* Gambit, On Meeting House Green, Ipswich, Connecticut, 1977.

Jaynes, Richard A. *Handbook of North American Fruit Trees,* Northern Nut Growers Association, Knoxville, Tennessee, 1969.

Johnson, Jerry Mack. *Country Scrapbook: All About Country Lore and Life,* Simon & Schuster, Inc., New York, 1977.

Josselyn, John. *New-Englands Rarities Discovered,* London, 1672, Reprint of the Massachusetts Historical Society, 1972.

Kalm, Peter. *Peter Kalm's Travels in America: The English Version of 1770,* Dover Publications, Inc., New York, 1937.

Kappel-Smith, Diana. "A Christmas Business," *Country Journal,* December 1980, pp. 39-44.

Ketchum, Richard M. *The Secret Life of the Forest,* American Heritage, New York, 1970.

Lam, Brenda S., Gary A. Strobel, Leslie A. Harrison, and Stephen T. Lam. "Transposon mutagenesis and tagging of fluorescent *Pseudomonas:* Antimycotic production is necessary for control of Dutch elm disease," *Proceedings of the National Academy of Science 84:* 6447-6451, 1987.

Lanner, Ronald M. *The Piñon Pine: A Natural and Cultural History,* University of Nevada Press, Reno, Nevada, 1981.

Lape, Fred. "The Greening of 'Granny Smith'," *Horticulture,* October 1984, pp. 38-43.

Lawrence, Elizabeth. *Gardening for Love,* Duke University Press, Durham, North Carolina, 1987.

Lehane, Brendan. *The Power of Plants,* McGraw-Hill Book Company, New York, 1977.

Leydet, Francois. *The Last Redwoods and the Parkland of Redwood Creek,* Sierra Club–Ballantine Books, New York, 1969.

Lincoln, William A. *World Woods in Color,* Macmillan Publishing Company, New York, 1986.

Little, Nina Fletcher. *Country Arts in Early American Homes,* E. P. Dutton and Company, Inc., New York, 1975.

Mabey, Richard. *Plantcraft: A Guide to the Everyday Use of Wild Plants,* Universe Books, New York, 1978.

MacFadyen, J. Tevere. "A Taste for the Cold," *Horticulture,* August 1986, pp. 46-53.

Madson, John. "Trees That Weep, Whistle, and Grow Kittens," *Audubon,* September 1985, pp. 46-56.

Manager's Handbook for the Black Walnut, General Technical Report NC-38, North Central Forest Experiment Station, U.S. Department of Agriculture, Washington, D.C., 1984.

Mansfield, Howard. "Elm Street Blues," *American Heritage,* October/November 1986, pp. 98-102.

McGee, Harold. *On Food and Cooking: The Science and Lore of the Kitchen,* Charles Scribner's Sons, New York, 1984.

McLean, Teresa. *Medieval English Gardens,* Viking Press, New York, 1980.

McPhee, John. *The Survival of the Bark Canoe,* Warner Books, New York, 1975.

Menninger, Edwin A. *Fantastic Trees,* Viking Press, New York, 1967.

Mercatante, Anthony S. *The Magic Garden: The Myth and Folkore of Flowers, Plants, Trees, and Herbs,* Harper and Row, Publishers, New York, 1976.

Miller, Heather. "Tradescantia," *Horticulture,* June 1983, pp. 20-21.

Miller, J. A., and E. C. Miller. "The metabolic activation and nuclic acid adducts of naturally-occurring carcinogens: Recent results with ethyl carbamate and the spice flavors safrole and estragole," *British Journal of Cancer 8:* 1-15, 1983.

Mitchell, Alan. *The Trees of North America,* Facts on File Publications, New York, 1987.

Morton, Julia F. "Plant products and occupational materials ingeted by esophageal cancer victims in South Carolina," *Quarterly Journal of Crude Drug Research 13:* 2005-2022, 1973.

Nearing, Helen and Scott. *The Maple Sugar Book,* Schocken Boos, New York, 1950.

Needham, Walter, and Barrows Mussey. *A Book of Country Things,* The Stephen Greene Press, Brattleboro, Vermont, 1965.

Norman, Geoffrey. "The First Apples of the Season," *Yankee,* September 1983, pp. 118-123.

Norton, Phillip. "Decline and Fall," *Harrowsmith,* April/May 1985, pp. 24-30.

Oppel, Frank, ed. *Tales of New England Past* and *Tales of Old New England,* Castle, Secaucus, New Jersey, 1987.

Orton, Vrest. *The American Cider Book,* Farrar, Straus, and Giroux, New York, 1973.

Orton, Vrest. *The Homemade Beer Book,* Charles E. Tuttle Company, Rutland, Vermont, 1973.

Outerbridge, David E. *The Hangover Handbook,* Harmony Books, New York, 1981.

Parker, Tom. *In One Day,* Houghton Mifflin Company, Boston, 1984.

Peattie, Donald Culross. *A Natural History of Trees of Eastern and Central North America,* Houghton Mifflin Company, Boston, 1948.

Peattie, Donald Culross. *A Natural History of Western Trees,* Bonanza Books, New York, 1953.

Peeples, Edwin. "Hickory — the American Tree," *Country Journal,* May/June 1989, pp. 35-38.

Peeples, Edwin A. "The Many Uses of Hybrid Poplar," *Country Journal,* April 1985, pp. 78-81.

Peeples, Edwin A. "Black Walnut — Bothersome Beauty," *Country Journal,* September 1988, pp. 37-40.

Pennington, Samuel. "The Antique That's Never Advertised," *Yankee,* March 1984, pp. 72-75.

Perényi, Eleanor. *Green Thoughts,* Random House, New York, 1981.

Perlin, John. *A Forest Journey: The Role of Wood in the Development of*

Civilization, W.W. Norton & Company, New York, 1989.

Perrin, Noel. *First Person Rural,* David R. Godine, Publisher, Boston, 1978.

Platt, Rutherford. *American Trees,* Dodd, Mead & Company, New York, 1952.

Platt, Rutherford. *This Green World,* Dodd, Mead & Company, New York, 1963.

Platt, Rutherford. *The Great American Forest,* Prentice-Hall, Inc., Englewood Cliffs, New Jersey, 1965.

Poole, Gray Johnson. *Mistletoe: Fact and Fiction,* Dodd, Mead & Company, New York, 1976.

Randall, Charles Edgar, and Henry Clepper. *Famous and Historic Trees,* American Forestry Association, Washington, D.C., 1977.

Reich, Lee. "Pines for Eating," *Horticulture,* February 1988, pp. 18-2.

Riotte, Louise. *Nuts for the Food Gardener,* Garden Way Publishing, Charlotte, Vermont, 1975.

Root, Waverley. *Food,* Simon & Schuster, Inc., New York, 1980.

Root, Waverley, and Richard de Rochemont. *Eating in America,* The Ecco Press, New York, 1976.

Rosenthal, Gerald A. "The Chemical Defenses of Higher Plants," *Scientific American,* January 1986, pp. 94-99.

Schorger, A. W. *The Passenger Pigeon: Its Natural History and Extinction,* The University of Wisconsin Press, Madison, Wisconsin, 1955.

Schultz, Kathleen. *Create Your Own Natural Dyes,* Sterling Publishing Co., Inc., New York, 1975.

Sekizawa, Jun, and Takayuki Shibamoto. "Genotoxicity of safrole-related chemicals in microbial test systems," *Mutation Research* 101: 127-140, 1982.

Shepherd, Jack. *The Forest Killers,* Weybright and Talley, New York, 1975.

Simpson, Beryl Brintnall, and Molly Conner-Ogorzaly. *Economic Botany,* McGraw-Hill Book Company, New York, 1986.

Simpson, Ruth M. Rasey. *Hand-Hewn in Old Vermont,* Poly Two Press, North Bennington, Vermont, 1979.

Skove, Cynthia A. "The Violin and the Fungus," *American Forests,* May/ June 1987, pp. 56-57.

Sloane, Eric. *A Museum of Early American Tools,* Wilfred Funk, Inc., New York, 1964.

Sloane, Eric. *A Reverence for Wood,* Funk & Wagnalls, New York, 1965.

Smith, Charles W. G. "What's Killing the Sugar Maples?," *Country Journal,* March 1986, pp. 46-49.

Snyder, Phillip. *December 25th: The Joys of Christmas Past,* Dodd, Mead & Company, New York, 1985.

Snyder, Phillip V. *The Christmas Tree Book,* Viking Press, New York, 1976.

Steinhart, Peter. "As the Old Oaks Fall," *Audubon,* September 1978, pp. 30-40.

Swain, Roger B. *Earthly Pleasures,* Charles Scribner's Sons, New York, 1981.

Swain, Roger B. *Field Days,* Charles Scribner's Sons, New York, 1983.

Swain, Roger B. "The Secret Life of the Familiar Evergreen," *New York Times Magazine,* March 12, 1983, pp. 78-82.

Thomas, Keith. *Man and the Natural World,* Pantheon Books, New York, 1983.

Tompkins, Peter, and Christopher Bird. *The Secret Life of Plants,* Harper and Row, Publishers, Inc., New York, 1973.

Trefil, James. "Concentric clues from growth rings unlock the past," *Smithsonian,* July 1985, pp. 47-52.

Trener, Robert. *The Tree Farm,* Little, Brown, and Company, Toronto, 1977.

Tresemer, David. *Splitting Firewood,* Hand & Foot, Ltd., Brattleboro, Vermont, 1981.

Tripp, Nathaniel. "Acid Rain: Now It's Threatening Our Forests," *Country Journal,* May 1983, pp. 63-70.

Walker, Winifred. *All the Plants of the Bible,* Harper & Brothers, Publishers, New York, 1957.

Wallace, David Rains. "The Oaks," *Country Journal,* November 1983, pp. 70-80.

Weiner, Michael A. *Earth Medicine, Earth Food: Plant Remedies, Drugs, and Natural Foods of the North American Indians,* Collier Books, New York, 1980.

Whittle, Tyler. *The Plant Hunters,* PAJ Publications, New York, 1988.

Wilkins, Malcolm. *Plantwatching,* Facts on File Publications, New York, 1988.

Wilkinson, Gerald. *Epitaph for the Elm,* Hutchinson & Co., London, 1978.

Williams, Ted. "Another Disease Might Save the American Chestnut," *Yankee,* January 1982, pp. 82-85.

Wilson, Brayton F. *The Growing Tree,* University of Massachusetts Press, Amherst, Massachusetts, 1984.

Wilson, Ernest H. *Aristocrats of the Trees,* Dover Publications, Inc., New York, 1974.

Wilson, Helen Van Pelt, and Leonie Bell. *The Fragrant Year,* M. Burrows and Company, Inc., New York, 1967.

Wintsch, Susan. "The Greedy Leaf," *Garden,* May/June 1986, pp. 26-29.

Yepsen, Roger B., Jr., ed. *Trees for the Yard, Orchard, and Woodlot,* Rodale Press, Inc., Emmaus, Pennsylvania, 1976.

Young, Allen M. "The Tasty Wars," *Garden,* January/February 1987, pp. 18-21.

Young, Judith. *Celebrations,* Capra Press, Santa Barbara, California, 1986.

INDEX

INDEX